The
Trainer
in You

How to
Design & Deliver
Dynamic
Workshops

by Hugh Phillips

This book is available at:
www.hp-trainingworks.com

Copyright 2004 by HP TrainingWorks Inc.

ISBN: 0-9736029-0-2

Canadian Books in Print Cataloguing-in-Publication Data
Phillips, Hugh
The trainer in you: How to design and deliver dynamic workshops
By Hugh Phillips
Includes bibliographical references and index
ISBN 0-9736029-0-2

Printed in Canada

Published by   HP TrainingWorks Inc.

13631 Buena Vista Rd
Edmonton, AB T5R 5R5

Ph: (780) 444-3420

Fax: (780) 489-7638

Visit our website at http://www.hp-trainingworks.com

Project Editor	Theresa Agnew
Substantive Editor	Theresa Agnew
Copy Editor	Brendan Wild
Indexers	Moira Calder, Nick Abboud
Cover Design	Gigi Meade
Interior Design	Gigi Meade
Printer	McCallum Printing Group Inc.

Printing   10 9 8 7   6 5 4 3 2 1

This book is printed on acid-free stock.

Dedication

This book is dedicated to two very influential people in my life.

To my dad, Harold Thomas Phillips

A mentor, motivator, and magnanimous giver,
God enriched many lives through him.

To Randy Weber

My friend in sailing, skiing, and matters of the soul,
My memories of him are a blessing.

Acknowledgements

Who achieves anything worthwhile without the help of others? Not me, that's for sure.

I am grateful to the people who helped inspire this book. First and foremost to my family. My wife, Faye, was a constant source of moral and inspirational support in helping me stick with the writing, whether in the comfort of my home office or on the training road across Canada. My daughter, Kim, encouraged me with her creative and candid comments, especially in choosing a title for the book.

And to all who helped bring this book from its initial collection of ideas to this finished form. Theresa Agnew, the Project and Substantive Editor: I hold her work in high esteem. She gave countless hours in consulting and editing, combined with stimulating and results-driven meetings. Brendan Wild, the Copy Editor, was a meticulous and caring editor who ensured continuity and consistency. Moira Calder and Nick Abboud, the Indexers, worked swiftly and accurately in the late stages of the process. And Gigi Meade, the designer, who combined a wonderful creative spirit with a practical and knowledgeable gift to "see" the book in print before it actually happened.

Finally, I'm grateful to the following people (listed alphabetically), each of whom either sponsored one of my workshops over the past several years or befriended me with advice and counsel along the way. Their support helped to create a living laboratory in which to test and refine the ideas in this book: Marni Allison, Gary Anselmo, Jackie Appelt, Brad Blocksidge, Cindy Bolton, Kathleen Byrne, Dianne Conrad, Mike Cooper, Peter Dalzell, Terry Davis, Don Dick, Anne Dingwall, Les Deezar, Gordon Dirks, Kenene Doherty-Fergusson, Dan Faber, Pamela Farron, Sandi Fedorchuk-Hrynda, Janet Fry, Ken Forsyth, Lonny Gabinet, Ross Gillespie, Indira Haripersad, Debbie Hensman, Wendy Harrison, Marilyn Hussey, Ray Johnson, Ed Kamps, John Klass, Beverly Lafortune, Claudine Lowry, Fran Lucas, Katherine MacKeigan, Arnold Matson, Medhat Mahdy, Linda Marcil, Judith McGechen, David Milner, Val Olekshy, Wayne Pasemko, Bernice Parent, Georgina Riddell, Bente Roed, Chris Sayer, Marg Schwartz, Jean-Pascal Souque, Sandi Stechisen, Dan Stoker, Devon Taylor, Keith Taylor, Sheri Tchir, Carmen Thieson, Jeff Warthe, Wil Watson, Penny Wilkes, and Tom Wispinski.

Table of Contents

PART THREE: DYNAMICS

PART FOUR: DEVELOPMENT

Introduction

Everyone who is fully trained will be like his teacher.

Luke 6:40b

Training works!

Welcome to one of the most exciting, challenging, and fulfilling opportunities in the world—the art and skill of training. Whether you're a novice or seasoned trainer, or just thinking about entering the field, this book is for you. In these pages, you'll find innovative, creative, and practical ideas for designing and delivering dynamic training.

This book will help you translate your subject-matter expertise, no matter the topic, into training events that are high content, high value, and high impact. As trainers, we have the responsibility of leading learners. When we view what we do as a privilege, an opportunity, an investment in others, then we'll leave a legacy of excellence in training.

By applying the ideas in this book to your training events, you'll become known as a person who can help others perform at a higher level. You'll be able to take any topic you are passionate about and turn it into a learning event that informs, inspires, and initiates change for a better work place, a better home, a better community—even a better world!

I've titled this book *The Trainer in You* because I believe we all have what it takes to help others learn; we just may not know how to transform our potential into promise. Whether the trainer in you is hovering near the surface or buried deep inside, this book will help you take advantage of your natural training ability. Through practical ideas, tips, and techniques, you will learn to lead learners with fresh, workable, and easy-to-implement training techniques.

The Trainer in You?

If you're new to training, you might be asking, do I really have a natural ability to train? Well, put yourself in this situation:

The phone rings. It's Tuesday morning and your colleague and friend is calling to ask you to conduct a half-day workshop next month with a group of company sales reps. The topic is how to close a sale. You are a successful sales representative with your company. Your friend values your knowledge in selling. The audience you would speak to would be new sales reps. You've mentored staff members before, and you've always enjoyed working with aspiring professionals. So, you agree to deliver the half-day workshop.

You hang up the phone and then it hits you! You're not a trainer. It's one thing to be good at something, but it's quite another to teach others about it. How will you ever be able to meet your friend's expectations?

Mild panic sets in. You pick up the phone to call your friend back. You want to let him know that you can help out, but you won't be able to lead the session. But, as you start to dial the number, a competing thought comes to you. A little voice in your head says, "I am a pretty good sales rep. And I do have some ideas about why I've been so successful. Besides, I've really enjoyed the mentoring I've done. Hmmm. Maybe I can do this." You put the phone down. Panic is replaced by enthusiasm. "Hey," you say to yourself, "I can do this. I will do this!"

Excitedly, you set aside the project you've been working on, pick up a pencil, and start to jot down ideas. After an hour or so, you've sketched out a rough framework for the half-day session that looks something like this:

- *Call participants to ask about the challenges they face in closing a sale. (Do tomorrow.)*
- *Start session with an ice breaker to make everyone comfortable*
- *Tell the group about my first sales adventure — and how I flubbed that one!*
- *Share some ideas on how to successfully close a sale*
- *Divide the group up and have them apply some of these ideas to a sales scenario*
- *Ask individuals to choose an idea that they can try out at work this week*
- *Leave them with that quote I like so much that inspires me after a tough day*
- *Touch base next week to see how everyone is doing*

There, the workshop outline is in place. And without any formal training in training, you've uncovered the eight key steps in designing a training event. Congratulations!

So, what's in this book for you?

Road MAP

Part One: **Design**

The first section introduces you to the eight stages of the training cycle, providing you with a method to plan and prepare for any kind of training event.

Part Two: **Delivery**

Over one hundred and twenty training tips and techniques are provided to help you implement the training cycle. I'll walk you through the process of how to conduct each technique and give you options for your particular circumstances. There's enough detail here that you can easily use a new technique tomorrow!

Part Three: **Dynamics**

With a training cycle and training techniques in place, you'll learn how to lead a group of learners. We'll explore the dynamics of group interaction and examine ways to help learners become mutually supportive, collaborative, and cooperative. I'll provide you with management ideas and tips to work successfully with all kinds of learners.

Part Four: **Development**

Learners learn in different ways. In this section, I talk about learning styles and demonstrate how they can be accommodated in every training event. I provide examples to make this easy and exciting to do.

The POWERtool

I close by integrating the four parts of the book—design, delivery, dynamics, and development—into an innovative and practical POWERtool. This workshop planning pad will help you get the results you and your learners want from training and reduce your development time by over 50 percent!

Seven Cornerstones
to Support the Trainer in You

I rely on seven cornerstones or principles to sustain me through the ups and downs, the triumphs and failures, the sheer ecstasy and sometimes the extreme frustration of training. Using these cornerstones will help you discover or affirm the trainer in you.

1. Strive for learner-centeredness

Your role as a trainer is not to empower learners, but to create a learning environment that encourages learners to empower themselves. To do this, workshops need to engage people mentally, socially and emotionally. Involvement at multiple levels leads to a commitment to learning. When you deliver a learner-centered workshop, participants will leave mostly impressed with themselves, not with the trainer.

2. Manage your status

To keep it simple, there are three kinds of attendees at workshops–participants, passives, and prisoners. Participants want to be at the training event, they enjoy getting and giving. Passives are fence sitters who use the workshop as a vacation from the normal work day. Prisoners, for various legitimate or imagined reasons, do not want to be at training.

We trainers also walk into training events with a certain status. We can be excited and invigorated by the training experience—participant; or we can be low-key, laid-back, and noncommittal—passive; or we may be training with an unwilling spirit—prisoner. Manage who you are. Model what you want. Assume the professional responsibility of being the best participant you can be.

3. Be purpose-driven

Trainers want learners to return to work, home, or the community better equipped to think, feel, do, or serve. Training is an investment in time, capital, and people. Specific outcomes need to be identified, worked through, and accounted for in our training. Each technique or method needs to advance learning. Set clear goals and make a commitment to achieving them.

4. Experience the joy of training and learning

A lot of books for trainers explain how to use certain prescribed techniques, methods, and media. This can be very serious stuff. Yet the blessing of working with people, sharing new ideas, and learning in the moment can bring immense joy to the trainer. Happy is the trainer who is centred by a sense of joy for the work they do.

5. Embrace a flexible process

Product is what you do in training, process is how you do it. Sharing your knowledge is product, how you share that knowledge is process. This book offers more than a dozen ways to customize your lecture. As you advance your product, you'll become more competent; as you expand your process, you'll become more confident.

6. Practice authenticity

What learners want most from you is not your knowledge, as needed as it may be, not your tips and techniques, as creative and stimulating as they will be, and not your tools and templates, as practical and time-saving aids for work. Learners want *you*. Work at gaining the respect and trust of your audience by being in the moment, by having the courage to be honest, professionally transparent and if need be, vulnerable.

7. Leave a Legacy

See the big picture. The entry level of training is informational – revealing relevant, timely, and well-researched knowledge and skills. As you gain experience you'll find that you'll add another layer to the information focus and that is motivation – helping people become inspired and excited about what they learn. And this will eventually lead to transformational workshops – where learner attitudes, values, and abilities are transformed. Your workshops leave a legacy of helping learners to make a difference. What a grand picture that is!

Let's Go

Let's begin our journey of discovering the trainer in you! And with this beginning, I invite you to capture the magic of the moment in this book. Become the best trainer you can be for the lucky learners that have you!

HUGHism

"You are an awesome trainer. Born to be and gifted to act."

Chapter 1:
The A's Have It!

When the student is ready the teacher will appear.
Old Chinese proverb

Training for me started in a boat!

Years ago I was asked to teach canoeing to a group of fifteen to eighteen year olds. As a recent graduate from several summers of canoe training, I was pleased to have the chance.

It was a beautiful Saturday morning at Blue Lake Centre, an outdoor education centre in the foothills of the Canadian Rockies fifty miles from the magnificent Jasper National Park. For two days, I would teach groups of teenagers basic canoeing skills.

The first group arrived at 9:00 am. In preparation for them, I laid out the paddles on each side of the dock, one behind the other. Next came the boats. Each one was hauled from the storage locker and placed near the shore. I then got the PFD's (personal floatation devices) and laid them out near the boats. Putting my foot in the water, I was reminded that the cool temperature of Blue Lake came from the nearby Athabasca Glacier. All was ready!

My plan? First, I would get the students to line up on the dock in a kneeling position. With paddle in hand, I'd teach them the four basic canoe strokes. Two of the strokes, the bow and the sweep, are done by the bow person or front paddler. The other two strokes, the J-stoke and the pry, are used by the stern person or rear passenger.

After twenty to thirty minutes of stroke training, the next steps in my plan would be to demonstrate getting in and out of canoes safely and using the PFD. They would then be ready to partner up and head out on the water to practice the four strokes.

All too soon it was 9:00 am. The kids were arriving. Laughing, joking, and yelling at each other, they ran down the wood chip trail and headed straight for the boats. I was excited, too. It was a perfect morning to teach canoeing, twenty degrees Celsius, calm water, and a bright, warm sun. A great start for my first canoe class!

Kneeling at the front of the dock, I invited the students to join me. "Come on over. Let's get you lined up on the dock here. We'll begin by teaching you four canoe strokes. Then you'll head out on the water and practice." Most joined me on the dock but a couple of the students, Judy and Martin, stayed by the canoes. I encouraged them to participate, saying, "Come on over. We'll get this dry land training done and then we'll head out on the water. Not to worry, the boats won't float away!"

Reluctantly Martin and Judy joined the rest of us on the dock. I began, "Welcome to our canoe class this morning. Glad you're here. This morning I want to show you the four basic strokes in canoeing. Then you'll be able to practice with a partner in a canoe. We'll also teach you some safety tips, like what to do if you should tip out there. Okay, let's get started."

I was keen to get started, but it didn't take long before the students were distracted. I felt like a broken record as I tried to keep the students on track: "Martin, please keep your paddle out of the water." "Judy, please pay attention. You need to see what I'm doing in order to learn the strokes." "Martin, you've got your paddle in the water again. Please take it out and hold it this way so I can coach you properly." "Please stop splashing your paddle in the water; it's annoying Bruce."

The students were too busy admiring the bird life and fooling around with the paddles to listen to my lecture on the four strokes. Eventually, I found myself raising my voice at one of the students. "All right," I yelled. "No practice, no canoeing. Got it? If you can't cooperate, we'll leave you on shore."

Well, my threat worked. Everyone started to practice. But no one was having fun. No more questions were asked. Just quiet compliance. I got my way but I got in the way of learning. After twenty more minutes of drill, the students had learned the four strokes. I partnered them off and got each pair assigned to a boat. A few safety tips were demonstrated before they excitedly headed out on the water.

Guess what happened? Lots of goofing around, laughing, and a few high-risk maneuvers. Very few were attempting the four strokes. What I had just taught seemed to be a waste of time. Again I found myself yelling at the students, but to no avail. The carefree attitude persisted and seemed to spread among most of the students. Before I knew it, noon had arrived. The class quickly returned back to shore, docked their boats, and ran up the trail towards the centre for lunch.

Discouraged and frustrated, I sat down on the dock. Realizing I had three more half-day classes to conduct, I tried to muster up a little enthusiasm. I knew I had to change some things – my attitude for one and my approach to drill teaching for another.

I decided to skip lunch. Maybe if I just started getting ready for the afternoon class, some good ideas would come. My creative right brain had gotten me out of jams before. But no great ideas were coming. I guess I was too overloaded with negative emotions from the morning.

All too soon it's one 1:00 pm. "Okay, let's just go for it," I tell myself. "Maybe some good ideas will come in the moment."

I wait for the students to arrive. By 1:15 pm still nobody has arrived. News must have traveled fast about the morning's class I thought. I decide to head back up to the Centre. Leaving the lake, I walked up the trail, only to be greeted with the distant sound of students coming my way. I returned to the dock area. I noticed right away that the wonderful initial enthusiasm of the morning class was not a part of this group. They must have heard what happened in the morning class. Oh boy, here goes another class. What to do?

At that point, my intuition took over. I gathered the students near the boats. I welcomed them to the afternoon canoe class and then demonstrated how to put on a PFD. I asked one student to repeat the demonstration to ensure understanding. So far, so good. Next, I showed the students how to get in and out of a canoe on shore. Working in pairs, students repeated this demo. I explained a few safety tips, asked the students to pair up, choose a canoe, and head out into the water. With a noticeable lift in spirits, the students partnered up and headed out.

I positioned myself at the end of the dock, ready to respond should there be any tipping or other unforeseen problems. Ten minutes pass. The joyous mood is slowly but steadily moving towards one of frustration. I notice many of the boats are going in wide circles and their vain attempts to control the canoes are not working. From one of the boats, I overhear, "Hey, look at all the water we've got in our boat. We're going to go down." In another boat, some critical coaching is going on: "Don't you know you're not supposed to paddle on the same side of the boat as me?"

Discouraged, the students look to me for some input. I respond with an intuitive shout, "If you want to learn how to keep your boat straight, dry, and going where you want, then join me at the dock." Quickly all canoeists head for the dock, but with their circular journeys it took another ten minutes before they arrived!

"Would you like to learn how to steer a canoe?" I asked. "Yes," comes the unanimous reply. So, I begin to teach them the four strokes. Surprisingly, all the students are tuned in. They watch and question my moves. They practice with intent, first the bow stroke, then the J-stroke, the pry, and finally the sweep. Twenty minutes later they're anxious to try out their new skills. So back out for some canoeing practice. It was wonderful to see them succeed at canoeing!

The class ended all too soon, but not before I congratulated their successes and suggested a few follow-up actions they may want to take such as purchasing canoe books from the Centre or picking up the local canoe club application forms.

The afternoon had been a splashing success! The students hung around, joking and talking with each other. A few asked if they could come back later for more canoe practice!

4 The Four Stages of Training

Yes, training for me started in a boat, but it was years after my canoe instructor experience at Blue Lake that I sat down and thought about why my morning session didn't succeed and my afternoon sessions did. I'd like you to keep this story in mind as I introduce you to the components that influence me every time I design a workshop.

I believe an effective training event is made up of four distinct phases: Attention, Acquisition, Application, and Action. Each "A" is a part of a logical, sequential, and easy-to-use process that guides trainers in the what, how, why, and when of a training program. My understanding of these components has grown steadily as I've gained experience as a trainer. I'd like to share my ideas with you regarding the significance of these four key stages of the training cycle.

The First "A":
Attention

In her book *The Sense of Wonder*, Rachel Carson writes, "It's not half so important to know as it is to feel. Childhood is the time to till the soil in which the seeds must grow. . . . It is more important to pave the way for a child to want to know, than to put him on a diet of facts he is not ready to assimilate."

Carson reminds us that learning begins with a desire to know more. Curiosity, intrigue, and inquisitiveness "pave the way" for real learning. This is what the first "A" is all about. Before we put learners on a diet of facts, figures, and formulas, the need or desire to learn must be present.

As trainers, we need to seize the moment when we begin training. We have to grab the learners' attention and encourage them to discover why they need this training at this time. We cannot assume that just because we are ready to train that our students are ready to learn. A trainer needs to lead the learner in asking and answering the question, "Why do I need to learn?" Only then has the desire to learn surfaced. We have got their attention. This is a vital first step.

How do trainers encourage learners to *want* to learn? By starting each lesson with an activity that ignites the desire to learn, you will successfully help learners become excited about learning. We will look at specific attention-gaining techniques in Chapter Six, but first I'd like to explore three factors that I believe make the attention phase such a vital first stage of training: Learner Luggage, Saturation Factor, and Affinity Index.

Learner Luggage

I've heard that the attention span of the adult learner averages about thirty seconds (the length of most television commercials). Why so short? One reason is because of what I call learner luggage.

Luggage refers to all our life experiences. We carry these experiences—both good and bad—in our memories. When a workshop begins, the learners' memories and day-to-day concerns are in constant competition with the trainer's words and actions. Because learners can think at four times the rate that a trainer can talk, they may be distractedly dipping into their luggage while giving the appearance of listening.

Adult learners are adept at handling this competition for their thoughts. They can look right at the trainer, use body language that suggests they are listening (nods, smiles, etc.), yet be thinking about something entirely different than the workshop. Sound familiar? Sometimes, something as innocent as a reference to Vancouver to illustrate a point will trigger a learner memory about a recent trip to the West Coast.

Adults get distracted by their luggage, by the events in their lives. The trainer needs to grab the learners' attention early in the session and pique interest in the session's topic. Gaining attention helps learners manage luggage distractions.

Making Connections

From a very young age, I remember my father saying, "Most of what I teach you is caught not taught." I have often considered this metaphor of a game of catch when developing the attention phase of a training plan.

In order for me to learn from my father, I first needed to be ready to catch. Some learners will make no attempt to catch ideas. They don't want to play the "learning game." Other learners may attempt to catch but are not confident in their abilities. Still others are keen and want to catch. The point of the attention stage of training is to get learners to want to play. Metaphorically, it creates the desire in the learners to lift their catching gloves and get ready to receive the ball of thought. If they don't even want to play, no learning will take place.

Saturation Factor

Every day our brains are bombarded with information. Someone once told me that the typical North American takes in over seven thousand messages in a 24-hour period. Because your learners are so saturated with facts and ideas before they even make it to your training session, you need to grab their interest quickly. The saturation factor occurs when learners are so overloaded with information that any new learning is lost.

To illustrate: I typically wake up at 5:30 am to the news and sports broadcast on my radio. For the next few minutes, before I actually get out of bed, I'll take in about 40 to 50 messages—everything from political updates to the weather forecast to the scores in last night's hockey games. Once I'm up, I go for a morning jog with the dog, shower, prepare any final details for the day's workshop, have breakfast with my family (if I'm lucky), and leave for work. In that time span, I've easily logged another 200 messages. Throughout the day, the total number of messages we each receive is tremendous!

The implications for training? First of all, remember that adults who are trained in the afternoon or evening have likely already been saturated with information, ideas, and intentions. They're not in prime condition to take in more ideas. As well, remember that you can confront the saturation factor by arresting their minds—by getting their attention as quickly as possible.

Affinity Index

The affinity index refers to the likelihood that learners in your session will develop an affinity for you and your presentation style. From my experience, I would generalize that approximately 15 percent of the people you encounter will develop an instant affinity with you, 80 percent will feel neutral, and 5 percent may dislike you.

The 15 percent who instantly like you may do so because of the way you walk, smile, phrase your words, or gesture. Often, affinity develops because you look, act, or sound like someone in a learner's "affinity circle." Maybe you remind the learner of a kind parent, a supportive sibling, a wise uncle or aunt, a gracious grandparent, or even of the learner himself.

On the other hand, the majority of your learners will begin the day feeling quite neutral toward you. They will make little, if any, immediate connection to you, but will hope you'll be a prepared and effective trainer. The size of this group makes it a powerful ally should you be able to get their attention early in the day.

The five percent who may not like you will associate you with someone they do not like: an overly strict mother, a lenient father, an irritable sibling, an annoying uncle or aunt, a humourless neighbour, a stodgy boss.

Of course, you can't take this lack of affinity personally. Trainers can influence, but not control, the impressions that learners have of them. These impressions are a part of the complex human dynamic at work when people meet and interact with each other. You can learn to minimize the possible negative effects of the affinity index. The attention stage of learning fosters curiosity about a topic, thereby encouraging learners to focus on the training, rather than the trainer. If you work hard at gaining learner attention, you can help your students move beyond natural affinities by getting them excited about learning.

The Second "A": Acquisition

The number one reason people come to workshops is to learn. They want to acquire current and relevant knowledge, skills, and attitudes that will enhance their value as a person, a professional, or a practitioner. The *attention phase* of learning has roused the learners' curiosity about the topic and made them aware of their need to know more. The *acquisition phase* responds to that need with timely, useful information.

Once you have gained the *attention* of your audience (the desire to learn has surfaced), then learners are ready to *acquire* the knowledge that will satisfy their curiosity. They want the information that will help them improve a skill or develop an idea. As trainers, we can now "throw" ideas with the expectation that learners will attempt to "catch" them. Throw by throw, we toss out more ideas and learners make attempts to catch or acquire this information. They are in the game!

Remember, though, the learning game must be played at the learner's pace, not your own. Play too fast and the ideas will be dropped before a learner has fully understood them. Play too slow and learners will get distracted and not catch the next thought coming their way.

When we begin to share information and ideas with learners who are ready to learn, we are perceived as leaders in our field. Generally, three elements—education, experience, and expertise (the three E's)—are necessary for a trainer to gain and maintain the learner's respect.

Education

As trainers, our educational backgrounds provide us with some of the knowledge we impart to our students. Whether you've attended college, technical school, or university, your schooling gives substance to your training program. And learners do want substance. They don't want to waste their time with "fluff." They want to acquire information that gives them the current and relevant knowledge they need to succeed at work.

Education doesn't end once you graduate. You still need to keep up to date in your field. Participating in training opportunities, conducting your own research, and reading recent literature are all examples of life-long learning.

Dear Hugh,

I'm a bit nervous about my next training session. What should I do if the learners know more about the topic than I do? What if I'm in a group of practitioners who have years more experience in the field than me?

Nervous in Newfoundland

Dear Nervous,

Rest assured you are not alone in your nervousness! Your fear is one of the most common concerns of a new trainer. But don't worry! If you take just twenty minutes a day to read about the topic(s) you teach, within a year you will know more about your topic than 95% of the population. Reading will keep you current and learners will be impressed by your ongoing efforts to stay on top of current trends and ideas.

Sincerely,
Hugh

Experience

Knowledge itself is not enough to gain the respect of your audience. Learners want your knowledge to be supported by work experience. The stories, illustrations, and anecdotes that you bring to a topic make it relevant to the learner. By sharing your own experiences, participants will be able to make connections with their own work. You'll love it when you overhear participants saying:

"She's talking at my level. It's not above or below me. It just right for me."

"This stuff really makes sense. I can see now why I've struggled with my problem."

"He's been reading my mail. It's like he works next door to me. This learning is going to be very useful when I get back to work."

Education provides the *content* for the learning environment; our experiences provide the *context*. Learners appreciate a trainer's stories. You gain credibility when you can illustrate what you teach with life experiences. The combination of our education and work experience give learners a balanced presentation. Experience broadens and enriches training.

Expertise

New trainers sometimes ask for my advice on how to start a training business. I always emphasize the importance of becoming an expert in your training area. This means "owning" what you teach. To become an expert, you need to do plenty of research, take the time to consult with other experts, set up interviews with practitioners, and make on-the-job observations. All of this study, research, and observation will yield a body of knowledge that characterizes your own unique interpretation, understandings, and wisdom.

Passion is one of the spin-offs of ownership. You will stand before your audience knowing that the information you have to share will, in most cases, be highly valued. Individuals will enjoy learning from you because you are an expert. It will be clear to them that you have internalized the subject to the point that it has become an extension of yourself both professionally and personally. You will deliver with passion because you are delivering, in part, yourself!

Learners want to know we are experts in our field. When you distill your education and experience—when you squeeze out what these two dimensions of learning have given you—wisdom emerges. Wisdom is the trainer's expertise. It makes you unique and memorable. While all trainers benefit from education and experience, the ones who use these elements to generate their own wisdom will have the biggest impact on their audiences. When trainers pass on their life lessons, they create change

Let me tell you how I gained expertise in public speaking workshops.

Many trainers teach public speaking skills, but I've made this field my own by developing the SMARTpad, a tool to help learners quickly and effectively plan their presentations. Before I came to "own" this area, I did a lot of reading about giving presentations. I watched professionals speak. I gave speeches. I searched the internet, visited many a bookstore, and consulted numerous training videos. As well, I videotaped and critiqued myself in action.

This immersion experience allowed me to develop and expand *my own* expertise in public speaking and led to the development of the SMARTpad. This tool has given me a strong identity in presentation design and delivery. If you will, I now "own" a unique piece of knowledge regarding effective presentations!

The Third "A":
Application

This third "A" distinguishes *training* from *education*. Typically the thrust in education is to *know and understand* while the focus in training is to *do*. This "know" and "do" dichotomy affects how we design successful programs.

To be remembered, knowledge must be used—and the sooner it is used, the better. In the *attention phase* we encouraged students to ask, "*Why* do I need this information?" In the *acquisition phase*, we want learners to say, "Okay, so *what* do

I need to know?" In the *application phase*, trainers respond to learners who ask, "*How* can I use this new idea?"

The application phase is the testing and validation phase for adult learners. They scrutinize the information that has come their way and want to apply it to real-life problems and challenges. Trainers validate the workshop experience by encouraging learners to apply their new-found knowledge to relevant work place issues, problems, and scenarios.

Five actions govern my use of the application phase in a training event: Adapt or Adopt, Customize, Assess Risk, Transfer Ownership, and Internalize Learning.

Adapt or Adopt

Most of the information we impart when we train will be *adapted*, rather than wholly *adopted*, by the learners. Let's think of this in terms of the ways we adapt information as trainers.

Much of what we train is not the sole domain of one person. For example, many trainers teach coaching skills. Each trainer conducts his own research and does his own coaching to develop his expertise. But many have read the same books, visited the same web sites, and spoken to the same experts. So what makes each trainer unique? It's the way he *adapts* the information in developing a training program.

Similarly, the learner will not fully *adopt* the ideas you share in training. They are much more likely to tweak what you have to say so that the information and skills will work for them in their own unique work situations. Sometimes workshop content can be immediately adopted, and requires no change. But, for the most part, knowledge needs to be adapted to specific situations. Good application exercises will help learners significantly increase the amount of information they can use.

Customize

The potpourri of personal knowledge and experience that shapes each classroom makes for a very rich learning environment. You need to be aware of your group's situation in order to make the application stage relevant and meaningful. With your customization of application exercises and activities, learners will make direct connections between the ideas you expose them to and their work place.

Keep in mind that certain training circumstances demand that the learner *adopt not adapt* what you say. If you are training a group about safety procedures, for example, you do not want the learner to re-work information. You are asking for complete compliance because certain methods and procedures must be carried out in a specific order and manner to ensure the safety of all involved.

For example, when I conduct the "Coaching for Peak Performance" workshop, some clients want me to focus on conflict resolution, while others want me to focus on mentoring. Many of the basic skills in these two areas are the same but their application is quite different. By customizing each workshop to meet learner needs, I help each participant answer the question: "How do the ideas I've learned in this training event apply to my work situation?"

Assess Risk

In the application phase, learners take risks. After all, they are applying new knowledge to familiar situations – not always an easy task. The trainer plays a key role in making sure everyone involved feels safe as they perform, practice, observe, respond, and evaluate new learning.

In some situations, learners are practicing a new skill. In other situations, they are re-learning a skill because of policy or practice changes at work. Whatever the case, the learner is generally putting more at risk than the trainer. It is up to you to assess these risks and, where appropriate, minimize them. No one likes to be embarrassed. If a learner feels stupid or slow (intellectual embarrassment), feels fear (emotional embarrassment), or is left alone for too long (social embarrassment), the risks are too high and learning won't take place.

This is not to suggest you should aim for a training environment where everyone is so safe that no risks are taken. Risk is an important part of learning. Having survived a risk makes for greater trust and rapport in the training room. But never

the Trainer's EDGE

Remember that risk is not static. An activity that is considered risky during the first day of training may be boring on the second day. The trainer needs to continually raise the bar for learners to ensure the class experiences appropriate levels of risk and adventure. Training is more effective when it focuses on challenging learners to meet their full potential, not on maintaining the status quo.

risk to the point where learners are in embarrassing or demoralizing situations. If learners are respected, they will feel safe and have the confidence to take risks and meet challenges with the best of their abilities.

Transfer Ownership

As the trainer, you are the subject-matter expert (SME) and come to a session "owning" the knowledge and skills that will gain the respect of your audience. In the application phase, though, the goal is for learners to become comfortable owning the knowledge and skills you've shared. The transfer of ownership from trainer to learner is one of the most exciting phenomena of training. This transfer begins in the acquisition phase and spills over into the application phase. You succeed when learners begin to identify with the ideas they've learned. The new information becomes *theirs* because it works for them.

Internalize Learning

The acquisition of knowledge is important, but as one workshop participant from Newfoundland reminded me, "Knowledge keeps no better than fish." His insight reinforces the importance of the application phase. If we don't use our knowledge, we will lose it.

Up to this point in a workshop, most of the learners' experiences have been external. You have whetted their appetites by piquing their curiosity, and you have provided them with the knowledge they need to respond to this curiosity. But these steps occur *externally*, through lectures, or flip charts, or videos. If learners aren't given the opportunity to *internalize* ideas, they will soon be forgotten. Let's consider the link between memory and knowledge.

Short-term memory can hold about six to eight ideas for about twenty minutes; long-term memory can hold many ideas for many years. The challenge in training is to move information from short-term memory to long-term memory. In a sense, the learner will be moving information from a temporary filing cabinet to a more secure and enduring storage system. When this occurs, the learner has internalized an idea.

The implications for training? First of all, be wary about passing on too many ideas without giving the opportunity to apply or internalize them. Unless we give learners time to become familiar with information and ideas, they will simply forget them and make room for other information coming their way. Short-term memory will be flooded and ideas will get lost. We need to carefully pace the flow of ideas during the acquisition phase to maximize the transfer of ideas to long-term memory during the application phase.

Secondly, be aware that moving information from short-term to long-term memory relies on repetition. Albert Mehrabian tells us that if you repeat something six times, you will increase retention by 90 percent. That's great payback. Repetition works not because learners are inattentive or slow, but because it helps learners to revisit a concept allowing them to deepen their understanding.

the **Trainer's** EDGE

> Creativity is key to the successful repetition of ideas. Repetition does not mean repeating the same drill six times. It does mean revisiting a concept, idea, or skill in different ways to ensure learners stay involved. The more we repeat an idea, the better chance we have of helping learners to transfer information from short-term to long-term memory.

The Fourth "A":
Action

In the *attention phase* of learning, participants are encouraged to ask "why;" in the *acquisition phase,* they ask "what;" and in the *application phase,* they ask "how." Now it's time to have them ask "when." When am I going to use what I've learned?

By asking this question, the learner enters the *action phase* of training. Unlike the application phase, where the trainer motivates, encourages, and provides constructive feedback, in the action phase, the learner is more independent. At this stage, the trainer encourages the learner to transfer knowledge from the classroom to the work place. The action phase is an extension of the application phase, but now the learner works independently. Responsibility for implementing new ideas shifts from trainer to learner.

Unlike the other three A's, which take place solely in the classroom, the action phase occurs both in the training environment and back at work. This shift in location suggests that our involvement as trainers does not stop simply because our session has come to a close. We may continue to be involved, but in more peripheral ways.

Why is the action phase so vital to effective training? These points come to mind.

Sense of Achievement

Change can occur quickly in the training environment for several reasons: learners observe new skills as they are performed by the trainer; learners have the support of other learners both during and beyond training; and finally, with practice sessions during the workshop, the learner immediately begins to develop a higher level of confidence.

In other words, the action phase cultivates a strong sense of achievement. Learners quickly see how their actions can lead to change in the work place. At all levels of responsibility, training assists an organization in achieving its potential and profitability.

Accountability

By incorporating the first three A's into their workshop plan, trainers acknowledge their responsibility for creating a positive and effective learning environment. The fourth "A" makes clear to learners that they, too, have a major responsibility. Learners are responsible for using what they've learned. In other words, the trainer and the learners share accountability.

For me, the beauty of the action phase lies partly in its built-in accountability. I do not *hope* things will change back at work, I *expect* things to change back at work.

Dividends

When you invest your hard-earned money, you will often use the Return on Investment (ROI) factor to determine the type of investment you make. For example, should you select a Guaranteed Investment Certificate (GIC) or an Equity Mutual Fund? If interest rates are high and income levels are modest, then the GIC may be your best choice. One thousand dollars can double in less than six years. On the other hand, if your income levels are higher, then the tax implications may be significant enough for you to choose a mutual fund. Here your dividends earned are given better tax treatment. Either way, your bottom line is the ROI, your return on investment.

In a similar way, personnel responsible for training consider the ROI factor. Is the training that a manager approves and sponsors going to give the ROI that will justify the expense in time and costs? (Some of the costs associated with a training event include release time for learners and support staff, facility charges, food and refreshments, AV equipment rental, and the trainer's fee.)

One of the key indicators for the manager will be the post-training experience. Are workers returning to the job with increased skill? Do they display a higher level of competence? Are they more confident in their own abilities? If the answers to these questions are positive, the manager will likely conclude that the payback for training has been well worth the investment.

When you collect your dividends from stock investments, they are usually modest. So it is with trainees who return to work. Their new actions may not seem to make a big difference, but, with continued and consistent efforts, new learning will have an impact not only on a trainee's work habits, but on her colleagues' work as well. Soon the benefits of training escalate in value from one person to many people. Clearly a very worthwhile dividend!

the **Trainer's**
EDGE

> If you want to figure out how much time a client has invested in training, try this formula I've developed. Multiply the total number of people attending the workshop by the length of the workshop itself. For example, if 20 people are attending an 8-hour workshop, then the total time invested is 160 hours for the day!

Self Esteem

Individuals with a strong sense of self-esteem make positive contributions to the work place. The action phase fosters learners' self-esteem because the successful implementation of new skills builds self-confidence and pride in the work place. The action phase affirms the value of learners' new skills and enhances their value within the work setting. It is a win-win situation for learners!

When trainees make a difference at work, they confirm that continued learning brings about change. Change can be constructive, creative, and contribute to the bottom line. To know that you help to make a difference at work can be the greatest reward of training!

Let's Review

I use this at-a-glance table to keep me focused when I design training plans.

The "A"	Purpose	Learner question answered
Attention	You ignite curiosity in the learner. You prepare them to learn.	Why do I need to know this?
Acquisition	You provide information to satisfy learner curiosity.	What do I need to know?
Application	You provide learners the opportunity to apply new ideas through relevant, learner-centered activities.	How will I use it?
Action	You encourage learners to commit to using their newly acquired skills	When will I use it?

Meanwhile Back at Canoe Camp

Let's return to my first training experience as a canoeing instructor. Why did the morning canoe session bomb and the afternoon session succeed? We can use the four A's to help figure this one out.

In the morning canoe session, I began right away with an attempt to teach the four canoe strokes. I lined the students up on the dock and began to teach. In other words, the process began with the second stage of learning: acquisition. The students are silently saying to themselves, "Who says I need to know these strokes? I think I can get along just fine without learning all this stuff. Besides, I want to get in the boat and see what I can do." By beginning with the "what" instead of the "why," the students were not prepared to learn. The purpose of the attention phase is to "pave the way," to create a desire to learn, to answer the question, "Why?" If I couldn't galvanize the students' attention, there's no way I was going to be able to rouse their desire to learn. I began by plying them with information that they didn't even care about or know was important.

In the afternoon class, I was able to catch the students' attention by getting them out on the water right away. Soon, most of them were frustrated. They found they could not keep the canoe pointed in the direction they wanted to go. In other words, the learners were in a situation where they discovered they *needed* to know more about canoeing if they were going to enjoy and pursue the sport. A need surfaced. A gap in their knowledge was identified. Students were asking, "Why does this crazy canoe keep going in circles?" "Why is it so tippy?" Because the "whys" had been established in the learner's mind, they were ready for the acquisition phase. The exercise raised questions in the learners' minds and roused their curiosity.

When this second group of students came back to shore, they did so with the desire to learn. They were ready to receive information. The acquisition phase now made sense. After twenty minutes of learning four new paddle strokes, they were ready to try to apply their new knowledge. The application phase was essential for them to retain their new knowledge. By getting back in their canoes and trying out the new strokes, they were able to practice what they had learned!

To finish the lesson, I encouraged action. I let students know about the canoeing books available at Blue Lake Centre and told them about opportunities through the canoe club. I'd like to think that one of my first learners has become a skilled canoeist and is enjoying the magnificent Canadian lakes and rivers and beyond!

HUGHism

"Train with a plan and you plan to train."

References

Carson, Rachel. 1956. *The sense of wonder.* New York, NY: Harper & Row, Publishers.

Chapter 2:
Expanding the A's

A person with the "why" can deal with any "how."

Friedrich Nietzsche

Every time you train you learn!

One day in the northern Alberta oil sands town of Fort McMurray I was conducting a Train the Trainer workshop. In the session, I introduced the group to the idea of the four A's. One learner asked me, "Hugh, do you limit yourself to the four A's when you plan a workshop? Isn't there more that guides you in the planning of training modules?" The fact that he had used the word "limit" suggested to me that he might be on to something. So I asked him, "What else might there be?" He replied that he wasn't sure. And then he stated, "Your workshops, Hugh, are more than just a learning event. You seem to put a lot of emphasis on people."

Up to that point, I thought the four A's gave me a pretty complete training plan. But when I returned to my hotel room that night, I gave myself the freedom to think outside of the four A's box. I asked myself, "What are the elements in my workshops that take place outside of the four A's? Where and how do I emphasize the people element?" And then it struck me: I carefully and intentionally focus on learner needs when I begin and end workshops even though these components are clearly not a part of the four A's.

This learner's question was a gift. It prompted me to think more deeply and more completely about how I plan a workshop. I needed to include stages that focus on effective beginnings and endings. Two new A's had to be added! Affiliation and affirmation were born!

Beginning the Workshop:
Affiliation

For me, Will Schultz's book *The Human Element* has proven to be a valuable reference with respect to the affiliation stage of planning a workshop. In thirty years of observing adults in a wide variety of social groupings, Schultz noticed three consistent and sequential "growth stages" that adults work through whenever they form a group: inclusion, control, and openness. Whether the group consists of two or two hundred, Schultz observed that in the first and most fundamental of these growth stages—the inclusion stage—most members of the group enter the situation intent on satisfying their need to belong.

I'm always fascinated by the different ways people achieve this need to belong. Some are outgoing and direct, others adopt a less public, more private, approach. The key for each of us, though, is to feel that we belong to the group. In other words, we will wonder if we have any *affiliations* with other group members. If we don't, we'll begin to question whether or not our membership in the group is worthwhile. Only when we feel included will we be ready to work, learn, have fun, and share with our group. In the training scenario, if affiliations are not fostered, chances are the learners will emotionally withdraw from the group and remain quiet or even leave.

Schultz's ideas about inclusion influenced my thoughts about training by prompting me to focus on the human element of training from the very beginning, when the group first comes together. I've learned that fostering connections means much more than involving learners in a few ice-breakers. As I prepare participants for their learning journey I consider three different levels of affiliation: learner affiliation, trainer affiliation, and topic affiliation. Let's take a closer look at what I mean by each of these terms.

Learner Affiliation

As we noted in our discussion of the acquisition phase, the number one reason people attend workshops is to learn. What is the second most compelling reason that people attend workshops? They want to meet people—to make connections and develop professional networks. With this in mind, I try to create the opportunity for learners to learn a little bit about one another. This "touching base" helps build a platform of congeniality between learners. It encourages the notion that they are in this training event together.

When I plan for a training session, I work to foster learner connections by creating an environment that puts everyone at ease and accommodates the need to develop relationships (i.e. affiliations). This includes consideration of the physical, intellectual, emotional, and social comfort of learners. By ensuring learners are comfortable on a number of levels, I make it easier for them to "connect" with others in the group.

Topic Affiliation

The affiliation phase also needs to consider how comfortable a participant is with the program content. For those in the class who are more task driven than relationship driven, topic affiliation occurs when one of their most pressing questions is answered: "How will I benefit from the knowledge and skills provided in this workshop?"

This question can be answered, at least partially, by orienting participants to the session. Early in the workshop, you will need to ascertain learning needs, describe course outcomes, present the session outline, and identify participant needs. Other "housekeeping" items that will orient participants to the session include break times, washroom and fire exit locations, and lighting and temperature controls. Usually trainers will discuss question-and-answer guidelines during the orientation. When time is limited, the orientation will necessarily be brief. Nonetheless, this introductory information will assist learners as they establish a sense of inclusion, both with you and their learning.

Trainer Affiliation

Learners also need to develop an affiliation with you, the trainer. They will be curious about this person they are about to spend time with. They'll wonder: Is this person experienced? Does she have professional expertise? Has the instructor handled groups of this size? Will she be open and easy to get to know? What does the trainer expect of me?

By introducing yourself to the learners early in the session, you will be inviting them to trust you and get to know you. The intellectual, emotional, and social comfort that you strive to establish in fostering learner affiliations carries over into the focus you give to developing strong trainer affiliations.

Why Is Affiliation So Important?

Why this emphasis on affiliation? Why make it another "A" in the training cycle? The answer to these questions comes from my conviction that training is primarily a human event, and secondarily a learning opportunity!

Ten years ago this statement would have meant very little to me. I was deeply committed to my material. Some would say I was married to it. I began each session hoping that the human aspects of training would not get in the way of what I wanted to train that day. I was the content expert. I thought, "I'm here because of what I know and the learners are here because of what they need to know."

Thankfully, my trainees in these early days were patient with me. They soon realized I was a content-first/people-second kind of guy. Sometimes they would even get very serious, like me, for the day. But this attitude did not contribute to a very warm or engaging learning environment.

With much practice, I've learned to balance the people element and the content element in my workshops. I now know that my role as trainer is to meet the needs of the group—both educational and social. I can't ignore one at the expense of the other. I simply need to find the right balance for the group. The affiliation stage, right at the beginning of the workshop, ensures you meet people where they're at and enables you to create a positive learning environment.

Remember, a training event is not about you—it's about your learners. This philosophy in no way downplays the content you have to offer; it merely sets a context for content. Client needs first, trainer knowledge and expertise second.

Closing the Workshop:
Affirmation

When my Fort McMurray student prompted me to re-think my training methodology, I first thought about the way that I opened my session. But this led me to examine the way I close a workshop, too. If beginning an event appropriately is vital, isn't ending one important, too? I wondered, "Is there another "A" to consider?"

From my thinking another "A" emerged: affirmation. This stage of the training cycle emphasizes the importance of closing a workshop just as you started it. You focus on the people.

The affiliation phase marks a new beginning and prepares learners to learn and to interact with one another; the affirmation phase supports learners as they "disconnect" from the group when the session draws to a close. You want to show the learners that you valued their presence, appreciated their contributions, and believe in their ability to incorporate change into the workplace. This phase focuses on bringing closure to the training event.

There are two key elements in the affirmation stage of learning: Disconnecting and Reconnecting.

Disconnecting

Just as you take time to "connect" at the beginning of a workshop by focusing on learners' and the instructor's needs and expectations, so too must you take the time to "disconnect" when the session is over. Disconnecting is a planned event at the end of the workshop where, for example, learners have the opportunity to review what they've learned, congratulate their fellow learners on their successes, spend a few moments assessing the merits of the workshop, or communicate any closing thoughts to the trainer.

As I write this, I'm especially mindful of the way I used to manage endings. Typically, I would work the group as long as I could, sometimes to within ten minutes of the finish time. Then I'd pass out evaluation forms, make a few concise closing comments, and send the group on its way. We could all see from the clock that it was time to go, but it soon became evident to me that the group was not emotionally or socially ready to leave. Yes, the topic had been covered, but evaluation forms and non-verbal behaviour suggested these learners needed something more than a simple, "Goodbye and good luck."

When I set out to address this gap in my training, I realized that the affirmation stage, in many ways, is simply preparing the learner to go back into the real world. The training environment stimulates the intellect and provides a supportive, respectful, and collegial milieu. But this is not always the world learners are returning to. One learner's evaluation really hit the nail on the head when she commented on my rushed endings. She said, "It's true, we're done the with topic, but we're not done with ourselves. We've taken learning risks together, appreciated what we have in common, and supported each other. To stop without helping us to disconnect as a group is incomplete for us."

These words still ring true and now form the essence of the affirmation stage in my training sessions. Learners need time to leave the group and prepare themselves for their work or home environment. As a trainer, you are in a position to foster closure, to inspire and invigorate learners for the challenges ahead, and to create opportunities for fellow learners to support one another outside the workshop walls.

Reconnecting

Learners need time to "disconnect" from the group but, when the clock hits 4:30 pm, the trainer still has work to do. In order to affirm the new learning that has taken place, trainers need to take the time to "reconnect" or follow up on the training. Some follow-up takes place right away, while some may happen days or even weeks down the road. When you (or workshop colleagues) reconnect with learners you play a role in their life-long learning pursuits.

Making Connections

On some level, I probably became aware of the importance of endings as a senior high student in Edmonton, Alberta. I had a social studies teacher who knew exactly how to build a sense of anticipation and create a dynamic learning environment.

Mr. Willy would begin class by telling a story. Part way through, he would, intentionally, interrupt the story and move on to the main teaching points of the lesson. Of course, my classmates and I greeted this with loud resistance— "Finish the story!" we'd plead. "What happens next? You can't do this to us!" With a smile, he would stick to his plan. When the lesson was over, he would return to the story and finish it.

At the time, of course, I didn't know that this technique was called "closing the circle," but I do recall just how masterfully he used it. The delay tactic made for a dramatic closing, and the main points of the lesson were better learned and remembered because of the way he presented the material and because of the sense of anticipation he aroused in the classroom. Thinking back to this early learning experience reinforces for me the importance of a powerful closing to any training session.

Interestingly, some of the biggest impacts you'll make as a trainer come not during the workshop but when it is over. I remember a five-day workshop I took in Toronto. As promised, the trainer personally called me one month later and we chatted for fifteen minutes about how I was doing with my action plan. I also had the opportunity to ask him some of the questions that I'd come up with post-training. Wow, what an impact that personal touch made with me! I didn't need any further convincing to develop this habit with the learners I've had the privilege to train.

Let's Review

With these two additional A's we close the learning circle. In the affiliation stage we begin with people; in the affirmation stage we end with people. We end and begin, with the most important element in training, people.

HUGHism

"Training is primarily a human event,
Secondarily a learning opportunity."

References

Schultz, Will. 1994. *The human element: Productivity, self-esteem, and the bottom line*. San Francisco: Jossey-Bass Publishers.

Chapter 3:
The Before and After A's

Feedback is the breakfast of champions.

Ken Blanchard

In 1989 I was invited to give a keynote address to 250 conference delegates in Red Deer, Alberta. It was a motivational presentation designed to encourage and inspire people in the "how to's" of business success. I worked very hard on the talk and it paid off. At the end of the speech I got my very first standing ovation! What a thrill!

Afterwards, as I was packing my gear into the van, a woman came running towards me. She congratulated me on the presentation and then said those words that every budding presenter loves to hear: "I'm looking for a speaker and you're the one. Would you be able to come back to Red Deer in three weeks and give the same presentation to my group?"

I agreed. She was delighted.

I'll never forget her parting words: "Hugh, please, don't change a word. Your presentation today is just what we need for our group." I thought to myself, "This hard work is already paying off. All I have to do is show up and do this same awesome speech again." I also thought I was going to make her a winner because by the time I'd finish speaking to her group—and received another standing ovation, of course—she'd look like a hero.

The three weeks passed quickly and show time soon arrived. In keeping with her request, I had not revised the speech. However, as I glanced out over the audience I realized that the average age of this group was about twenty years younger than that of the previous audience. "No sweat," I thought. "This speech is quite broad in appeal. It's sure to be a hit with this group, too."

Within minutes of starting the speech, I felt a lack of connection with the audience. My humorous opening quip met with a couple nervous giggles—nothing like the uproar of the audience three weeks ago. My first heart-moving story received a cold response.

I was in big trouble. It felt like I was digging a hole and slowing disappearing before the audience. It didn't take me long to realize I was wasting their time and boring them to boot. I was devastated.

Of course, I didn't receive a standing ovation that day, only polite applause from those who stayed to the end. Looking over at my contact person, I could see the disappointment in her face.

It took me a while to recover from the disastrous presentation I gave to this second group in Red Deer. But, as I reflected on the experience, I thought that maybe, just maybe, something good could come of it. After dealing with my client's disappointment and my own discouragement, I was able to think more clearly about this disaster. What had I done or not done that led to this terrible experience?

I soon realized that I had made one fatal mistake. And it was made even before the speech began. I listened to my contact person's advice: "Hugh, don't change a word. It's great the way it is." But, of course, you can't use the same presentation for two completely different audiences. For the first audience, with people in their thirties and forties, my stories and baby boomer mentality were totally relevant. But in front of the second, generation-X audience, my stories, humour, and examples had little to do with their twenty-year-old lives. Had I taken the time to find out more about the second audience I would have known that I needed to change the speech in order to really talk to them, to acknowledge their values and perspectives.

Lesson learned? Your first impression of the audience should not take place when you stand before them; it should take shape as you prepare for the session by conducting an audit. Accurate information about the needs, values, and interests of the audience enables a trainer to design a targeted program specific to a group, at a time, in a place.

And so, from the ashes of my Red Deer misadventure, a new "A" arose: the audit.

The Audit

I believe a thorough knowledge of the needs and interests of the audience are essential to any successful training plan. In the audit stage, you identify those needs and interests through contact with your client or with the participants who will be attending the training session. The information you gather will allow you to customize materials and, in this way, meet the unique needs and circumstances of each training event. Most unexpected and unpleasant circumstances in a workshop (like my experience in Red Deer) can be prevented by conducting a thorough audit.

The next five sections contain the information and focused questions that I use to shape the audit stage of my own workshop preparations. They will help you collect appropriate data and identify relevant input for creating customized programs. I focus on five areas when conducting an audit: Demographics, Workplace and Training Experience, Factors Affecting Group Dynamics, Expectations, and the Venue.

I'd like to note that I base much of the information in these sections on observations from my own workshop experiences. These comments are not meant to reinforce stereotypes or to serve as labels. I am aware, though, that making personal commentary necessarily reveals my subjective side. Nonetheless, I've tried to be as objective as I can in my assessments.

Demographics

When you conduct an audit for an upcoming workshop you will want to find out if your group is homogenous or diverse. Ask your contact person for information about the following demographic areas.

1. Number of participants

The number of learners in your session will affect both product and process. Often you can cover more ground with a smaller group (product), while your presentation style will be influenced by the size of your audience (process). Some trainers like larger audiences. They enjoy the drama and excitement of a big event that gives them the opportunity to engage in "edu-tainment," a delightful blend of entertainment and educational content. Other trainers prefer the intimacy of a smaller group, wherein learners can benefit from individual attention and group rapport can be developed.

Making Connections

Holiday Inn trains its employees using the motto "No Surprises." These two words are regularly repeated throughout their staff training. Translation? We don't want our clients to have any unexpected or unpleasant surprises when they stay at our hotels. A surprise could be "Sorry, breakfast is not served until 7:00 am" "Sorry, you're room is not ready yet." "Sorry, you can't check out at noon." Client surprises like these are remembered and result in lost business.

2. Male/female ratio

How many trainees are women and how many are men? Gender makes a difference. In general, I've found women are more reflective and participative. Men are more goal driven and competitive. A mixed audience blends these qualities.

3. Age

Knowing the average age of your audience helps to frame expectations. For example, I've often found younger audiences to be more idealistic, while older audiences are more skeptical. You'll also want to consider where you fit into the group in terms of age. Younger groups or individuals may perceive you as the "wise old sage," while older groups may think of you as "Sonny." Consider how these perceptions shape your interactions.

An age range reflects diverse experience levels in the room. With wide age ranges, you'll likely have some participants who are novices and others who are experts. Knowing this will help you select appropriate activities. In a mixed group, you can balance the expertise of the experienced worker with the novel thinking of the new employee.

4. Education

Knowing the education range of your audience helps you decide the level at which to pitch your session. For example, if you are training a combination of high school and university students, you will need to incorporate enough challenge and credibility for the university students even as you emphasize the practical ideas that the high school students will want to hear. Sometimes, you will be in front of a more homogeneous group.

5. Cultural and ethnic backgrounds

Will there be a variety of cultural backgrounds among the participants? If so, which cultures will be represented? What do you need to know about cultural norms that could affect the content and process of the workshop? For example, in some cultures, eye contact is highly valued, while in others it is a sign of disrespect.

Workplace and Training Experience

When you speak with your contact person, you will want to find out as much as you can about the experience your participants have, both in their workplace and with the training topic. This information helps you to customize materials to meet participants' needs. Be sure to ask if you can interview a sample of the participants themselves. Their understandings can provide valuable insights during the audit process. Seek input in the following areas.

1. *Topic knowledge and experience*

   What does your audience already know about the training topic? Have they attended other similar workshops? Is there a mixed level of knowledge—some experts and some novices? If so, what is the ratio? Assess whether or not differences in experience will likely lead to cooperation or competition among participants.

2. *Workplace knowledge and experience*

   When you speak with your contact person, ask how long most participants have been with the organization. You will pitch your session differently if it is part of an orientation seminar for new employees than you will if it's for a group that has been with the business for years.

   Depending on the size of the group, you also might want to find out who has been around the shortest and longest time. This can guide your decisions about creating small-group sessions. Do you want to mix experience with inexperience? Some other factors to consider in this area: Are long-time employees respected and valued by colleagues? Are trainees a mix of middle management and front-line workers? Are they all engineers? Knowing the nature of the work performed by the attendees helps to determine workshop content and focus.

3. *Sensitive issues*

   Ask your contact person to make you aware of any sensitive workplace issues. Should any issues be avoided? A thorough audit will reveal political and organizational matters that should not be raised at the workshop. By avoiding sensitive issues, you respect the wishes of the contact person and keep the workshop purpose clear.

Factors Affecting Group Dynamics

A variety of factors will influence the manner in which your learners interact with one another. In order to be fully prepared for your workshop, you will want to have an idea of existing learner relationships. Consider these factors.

1. *Decision makers*

   Will there be any decision makers in the workshop? How will their presence influence the other trainees? Will they be respected or rejected by the rest of the group? Can they assist in follow-up and implementation of workshop ideas?

2. *Decision making*

   How are decisions made within this particular group? Is decision making a hierarchical process or do interdependent teams have decision-making responsibilities? Are decisions made slowly or can the group respond quickly to new ideas proposed in the training? When you understand decision-making processes that exist within the group, you will be able to use small-group feedback more effectively, choose appropriate activities and exercises, and encourage constructive feedback among participants.

3. Benefits of attending

Find out who has requested the workshop. Is it solely the idea of the management, or have the workers asked for training? Do the employees have a vested interest in the workshop topic? Will it matter to their careers? How directly or indirectly? What benefits are important to them? If employees are "forced" to attend, you can plan on minimal motivation and, possibly, negative attitudes toward the training. However, if employees have had input into the session topic you can expect them to be more motivated and committed to the learning.

4. Job successes and concerns

What successes have employees achieved that are relevant to the workshop topic? What challenges have they encountered? How can you weave these examples into the workshop without violating the privacy of the attendees? The way the group interacts will be affected by the success or lack of success individuals have experienced with the subject matter.

5. Group uniqueness

What makes this group unique? Perhaps they all commute to work, all have families, have never attended an on-site training session, or are proud of their annual Christmas project for the community. How can this information be appropriately integrated into the workshop? By finding a common thread that binds the group, you will be able to encourage a healthy group dynamic more easily.

6. Morale

Is group morale high, or do employees have unresolved issues? Recently I conducted a workshop in which most of the employees were going to be released within six months. The management considered the workshop a perk for them. Knowing this, I focused on their futures and how the workshop could help them make the transition into new work situations.

7. Existing relationships

Has this particular group trained or worked together before? How often? Have they shared experiences that are relevant to the training? Do they support each other, or is there a more competitive atmosphere? Can they work independently and interdependently? Is there anything that the trainer or contact person can do to increase participants' comfort levels?

Expectations

Whenever you prepare for a training event, you will be guided by the management's or sponsor's expectations (usually indicated through your contact person), the trainees' expectations, and your own expectations. Ideally, all three sets of expectations will be similar. By conducting an audit you will be able to address, prior to a training event, any discrepancies in expectations. As well, you will be able to make sure you understand your client's expectations of your role as trainer.

1. Organizer's top three priorities

The organizer of a training event usually has quite specific ideas about the training session. When I speak with my contact person, I ask, "What are your top three priorities for this workshop?" Or I might ask, "When training is complete, what three skills or abilities do you want participants to walk away with?" This is one of my favourite questions because I tend to get well-articulated responses.

2. Organizational culture

Does the organization have a vision statement? Does it have clearly articulated values? If so, is the vision congruent with the training that is proposed? Is training seen as one element of the learning environment? Does the company or group manifest itself as a learning organization? Often, an organization's expectations have been directly influenced by the organization's vision, values, and goals.

3. Company support

Does the organization support and value training for its employees? Will the company support employees after the training is completed? It's one thing to give employees time for training; it's quite another for the company to commit to on-the-job reinforcement of training. What are the organization's expectations of employees and the trainer regarding post-training activities?

4. Workshop topic and program theme

Is your session one of several being offered to the group? If so, how does your workshop relate to the larger program theme? For that matter, is there a program theme? How does your client see you and your session fitting into the larger scope of the training event?

5. Dress code

Will the dress code be casual or professional? As the trainer, you should dress closer to the "upper end" of the workshop dress code rather than the "lower end."

6. Participants' top three priorities

What expectations do participants have for the workshop? By finding out their top three priorities, you will get to know your trainees before a session even begins. Call some of the participants during the planning of the workshop. Indicate you'd like three to five minutes of their time. Ask them, "What three questions do you want answered in the workshop?"

Sometimes you'll find a difference between what the contact person expects and what the sampling of trainees expect. When this happens, I usually have another meeting with the contact person to discuss ways to handle both sets of expectations.

7. Trainer's top three priorities

Based on the responses you receive from your contact person and the participants, determine your own top three priorities. Ask yourself, "Based on the input I've received, what workshop messages will have a lasting impact for this audience? How can I adapt the workshop to support the key messages I've heard? Do my top three priorities support the expectations identified by the client? Are my expectations realistic in light of the time provided, the number of participants, and the working conditions?"

8. Trainer philosophy

Once you've determined your top three priorities, it's time to look at the bigger picture. Are the vision and values of the group congruent with your own? Are you comfortable working with the group? Have you been able to build a professional relationship with the client prior to the training event? If the answer to any of these questions is "no," you may want to consider whether or not you are the best candidate to provide training for this group.

Venue

Before your workshop begins, you will need to consider many factors related to the space you will be working in. The venue affects your workshop in many ways.

1. Room size

Crowded rooms have a stuffy atmosphere, literally and emotionally. Small rooms make movement awkward; heat and stale air build up quickly and people feel constrained. If you limit the physical and social movements of people, their emotional freedom is restricted as well.

As a guideline, I request 25 square feet per person. So, if I'm conducting a workshop for thirty people, I request a room that is at least 750 square feet. With these dimensions, I can devote the front two-thirds of the room to workshop space—the participants' chairs and tables, AV equipment, and work tables—and leave the back third of the room for mingling. Here, trainees can chat with a coffee or juice in hand, view the resource books on the display table, or sign-in on the Internet and check out trainer resource Web sites.

During the workshop, I use this "connecting space" for role-plays, games, challenge events, and other activities.

I also request a minimum ceiling height of 4 metres (12 feet). This gives enough vertical space for visuals to be projected high enough for all to see. The larger the group, the more important the ceiling height guideline becomes. I've trained in hotels rooms with 2.5 metre (eight foot) ceilings. With groups larger than twenty, this low ceiling becomes a hindrance when showing visuals on a screen because the screen can never be positioned high enough for learners at the back to see over the heads of the learners at the front.

the **Trainer's** EDGE

> Twenty-five square feet per person is a guideline only. Sometimes less room is required. For example, a theatre-style room (i.e. chairs in rows) requires far less space. If you require less space, consider the group size and workshop duration. The longer the workshop, the more important it is to have room that comes close to the square feet per person ideal.

2. Room location

Prior to your session, take the time to find out where your room is located. Are washrooms nearby and accessible? Are the emergency exits well marked? Where is the closest smoking area? Is it far enough away that the smoke won't spill over into the workshop room? Is it close enough that smokers can manage the eight-minute breaks? Are break-out rooms close by for subgroup activities? (In some workshops, where the main meeting room is not large enough, or where subgroups need to be separated to conduct practice exercises and role-plays, break-out rooms provide necessary space.)

3. Light and temperature controls

Are temperature gauges locked up or are they easily accessible if adjustments are needed? If they are inaccessible, find out who can make adjustments and how long it will take them to

insidescoop

In 1996, I attended a National Speakers Association conference where one of the speakers was Ken Blanchard, author of the book *The One Minute Manager*. When he was asked about the three most important aspects of a successful workshop, he replied, "The three most critical elements that help make for success in a presentation are: number one, room size; number two, room size; and number three, room size."

respond to your request. Are the temperature controls for the workshop room only, or do they affect other rooms?

Are there windows in the training room? If so, are they positioned so learners can benefit from natural lighting without being distracted by the sun's glare or by light on video or overhead screens? Do windows have shades that can be drawn?

4. Table arrangements

Room set-up influences how people perceive you and how they work together. Therefore, it is important to think about the way tables will be arranged. You want an arrangement that encourages interaction, not one that suggests a "talk and gawk" scenario. To ensure a room is set up according to my expectations, I often send the client a room layout map (see below) that shows how I want tables to be set up and indicates where audiovisual equipment and refreshments should be located.

When you're deciding on the room layout for your session, you'll need to consider a variety of factors. Appendix One outlines several table arrangement options and identifies the pros and cons of each arrangement.

Room Layout Map

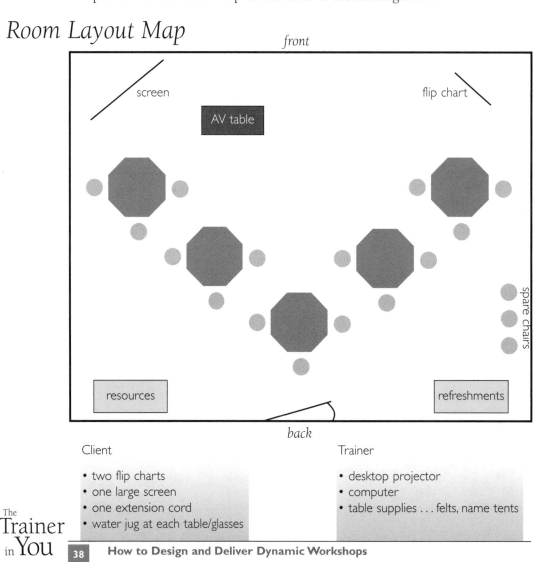

Client	Trainer
• two flip charts	• desktop projector
• one large screen	• computer
• one extension cord	• table supplies . . . felts, name tents
• water jug at each table/glasses	

5. AV equipment

At the bottom of the room layout map, list the AV equipment you require for your session. On one side of the list identify what the organizer needs to provide, and on the other side list the items you will bring. Typically, I provide a desktop projector and computer. The client provides the flip charts with paper, extension cords, and one large screen (at least 2 x 2 metres).

6. Time allotments

Confirm start and finish times with the contact person, along with the length of the lunch hour and any breaks. If lunch is provided, I'll sometimes negotiate with the class to shorten the lunch period and thus end the session sooner (by the same period of time saved at lunch).

In some workshops, I suggest two short breaks (eight to ten minutes) per half day rather than a single fifteen to twenty minute break. The shorter breaks give a better pace to the workshop, especially if participants are normally on their feet a good part of the working day. I don't recommend the more frequent short-break approach with larger groups because it can be difficult to get everyone back on task in a timely manner. Customize each workshop according to trainees' needs.

7. Microphone

I require a microphone with groups over fifty; for you it may be different. Room shape, location, and décor (e.g. rug-covered floors) also influence microphone use. Lapel mikes work great; they allow your hands to be free and give you greater movement throughout the room. Take the time to test all equipment prior to the event.

8. Competing events

It's always a good idea to check out the types of events taking place in neighbouring rooms. You don't want to be competing with a choir practice, a dance class, or a noisy party.

insidescoop

I remember conducting a seminar in Toronto. The hotel I booked had a very good workshop room available, so I booked it without checking out the details. Shortly after we began, we heard singing coming from another room. It turned out that a group had rented the room next door for a retirement party. They partied for over two hours. They seemed to be having a great time, but that wasn't the case with my group!

Additional Tips

Here are a few more tips to consider when conducting the audit.

1. Contact Person

Ensure you have a reliable contact person for the audit. You want to collect objective and insightful information about the group. This information provides the background needed to develop a customized training event that addresses individual and organizational needs.

If you do question the reliability of the information you receive, you can request permission to interview other people to complete the audit. It is important that the trainer embarks on the training event with objective and reliable information about the learners.

You should also find out if your contact person will be the same person before, during, and after the event. How do you get a hold of her before and during the workshop? If the contact person is not available, who is the alternative and what is her contact information?

2. In-house trainer

If you are an in-house trainer, it may be tempting to assume that you know your fellow workers so well that you do not need to conduct an audit. I recommend that you still take the time to ask questions, rather than make assumptions. Supervisors and managers can provide very useful insights. Also, by seeking to understand the audience, your managers will see your commitment to the workshop. This will establish your credibility, especially when you conduct follow-up with managers when the training is complete.

3. Using e-mail

I prefer phone calls to e-mail messages when conducting audits. Phone conversations allow me to interact on a more personal level with trainees or contact people. However, the demands of a trainer's timetable, combined with that of the client, sometimes make it difficult to schedule an audit by phone. The big advantage of e-mail is that it allows respondents to answer questions at their convenience.

Benefits of an Audit

It's been many years since my disastrous experience in Red Deer. Since then, I've benefited from the audit stage of the training cycle in several ways. Audits help me to accomplish the following:

Acquire Pertinent Training Material

The contact person and participants you touch base with will often share interesting, work-related stories. With permission, these stories can often be effectively integrated into your session.

Form Realistic Expectations

An audit allows you to develop realistic expectations for the training session. You may discover that the group you'll be working with is facing job insecurity, union and non-union conflicts, a dictatorial boss, or all of the above! On the other hand, you may find out that the group is coming to the session as a highly motivated, cohesive unit with a strong interest in your topic. Whatever the situation, when you know the group you can better set realistic expectations for yourself. I've found that when I'm working with a dysfunctional group it's better to focus on the present. Get them to talk constructively about their workplace situation in a spirit of mutual understanding. With a functional team, I focus more on the future and help them to develop proactive skills.

Think Audience

The audit is all about putting the workshop's focus where it's supposed to be—on the audience. Audits immerse the trainer in the group's culture, values, and norms. We learn, in advance, how our audience sees the world.

Interestingly, when we focus on our audience, not on ourselves, we become less anxious about our own performance in the workshop. One of the main reasons we fear public speaking is that we focus our energy inward instead of outward. The fear comes from thinking too much about ourselves. We forget about those we have the privilege to train because we're filled with questions about our own performance. What if I forget some of my stuff? What if I can't answer their questions? What if I'm not accepted by the group? A well-conducted audit teaches us to "think audience" rather than "think self."

Build Excitement

Audits help the trainer develop a relationship with a group before a session even begins! When I interview participants and my contact person, I become genuinely interested in the group. I look forward to meeting and working with them. It's almost as if I already know the individuals who will be participating, which increases my confidence in creating a session that will directly meet their needs. This anticipation is a wonderful way to enter the first day of training! Anticipation is one of the most exciting elements of training. You accelerate a sense of joy and purpose when you take time to meet the audience through the audit.

Develop Relationships

I believe the greatest benefit of the audit is that it allows the trainer and the contact person the opportunity to build a relationship. We all appreciate it when someone takes the time to understand our needs, wants, and interests. Taking time for an audit tells the client that you want to get to know the sponsoring organization and the trainees.

Contact Person

- Name and title _____
- Address and city _____
- Phone/Fax/E-mail _____
- Length of time with company _____
- Business card _____

- Decision-making capability _____
- Assistant's name and position _____
- Emergency numbers (names/titles) _____
- List of participants' names (if available) _____

Preliminary Factors

- Topic(s): Am I qualified? _____
- Date(s): Am I available? _____
- Location: Travel time involved? _____

Workshop Budget

- Allocated for event/program _____
- Honorarium, GST, rate/day _____
- Travel (car/air) _____
- Accommodation and meals _____
- Customized manual _____
- Workshop instruments _____
- Cabs, parking, other _____

Demographics

- Number of participants _____
- Where are participants coming from _____

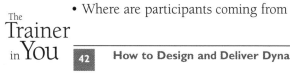

- Male/female ratio _____

- Average age/age range _____

- Range/level of education _____

- Cultural/ethnic representation _____

Workplace/Training Experience

Note: Ideally, you will be given the opportunity to ask participants about the topics covered in this and the following section (Factors Affecting Group Dynamics), not just the contact person.

- Participant's knowledge of topic _____

- Participant's experience with topic _____

- Other topics trained in _____

- Nature of participant's work _____

- How long with organization _____

Factors Affecting Group Dynamics

- Management personnel attending _____

- Management-employee rapport _____

- Decision-makers present _____

- Work in teams or independently _____

- Benefits of attending _____

- Who requested event _____

- Attendance voluntary or mandatory _____

- Examples of job successes _____

- Examples of job challenges _____

- Do learners know each other _____

- Common background/experience _____

- Who is most influential in group _____

- Who is most resistant _____

- Late comers/early departures _____

Organization Expectations

- Organizer's top three priorities   _____

_____

_____

- Organization vision/values   _____

- How does the company support training?   _____

- Sensitive issues   _____

- Dress code   _____

- Course advertising (Can I obtain copy?)   _____

- How much training per year   _____

- What kind of training/by whom   _____

- Other training during this event?   _____

- If so, other speakers   _____

- Program theme   _____

Participant Expectations
(Note: Ask participants only.)

Participants' top three priorities   _____

_____

_____

The Venue

- Room dimensions   _____

- Ceiling height   _____

- Lighting controls   _____

- Temperature restrictions   _____

- Table sizes/shapes   _____

- AV equipment already in room   _____

- AV equipment provided by trainer   _____

- Times of workshop: beginning/ending   _____

- Location of event/room   _____

- Workshop location familiar to attendees   _____

- Get in early for set-up $\rule{6cm}{0.4pt}$

- Events in neighbouring rooms $\rule{6cm}{0.4pt}$

- Refreshment arrangements $\rule{6cm}{0.4pt}$

- Meal arrangements $\rule{6cm}{0.4pt}$

- Parking $\rule{6cm}{0.4pt}$

Business Culture

- Copy of mission statement $\rule{6cm}{0.4pt}$

- Company achievements $\rule{6cm}{0.4pt}$

- Primary focus of time and energy $\rule{6cm}{0.4pt}$

- Values held by employees $\rule{6cm}{0.4pt}$

- Copies of newsletter/annual reports $\rule{6cm}{0.4pt}$

Questions for Self

- Has the audience met me before? Where?

- Why was I selected to do this workshop?

- My top three priorities

- Target message

- Best way to build rapport

- Goals to be achieved with group

- Company philosophy congruent
  with mine

- Links to participants/topic/time/place

- This event will be successful if ...

- Appropriate follow-up with group

The Assessment

Of course, all of the planning that takes place in the audit stage should lead to a successful workshop. But in the training business there are no guarantees. Let's skip ahead for a moment. The workshop is complete. Folks are leaving. But is it really over?

Not quite. I'd like to add one more step that is of prime value to the trainer and sponsor: the assessment. During the assessment, you reflect on what happened, what could have happened, and, in some cases, what should have happened. In other words, after all has been said and done, we need to take a look at what was said and done.

Generally, I conduct three types of assessments: In-the-Moment surveys, End-of-Session evaluations, and Follow-up Questionnaires.

In-the-Moment Surveys

In-the-Moment surveys are conducted during the training session itself. At appropriate times throughout the day—just prior to a break, for example—learners take a couple of minutes to complete the survey. Then you summarize the results, either on flip chart paper, a white board, or an overhead transparency. Together, the trainer and participants review the survey results during a reporting session conducted either when participants come back from a break or when they return the next day. In a one-day workshop, I would suggest administering the In-the-Moment survey just before lunch. In a two- or three-day workshop, administer the survey at the end of the first and second day.

I like using these surveys because they keep me abreast of both positive and negative reactions to the workshop as it proceeds. I'm able to be proactive, rather than reactive, in addressing learners' needs. In other words, In-the-Moment surveys enable the trainer to assess both "hot spots" and "happy spots" as they surface in the workshop. If I receive several negative responses to the workshop, I discuss them with the group at the commencement of the next part of the session. By identifying concerns "in the moment," rather than letting them fester, both the trainer and the learners have the opportunity to work through the issues. Ignoring problem areas or delaying responses to concerns only exacerbates the situation and may put reconciliation out of reach.

When the overall tone of the workshop is positive (i.e. filled with happy spots) the trainer can continue with the planned agenda. In these situations, the reporting time is usually brief. The class proceeds aware that its needs are addressed, the training is working, and the time is well spent.

By responding immediately to learner feedback, learners can see that I value their input. I'm also given the opportunity to emphasize that the success of the workshop is not just up to me. It is a shared responsibility. By periodically taking the pulse of your group and responding immediately to their needs, both trainer and learners become accountable.

Sample In-the-Moment Survey

The Workshop So Far

Instructions: Circle the number that best indicates how you feel about today's session thus far.

I'm finding the session to be:

On the mark	1	2	3	4	5	Not relevant
Interactive	1	2	3	4	5	Talk and Gawk
Organized	1	2	3	4	5	Disorganized
Relaxed	1	2	3	4	5	Tense
Appropriately paced	1	2	3	4	5	Too fast/slow
Interesting	1	2	3	4	5	Boring
At my level	1	2	3	4	5	Overwhelming
Worth my time	1	2	3	4	5	Not a good choice

Specific concerns I have at this time are: _____

_____

_____

_____

_____

_____

For your compliment bin: _____

_____

_____

_____

_____

_____

If your concerns need my attention, please leave your name and I will touch base with you as soon as possible.

_____

Name

Modifying the Survey

The sample survey provided is just one way to gather class feedback during the actual session. You can modify the survey by trying out some of the options described here.

1. Sentence Stems

Ask participants to complete sentences such as "The best idea so far is . . ." or "I am still confused about. . . ."

2. Verbal Feedback

Collect verbal feedback by asking open-ended questions. Take a few minutes at appropriate times (for example during breaks) to ask questions like these:

> What is working for you now?

> What would you like more of/less of?

> What questions are still unanswered for you?

> How is the pace of the workshop for you?

> What opportunities have you had to connect with other learners?

> Is enough time being given for Q&A?

3. Group Representatives

If you are working with a large group, individual feedback may not be an effective way to gauge the group's frame of mind. Instead, have the class appoint several representatives who will meet with the instructor at predetermined times to share their reactions. The questions suggested in the Verbal Feedback section (above), can be used to guide your discussion with the representatives.

End-of-Session Evaluations

As the name implies, End-of-Session evaluations are completed at the close of a workshop. They can be used along with In-the-Moment surveys, or, especially for short sessions, on their own. These evaluations are usually brief because, at the end of a session, trainees often don't want to spend much time on assessments. They may be tired from a long day (or a few days) of training, keen to get home to their families, or have other commitments to attend to. Here are some points (both good and bad) to consider when choosing to use End-of-Session evaluations.

☹ End-of-Session evaluations are sometimes called "smile sheets" because of their brevity and the impulsive responses they can generate. Some trainers find that adequate time is not provided to receive quality responses from the participants.

☹ Some people who use this type of assessment find they tend to get feedback that reflects either the euphoria of the moment after a good workshop or the negative comments that accompany a poor one. In other words, the comments made may be shallow and influenced too much by the emotion of the moment.

☺ This may be the only feedback the trainer will receive from some participants. Not everyone will be interested in or take the time to complete lengthier Follow-up Questionnaires that come two to three weeks after the workshop. For some participants, the best time to provide feedback is right now.

☺ Some participants give candid and practical comments in the End-of-Session evaluations. Their brevity and boldness is refreshing and the trainer benefits from the insights.

☺ Feedback is immediate for the trainer. When you've had a good session, handshakes, smiles, and enthusiastic comments will be shared with you in the wrap-up. But, for some trainers, there's nothing like seeing positive comments in writing. It is a wonderful endorsement of the strong and effective efforts you've made. And when the comments are critical or negative, you are given the opportunity to reflect on how you could have done things differently. In other words, both positive and negative comments have value.

☺ Some of the best quotations I've ever received for marketing my business have come from the "smile sheets." People are attracted to testimonials. Having an ample supply of these quotations adds credibility to a trainer's brochure, Web site, and business letters. Trainers can ask, typically at the bottom of the End-of-Session evaluation form, to use the comments for marketing purposes.

Sample End-of-Session Evaluation

End of Session Evaluation

Name _____

Rated Responses

Directions: Circle the number that best indicates your response to the following categories..

	Poor	Average	Above Average	Excellent
1. My level of knowledge increased..................................	1	2	3	4
2. Questions were handled adequately..............................	1	2	3	4
3. The workshop was well organized..............................	1	2	3	4
4. The learner manual was helpful.…….........................	1	2	3	4
5. What I learned will be useful..1		2	3	4
6. I would recommend this workshop to colleagues.......... 1		2	3	4

Written Responses

The two things I liked best about this workshop are:

The two things I would change about this workshop are:

Thank you for completing this workshop evaluation form. Your feedback is highly valued!

Would you like information on other training opportunities our company offers?

Name: _____

Address: _____

Position: _____ Company: _____

City/Prov: _____ Postal Code: _____

Permission is granted to use my comments and name in public brochures: yes ☐ no ☐

Additional Tips

In order to encourage reflective, useful feedback with End-of-Session evaluations, consider the following:

- Before passing out the End-of-Session evaluations, let learners know who will be reading their comments. If they know the comments are just for you, they may respond differently than they would if management was to read them.

- You may receive more straightforward comments if you make the End-of-Session evaluation form confidential. Give learners the option of not including their name on the form. This confidentially option may prevent self-censoring of comments.

- Emphasize the value of the feedback. Let the group know their ideas will encourage continual growth and enhancement of the program and the trainer!

- Give the End-of-Session evaluation prominence as *one of several* concluding activities. If you make it the last item in the workshop you can implicitly diminish its value.

- Plan adequate time for learners to complete the evaluation without rushing. This will provide an opportunity for reflective, synthesized responses.

- Avoid sacrificing the evaluation just because you want to get the last word in. Sometimes you'll find the end of the session is approaching and you really want to finish the last module. This pushes the course evaluation to the very end of the day. Don't be surprised if the quality of comments significantly declines.

- Wait to compliment learners until after the End-of-Session evaluations have been completed. It may be seen as self-serving if you compliment the learners prior to giving out the evaluation.

Follow-up Questionnaires

This assessment occurs three weeks to three months after the workshop. The Follow-up Questionnaire assesses the organizational aspects of the workshop and perceived learner value. It can be sent to the participants, the contact person, and/or the manager.

Follow-up Questionnaires are valuable because the responses give information not about what each participant *intended* to do but about what they are *actually doing*. The Follow-up Questionnaire will give you an accurate picture of how–if at all–learners are using the ideas they've learned. It will also reveal the obstacles they encounter when they seek to incorporate new knowledge and skills in the work place. This information will guide you in planning future workshops.

I like Follow-up Questionnaires because the feedback I receive is insightful and thought provoking. The comments come after reflection on what can realistically be used from training. This is trainer's gold! Great nuggets of wisdom are provided for use in future programs and trainer performances.

On the next few pages I've provided a sample Follow-up Questionnaire. You'll notice that I give Part One to the learners during the workshop and ask them to fill out pertinent sections. They keep one copy in their learners' manuals and give another copy to me.

Then I mail (or e-mail) the partially completed Part One and the not yet started Part Two to the learners approximately three weeks after the workshop. The learners finish Part One and respond to the participant section of Part Two. Then they forward these to the manager who completes the manager section of Part Two and returns both forms to me.

Sample Follow-up Questionnaire

Follow-up Questionnaire: Part One

1. Now that I've reviewed the modules we've covered in the workshop, please complete the Workshop Module column below.

2. Then, determine how you will apply your new knowledge/skills to the work place. Include this information in the Action Plan column.

3. Now, rank your actions, 1 indicating the most important.

4. Submit your questionnaire to me and make a second copy in your learning manual.

5. In about three weeks, I will follow up on this activity to see how you've progressed in accomplishing your goals. At that time, you can complete the Status Column.

Workshop Modules	Action Plan	Priority Ranking	Status (3 wks. later)
A. _____ _____	Work Challenge: _____ _____ What I'll apply: _____ _____ _____	_____	Done Half Way Not Done
B. _____ _____	Work Challenge: _____ _____ What I'll apply: _____ _____ _____	_____	Done Half Way Not Done
C. _____ _____	Work Challenge: _____ _____ What I'll apply: _____ _____ _____	_____	Done Half Way Not Done
D. _____ _____	Work Challenge: _____ _____ What I'll apply: _____ _____ _____	_____	Done Half Way Not Done

Sample Follow-up Questionnaire

Follow-up Questionnaire: Part Two

Participant Form

Follow-up Instructions

Hello and thank you for taking the time to complete this part of the Follow-up Questionnaire. It has been about three weeks since our session and I'm wondering if you've had the opportunity to apply your new learning in the work place.

When we last met, I asked you to complete the first three columns of Part One of the Follow-up Questionnaire (see attached). Now, I'd like you to take the time to see how you've progressed with meeting your goals. Please take a few minutes to review Part One of the questionnaire; focus on the Action Plan column and complete the Status column. If you were able to complete your plan, circle "Done." If you have been partially successful in completing your plan, circle "Half Way." If you were not able to apply your plan, then circle "Not Done."

Could you now take a few minutes to complete the following questions? Your responses will provide me with insights into the effectiveness of the workshop.

Follow-up Questions

What situations and/or people at work helped you to complete your plan?

What roadblocks prevented the successful completion of your plan?

Do you have other comments about the workshop or your current situation?

Sample Follow-up Questionnaire

Follow-up Questionnaire: Part Two
Manager Form

Thank you for your support in allowing _____ (name of participant) to attend the _____ (name of workshop) that finished on _____ (date). I appreciate your interest in this individual's professional development.

During the last three weeks, _____ (name of participant) has been working on completing an action plan begun on the last day of the workshop. Could you take a few minutes to complete the questions below regarding _____ 's (name of participant) progress.

1. Did you observe any changes in the behavioural skills, attitude, and/or performance of the employee? Please be specific (refer to their action plan as needed).

2. Were you able to support this person in implementing the action plan? If so, what support did you give?

3. Any additional comments

_____   _____
Instructor's Name   Course

Please e-mail this completed form back to me. Your responses are confidential, highly valued, and will play a central role in the ongoing development and improvement of our workshop programs. Thank you!

Additional Tips

Follow-up Questionnaires are a good idea for several reasons. They provide learners with the opportunity to gauge the effects of their learning; they provide trainers with valuable information for ensuing workshops; and they encourage managers to support ongoing learning in the workplace. To get the best results from the Follow-up Questionnaires, trainers should take the following steps:

- Involve managers in the Follow-up Questionnaires whenever possible. They are usually the ones who released the dollars and granted employees time to attend the workshop. Involving them is usually well received and helps managers assess the value of training.

- Make sure the Follow-up Questionnaire provides the opportunity for feedback on both product (i.e. ideas, skills, and values learned) and process (i.e. the learning environment, and elements such as pacing, involvement, and comfort).

- When you receive feedback, review and summarize it carefully. Ask yourself: What patterns or trends are revealed? What does the feedback mean in terms of my delivery of the session? Record these observations for use in future workshops. (A sample trainer's summary is provided at the end of this chapter.)

- I've found the response rate to Follow-up Questionnaires improves if I let learners know in advance that I'll be in touch with them after the session. I let them know when I will send the questionnaires and how they will be sent (mail or e-mail). Sometimes I remind learners about the follow-up by sending e-mail messages one week prior to sending the Follow-up Questionnaires themselves. I've also found that I get a better response to Follow-up Questionnaires sent by e-mail. E-mail also has the advantage of allowing returned data to be easily transferred into a summary document.

- If you do not have the time or resources to do Follow-up Questionnaires, but still have a desire to assess learner progress, take a few minutes to compose one e-mail message that can be sent to all learners. Send this out three weeks after the workshop. Or, if you have a bit more time, make a phone call to either a sampling of the learners or all of the learners.

The Value of Assessment: Change, Challenge, and Choice

No matter which type of assessment you choose, I am convinced you will find this component of the training process invaluable. It is important to follow up at whatever level you can manage. Here are the three areas that have added value to my training since I started incorporating the assessment stage into my training plan.

Change

Quality feedback received during, upon completion, and several weeks after a training event provide the basis for ongoing change in the workshop. Astute observation and recommendations from participants will "teach" the trainer. Whether comments are positive or negative, you should recognize feedback as a gift.

Challenge

I'm convinced that the best research you can conduct to develop your business is found in the feedback and fruitful comments of the learners who watch you in action. Trendy newsletters and professional development may provide useful tips and strategies, but they pale in comparison with the direct, relevant, and specific comments that will challenge you to improve your sessions.

Choice

Because of the wealth of information you receive in the assessment stage of the training process, you will be able to make choices that improve future programs. You can use feedback to modify your style, your content, your organizational approaches, and your expectations. When I launched full-time into the training business in 1990, I had one flagship program. Now I have five. This expansion has been inspired, in good measure, by learner feedback. By increasing the choices for the learner, you make your training messages even more practical and powerful!

Sample
Summary of Feedback Form

Summary of Feedback

Product Summary

What did feedback teach me about course content? Was it complete, at the group's level, and practical? Are the knowledge and skills being used?

Process Summary

What did feedback teach me about the workshop environment? Were learners comfortable? Was there enough involvement? Did their questions get answered? Did the workshop inspire them? Were their social and emotional needs met? How did I feel?

Possible Changes for Future Workshops

List, in order of priority, aspects of the workshop that I want to add, change, or delete for the next delivery.

HUGHism

"Audits ensure workshop success today.
Assessments guarantee workshop success tomorrow."

References

Pike, Robert W. 1989. *Creative training techniques handbook: tips, tactics, and how-to's for delivering effective training.* Minneapolis, MN.: Lakewood Books.

Shula, D., and K. Blanchard. 1995. *Everyone's a coach: You can inspire anyone to be a winner.* Grand Rapids, MI.: Zondervan Publishing House.

Chapter 4:
Purpose-Driven Training

Second only to freedom, learning is the most precious option on earth.
Norman Cousins

Training must get results.

In chapters 1, 2, and 3, we learned about the eight-A training cycle: Audit, Affiliation, Attention, Acquisition, Application, Action, Affirmation, and Assessment. However, these A's do not establish the purpose or goals for the workshop. The questions remains: What do you want to accomplish in the training event? What are the training outcomes you want to achieve?

In determining your outcomes, remember, "The critical question is not what topics to cover but what do you want the participants to value, understand and do with those topics?" (Silberman, 27).

Developing Training Outcomes

Let's return to the audit phase of the training cycle to guide us in the development of training outcomes.

The information gathered in the audit enables you to tailor a program that meets the specific needs and interests of your learners. By using a series of questions like those outlined in the sample audit (page 42), you learn about the unique and common interests of your group.

Once you've gathered and assessed all of this information, you will find you have the answers to three basic questions. Based on the results of the audit, ask yourself:

- What do I want participants to *understand?*

- What do I want participants to *value?*

- What do I want participants to *do?*

I summarize the actions associated with each of these questions—understanding, valuing, and doing—using three "H" words: head, heart, and hands. When we understand, we use our heads to think through processes and ideas; when we value, we use our hearts to develop attitudes toward the training topic; and when we do, we use our hands to perform actions. I use the head, heart, and hands concept to guide me in the development of strong training outcomes.

Types of Training Outcomes

Head outcomes

Head outcomes represent the knowledge that will be obtained at a workshop. Head outcomes focus on the academic aspects of training. As the subject-matter expert who shares knowledge and wisdom with the group, you are responsible for ensuring participants leave the session knowing more than they did when they arrived. Outcomes in this area address the cognitive or intellectual needs of a learner and reflect the concepts that participants need to know and understand to perform more competently.

Heart outcomes

Heart outcomes refer to the attitudes and values that shape the training scenario. When you develop heart outcomes, your goal is to cultivate desire, motivation, and inspiration in the learners. This type of learning, referred to as affective learning, focuses on attitudes, feelings, beliefs, or preferences. Heart outcomes need to outline the types of attitudes you want your learners to value and appreciate by the end of training.

Hands outcomes

Hands outcomes ensure participants are given the opportunity to practice new skills. In the hands-on sessions, learners gain direct experience by performing and refining their skills. This psychomotor or behavioural learning teaches trainees who lack a skill to perform a new skill confidently and capably at work. Your outcomes need to refer specifically to the techniques, methods, procedures, and operations you want trainees to learn.

Sample Training Outcomes

When you create training outcomes, use a format that is clear and concise. I often write outcomes by completing the phrase: "By the end of the training event, learners will be able to . . . "

Let's take at look at the outcomes I developed for my national seminar Speaking with Class.

Outcomes	Type
By the end of the workshop, attendees will be able to	
• Reduce planning time by 50 percent using the new SMARTpad system	Head
• Develop clear, concise, and credible self expression	Hands
•Target or customize a presentation for each audience	Head
• Design high-impact openings and closings	Hands
• Learn to maximize PowerPoint visuals	Head
• Deal effectively with difficult questions	Heart
• Develop skills that persuade and motivate an audience	Hands
• Value the need to adapt their style for each audience	Heart
• Receive customized coaching through interactive practice sessions and video	Head
• Set an action plan for continued improvement	Hands

Preparing Effective Training Outcomes

Preparing effective training outcomes takes time. You cannot just jot down ideas and hope they'll work. Use these tips to create concrete, meaningful outcomes for each session.

 • Use action words or verbs to make your outcomes come alive. (The verbs will often occur at the beginning of the sentence, as in the sample above, but this may not always be the case.)

 • Keep your outcome sentences short and crisp. Be specific, not general. Avoid overworked phrases or jargon. Say it in plain English.

 • Usually a training design that incorporates all three kinds of outcomes—head, heart, and hands—has the best chance to result in lasting change. With highly technical topics, you will automatically want to focus on head outcomes, that is, the information participants need to know. But to limit yourself to just one kind of outcome can, in the end, do a disservice to the trainees and to the organizers of the training. With technical topics, learners need to know more about the topic (head outcomes), but they also need to know how to apply the new knowledge back at work (hands outcomes).

• Because heart outcomes are harder to measure, it may be tempting to avoid using them. Heart outcomes, however, provide much of the driving force behind what is accomplished in training. In order to make heart outcomes work in your session, model the values, attitudes, and beliefs that you want your learners to exhibit.

• In some training events, particularly in the non-technical or people-oriented fields, training outcomes can be developed together with participants during the opening session. Learners determine what they need and want from the course. Combine this with your views to develop a set of agreed-upon outcomes.

• In order to avoid having too many outcomes for the length of a session, make the distinction between what learners *need to know, value, and do* and what would be *nice to know, value, and do*. You might even want to discuss this distinction with the organizers. What do they deem to be a *must* for trainees to perform more effectively? Remember, you only have so much time for training. You need to determine what is fair and reasonable for the trainer *and* the trainees.

• Avoid "over-working" the training outcomes or relying on them too heavily. This is particularly true for non-technical workshops. For example, when teaching leadership skills, don't focus on the hard and fast, the black and white, the right and wrong. Learners need the freedom to interpret the trainer's knowledge, values, and models of action in their own ways. Focus on getting learners to think through issues and apply principles, values, and appropriate actions. Outcomes should serve more as guidelines than rigid specifications.

the Trainer's EDGE

Useful Action Verbs for Training Outcomes

Head verbs	define	describe	differentiate	formulate
	illustrate	learn	list	measure
	name	reduce	remember	restate
	review	select	understand	update
	write			
Heart verbs	appraise	appreciate	assume	assure
	collaborate	compare	contrast	control
	deal	endorse	evaluate	feel
	interpret	maximize	place	recommend
	share	stimulate	value	verify
Hands verbs	administer	adopt	collaborate	conduct
	coordinate	delegate	design	develop
	disseminate	execute	exercise	implement
	instruct	manage	measure	notify
	plan	practice	prepare	set
	solve	supervise	train	

Benefits of Training Outcomes

Over the years, I've learned first-hand about the many benefits of carefully developed training outcomes. Here are a few of the ways I believe they will improve your training sessions.

1. When you develop training outcomes, you identify *trainer* expectations for the training session. As well, clearly stated outcomes provide *learners* with a list of course expectations. This helps establish *trainer and learner* accountability because outcomes make clear what we will understand, value, and do at the end of training. The value of preparing outcomes leads to greater commitment from both the trainees and the trainer.

2. Sometimes learners come into a training session with unrealistic expectations of the amount that can be accomplished in a one- or two-day training event. By setting reasonable outcomes, trainers and learners are able to determine realistic expectations and learners will not be overwhelmed or vexed by excessive amounts of information or ideas. Learners will see that the goals set are attainable.

In one of my "Train the Trainer" workshops in Calgary, we had to make the distinction between "need to know" and "nice to know" early in the workshop. Trainers were inundated with massive amounts of information to transfer to new employees. The manual we were given weighed over three kilograms, and we were expected to cover it all in only five days.

Obviously, our initial goal was not to figure out how to pack it all in quicker, but to assess what was "needed" and what was "nice." Fortunately, the trainers all had the experience required to make those determinations. The end result was a program that comprised only the information that learners *needed to know*. The *nice to know* was allocated to reference and background material.

3. Determining training outcomes helps to ensure that learners will receive all the essential information about a training topic. Time will be invested, not wasted. Topics will focus on the material that is essential for the trainee to understand, value, and do so that they perform more effectively and efficiently when they return to work.

4. When you thoughtfully prepare and write training outcomes, learners will notice the high value you attach to the training event. Your actions say, "We're all here with at least one thing in common—becoming better at what we do."

5. When you have well-articulated outcomes, many learners will use them to set goals for themselves during training and after training. You are giving learners the tools necessary to accept responsibility for their training. Shared goals give direction and purpose to the training event.

With the eight A's leading the way and strong training outcomes to guide us, let's look at some practical techniques for incorporating the A's into your sessions and enhancing your training results.

HUGHism

"The A's give us a plan
The H's give us a purpose
8 A's + 3 H's = Success 4 You!"

References

Silberman, Melvin L. 1990. *Active training: Handbook of techniques, designs, case examples and tips.* Lexington, MA: Lexington Books.

Chapter 5: Affiliation Techniques

Artistry, intuition, and quick emotional and intellectual reflexes are what help teachers survive–not rigid adherence to a particular set of techniques.

Jonathan Azp

There are days you never forget.

August 3rd, 2001, was one of those days. After five months of endless drills and tedious memorization of routines in rain, sun, wind, and even some hail, our daughter, Kimberly, and 4,000 other volunteers welcomed the world to Edmonton, Alberta, at the Opening Ceremonies of the 2001 World Championships in Athletics. And what a fabulous gala event it was!

Over three billion people tuned in to watch the arrival of more than 4,500 athletes from 63 countries. With great pride, a crowd of more than 60,000 sang *O Canada* as the athletes marched into the stadium. Then, to everyone's delight, at the crack of a pistol, the men's marathon kicked off the celebration. More than two hours later, at the conclusion of the opening ceremonies, the winner of the marathon would cross the finish line. Our daughter was one of the many dancers who welcomed the athletes and spectators to this grand event.

Now, imagine the Worlds with no opening ceremonies. What if the event just began? No hoopla, no fanfare. No special recognition of the years of dedicated training by the athletes. No welcome to the world watching.

Perhaps a training workshop doesn't rate the attention of the Worlds, but it does require, like any human event, a welcome. Participants are taking time out of their

Dear Hugh,

I've heard that, at the outset of training, many learners will feel quite anxious until a number of pressing questions have been addressed. What could they possibly be wondering about?

Regards,
Baffled in Barrhead

Dear Baffled,

Yes, your learners will have a number of critical and urgent questions they'd like to have answered early in the workshop. Here are just a few things they may be wondering about.

What are the instructor expectations?
Am I going to be put on the spot?
When are the breaks and for how long?
What is being covered? Does it match the brochure?

Is there anybody here that I know?
How am I going to benefit from this training?
Is there a smoking area?

I wonder where I fit academically and experientially with this group?
Will the instructor ask that cell phones to be turned off? I sure hope so!
Is this instructor experienced and qualified?

Try to address some of these common questions in the affiliation stage of your workshop and you'll be off to a fine start!

Sincerely,
Hugh

busy lives to learn and enhance their skills, and this needs to be acknowledged. And the welcome needs to be more than, "Hi, glad you're here." Like all other parts of the workshop, the affiliation stage needs to be carefully prepared, so participants can share in a worthwhile and memorable event.

So, take time to plan your workshop welcome—that is to say, your affiliation event. Whether you're teaching a half-day or a five-day workshop, think carefully about how to begin. The following techniques help to foster strong *learner affiliations, trainer affiliations,* and *topic affiliations.*

Learner Affiliation

Learner Affiliation techniques, also called warmer-uppers or ice-breakers, help to establish a friendly environment at the beginning of a program. They are meant to relieve learners' anxieties, address learners' questions, and encourage comfortable and mutually beneficial interaction. Learner Affiliation techniques in this section include:

Name Tents
Ray of Sunshine
Partner Intros
I Am
Solo Intro
Group Résumé

the Trainer's EDGE

While I use the terms "warmer-upper" and "ice-breaker" in this book, you may want to avoid them in the actual session. For some participants, these words have negative connotations. Instead, use terms like "opening activity" or "welcome exercise" to introduce learner affiliation activities.

Name Tents

Ready

Purpose:	To enhance the comfort level of participants by building participant rapport and initiating participant interaction.
Time:	Approximately seven minutes
Group size:	Up to fifty
Learner risk:	Low
Materials:	Name tents, markers

Set

• Distribute name tents and markers to each table.

• Ahead of time, create five open-ended questions that you will have participants respond to on the back of the name tent. Prepare a sample name tent with the five questions. (See sample on the next page.)

Go

• Begin by asking participants to write their names on the front of the name tent with the markers you've provided.

• Ask participants to turn the name tent over and write the numbers one to five down the left hand side of the back of the name tent. Show the participants a sample name tent with the numbering.

• Indicate that you'll be asking five questions and that you'd like them to write responses to the questions beside the corresponding number. Then ask five open-ended questions. For example: Where is a place you like to spend time? What two things are you good at? What three things are important to you? In four words or fewer, describe yourself five years from now. In five words or fewer, describe your expectations for this workshop.

• Once the learners have responded to the questions, ask them to take their name tent, leave their seat, and meet four people in the room. (Note: If you don't instruct them to leave, they'll often remain seated.)

• As they pair up with other participants, they should introduce themselves and then ask the other member to share his or her answer to one of the five questions. For example, when Jane walks up to Jim, she introduces herself and then asks Jim what his response is for, let's say, question number 3. When Jim has completed giving his response to question 3, he introduces himself and asks Jane her response to, say, question number 1. Inform participants that they do not need to record the information you learn. Simply listen to the other learner and move on to a new pairing.

- Repeat the exchange of first names and responses with three other people. Let participants know they have four minutes to meet four people.

- When participants have each met four people, they return to their seats.

Sample Name Tent

1.
2.
3.
4.
5.

reverse side
of name tent
*Have participants print
numbers 1 to 5 here at
the left hand margin.*

Rewards

- This is a non-threatening activity with virtually no intimidation factor. When participants leave to meet four people, they already have their responses prepared. Plus, they are only meeting four people, not ten. This activity will be over quickly.

Risks

- Some learners will want to meet more than four people. So be clear on your instructions.

Options

- Customize your questions to meet the interests of the group. With short workshops, you may want to link the questions directly to the workshop topic.

- On the back of the name tents, print workshop guidelines. Learners will have had the opportunity to read the guidelines before class begins. You could include expectations regarding punctuality, confidentiality, and participation. As the session begins, you can review and expand upon these guidelines.

Ray of Sunshine

Ready

Purpose:	To facilitate introductions and guide participants in getting to know one another better.
Time:	Approximately five minutes
Group size:	Up to fifty
Learner risk:	Low
Materials:	Ray of Sunshine Activity Sheet, pen or pencil

Set

• Conduct some research on the group to discover areas of special or shared interest.

• Design questions for the activity that reflect your findings. For example, when working with a group of architects in Vancouver, I dug up a few Internet articles on that city's architecture. Some of the questions included on that Ray of Sunshine sheet were based on this information.

• Choose questions that are short and sweet and that can be answered quickly and without offence. Some questions can focus on personal information (hobbies, interests) while others can be professional or job focused.

• Prepare your Ray of Sunshine sheet by incorporating the questions or comments you have researched onto the rays radiating from the sun's face. One question or comment is allotted to each ray. (See sample on the next page.)

Go

• Provide each participant with a Ray of Sunshine sheet. Ask them to read the question or comment on each of the rays.

• Tell trainees that they will be asked to leave their seats and ask another participant to respond to the question/comment on one of the rays. The person they approach should not be from the same subgroup. They can only get one answer from each person they approach. When they receive a response, they need to record it just below the question, along with the person's first name.

• Trainees continue to meet other learners for responses to the questions/comments on the other rays. Let participants know they have five minutes to complete the Ray of Sunshine sheet. When the sheet is complete, participants return to their seats.

Sample Ray of Sunshine

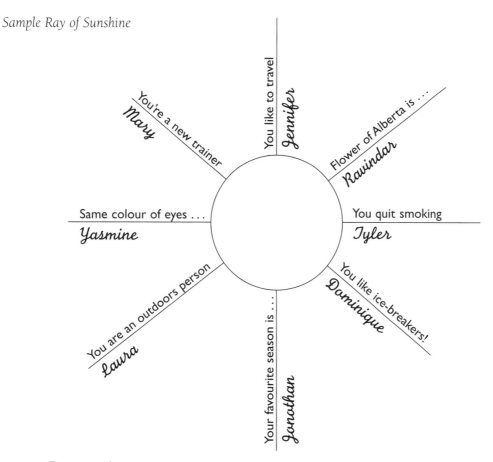

Rewards

• With this exercise, you can discover both personal and professional aspects of an individual in a non-threatening environment.

Risks

• Some people do not like having to complete a worksheet. You can limit the number of people these individuals have to meet.

Options

• Encourage participants to get several responses from the same person.

• Use riddles or quotations instead of questions. Quotations may be related to the company or organization.

• After the responses have been gathered and everyone is back with their subgroup, ask volunteers to share answers for each of the ray's questions. This works well either as an exercise for the whole group or within each subgroup.

• The sample above has eight rays. With larger groups, use twelve to sixteen rays.

Solo Intro

Ready

Purpose:	To help participants get to know each other quickly and have fun.
Time:	Approximately ten minutes
Group size:	Up to thirty
Learner risk:	Low
Materials:	Flip chart, felt pens

Set

• Prepare a flip chart ahead of time with these four headings:

Birthplace, Position, One Hobby, Name.

Go

• Draw the group's attention to the flip chart and ask participants to introduce themselves to the group guided by the outline on the flip chart. It does not matter in which order they choose to answer the questions.

• Let them know that they will each have up to fifteen seconds to respond to all four headings. You may want to introduce yourself to demonstrate the 15-second time frame.

• Ask participants to stand when they introduce themselves and to position themselves so they can see the rest of the group. This does not mean they have to come to the front of the room. (Note: During this exercise, the trainer should sit at the side or back of the room so the focus remains on the participants.)

Rewards

• This activity avoids putting people on the spot by letting them speak using a short and interesting outline.

Risks

• These four headings may seem straightforward, but don't assume everyone will know what you're getting at. The first time I did this activity I didn't explain what "position" meant. One man got up and said, "Birthplace: Melville, Saskatchewan; Position: I like being on top." The crowd burst out in laughter and took the humour as it was intended. But his quip reminded me to never assume my meaning is clear!

• I've found that if the first one or two participants keep to the 15-second timeframe, then most will keep it short. If the first one exceeds the 15-second time fame, however, you should tactfully remind the group of the time allowance so the activity doesn't consume too much time.

Options

• Some trainers use this activity in the opening. I like using it a little later in the workshop when comfort has been established and there is a genuine interest and need to connect with other participants.

• After the introductions have been made, go around the room and ask participants to recall the hobby of each participant. When I do this, I randomly choose learners instead of going table by table. I call this a "memory jog" and, besides being fun, this adaptation helps you and the trainees remember participant names.

• When all of the introductions are complete, include yourself in the exercise.

Sample Solo Intro

Birthplace
Position
One Hobby
Name

Group Résumé

Ready

Purpose:	To provide concrete examples of the talent and resources that exist in the group.
Time:	Approximately twenty-five minutes
Group size:	Up to forty
Learner risk:	Low
Materials:	Flip chart, felt pens

Set

• Determine how many learners will be attending the session and plan accordingly. If your group has more than ten people, I suggest dividing them into subgroups of about four to six participants.

• On a flip chart or white board, list the following:

   • *Educational background*　　　　　• *Years of work*
   • *Types of work experiences*　　• *Hobbies*
   • *Adult education courses*

Go

• If you've done this activity before, then draw the group's attention to a sample group résumé from a previous workshop. If not, advise the group that they will be compiling a résumé for each subgroup based on the headings provided. Indicate the headings which you wrote ahead of time on the board or flip chart.

• To construct the résumé, have each subgroup collect information on each other that would build an impressive group résumé. Within each subgroup, the information is recorded on a flip chart. Names are optional.

• Once the information is gathered, have each subgroup hang its flip chart page for the rest of the group to see.

• Have each subgroup appoint a spokesperson to summarize the group's résumé.

Rewards

• This is a very affirming exercise, and the group will often be quite amazed at the wide spectrum of interests, talents, and professional resources they come up with. After all, when you start to add up work experience, you can easily find your collective experience in the hundreds of years!

• You can refer to the broad base of experience throughout the workshop.

Risks

• Group size is particularly important in this activity. When subgroups are larger than four or five, this activity gets long and a bit laborious. With subgroups smaller than four, the group résumé starts to look like it could represent one busy person.

• Sometimes you may get a subgroup where most of the members hold management positions and have a whole raft of university degrees. The remaining member may be a new staff member just out of university with little work experience. This member may feel isolated or intimidated, but you won't be able to detect their feelings on the group résumé data. Keep a listening ear open as subgroups complete this activity and do your best to ensure that each person is comfortable.

Options

• You may wish to customize the résumé by having participants answer questions that pertain directly to the workshop topic. For example, with a people-skills course, the content of the résumé could focus on the following headings:

- *Courses taken that relate to people skills*
- *Situations where people skills were used*
- *Most common conflict areas at work*
- *Coaching or mentoring experiences*

• You may wish to simply hang the completed charts with no reporting by the subgroups. Member curiosity often encourages visits to the charts during breaks. This variation is particularly useful to save time with large groups.

• Refer to the charts during the training. When you need an example, you can base it on the group's experiences and expertise.

The learner affiliation techniques in this section aim to put learners at ease with one another. But remember a learner is more likely to be socially comfortable if she is physically and emotionally comfortable, too. Here are some "best practices" I've discovered that enhance learner affiliations.

1. Refreshments

Ideally, refreshments should be available about half an hour before the workshop begins and throughout the day until about 3:00 pm. When choosing refreshments, I opt for herbal tea and juice along with the traditional coffee and tea. I also ensure participants have healthy snack options, like muffins and fruit. People's tastes have changed over the years—and probably for the better.

2. Lunch

When workshops last longer than one day, and when the workshop organizer has not provided lunch, I usually inquire whether the group would like to eat together at a local restaurant. When booking the restaurant, I indicate that the group is attending a workshop and that they need to return to the classroom by 1:00 pm Usually the restaurant owner will suggest ways in which this can be done with the number of people coming to lunch.

3. Music

Music and learning belong together. I often play music half an hour before the workshop begins, during the lunch break (if participants are in the room), and at the end of the workshop. I also play music during the quiet, more reflective moments in a workshop. I've found classical music, New World music, and light jazz relax learners and put them at ease. With CD players or with music storage programs built into laptop computers, I accomplish this very easily. No need for carrying around CDs any more!

One note of caution: If you want to use a particular piece of music as your theme song, be sure that you are not violating copyright; secure permission from the publisher. Original music needs to be composed for the trainer or permission must be granted from the recording company because the music selection is being used to trademark the trainer. Another option is to purchase music made for trainers that is royalty-free music.

4. Customized welcome

Approximately five minutes before the commencement of the workshop, I turn off the computer program that has been displaying a sequence of inspirational quotations onto an overhead screen. Then I turn on the customized welcome program I've created for this particular workshop. The welcome program starts with the workshop title, the name of the hosting company or organization, my company identification, and then the name of each participant is displayed on the screen (one per frame). When time is available, I intersperse digital photos of the workshop site with participant names. Or, I may use photos of the participants and organizing staff. At the close of the name and photo display, I include a few slides that address the workshop's guidelines, topic background, and a closing quotation.

Topic Affiliation

The techniques in this section explore the needs and expectations of the learners and the trainer with respect to course content. During topic affiliation activities you are given the opportunity to review, clarify, and agree upon the training outcomes you've developed. This will ensure your expectations and those of the learners are met.

Unlike the formal list of your needs as expressed in the training outcomes, participants who attend the workshop arrive with unwritten but "felt" needs. They have signed up for training based on the course description, the perceived workshop benefits, or the opportunity to network with colleagues. Or they may be having some difficulties at work and the workshop topic addresses their concerns. These "felt" needs are real and they need to be addressed.

By juxtaposing training outcomes (i.e. the trainer's needs) with the participants' expectations, you can build bridges of understanding and acceptance. You can accomplish this by specifying an agreement between yourself and the group concerning the anticipated knowledge and skill outcomes, the expected behaviour of trainer and participants, and by working out some of the finer points of the workshop, such as time allotments and the different competency levels within the group.

I use the following techniques to encourage topic affiliation:

Needs
Progress Chart
Welcome Letter
Live Audit

Needs

Ready

Purpose:	To address the felt needs of the group and to clarify training outcomes.
Time:	Approximately fifteen to twenty minutes
Group size:	Up to forty
Learner risk:	Moderate
Materials:	Flip chart, felt pens, program outline on flip chart or overhead

Set

• Prepare a flip chart with the headings shown on the next page. You will need a flip chart for each subgroup. (A subgroup should consist of five to six participants.) I usually post the flip charts close to each subgroup.

Go

• Tell the group that this exercise focuses on identifying and accommodating learner needs for the workshop.

• Ask each subgroup to use bulleted statements to respond to the three questions on its flip chart. Remind them to print neatly and large enough for the entire group to see. Allot four to five minutes for this part of the exercise.

• Invite participants to leave their subgroups and view the responses recorded on the other flip charts. Encourage them to compare and contrast their comments.

• After the subgroups have visited the other flip charts, direct participants to return to their tables. Compare what the participants have recorded with the prepared program outline you've posted. Are the differences unique to one subgroup or do they show up on several subgroup flip charts?

• Where possible, adjust the program outline to reflect participant needs/expectations. First, make adjustments to those areas that have the greatest consensus within the large group. Leave single subgroup differences to deal with near the end of this exercise. Making changes will demonstrate your commitment to meeting participants' needs.

• Remember, you are the primary subject matter specialist. You need to be in full support of the suggested changes. When necessary, you will need to acknowledge that some expectations lie outside the parameters of the workshop. For expectations that go unmet, suggest alternatives such as book references, other workshops, and experts.

Sample Needs Survey

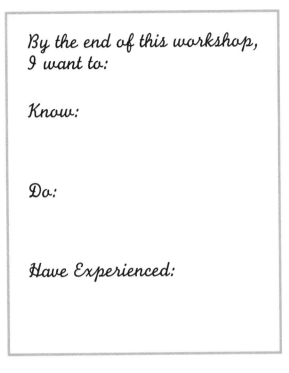

By the end of this workshop, I want to:

Know:

Do:

Have Experienced:

Rewards

• When it's possible to adjust the program to more closely meet the needs of the group, customization has gone to a higher level and course satisfaction will increase significantly.

Risks

• There are many reasons why programs cannot be adjusted to meet all participants' wishes. Your knowledge and familiarity with a topic, time restrictions, and company limitations each play a role in whether or not you can adapt the training outcomes.

Options

• Rather than bringing a prepared instructor agenda to the session, build an agenda based on the input you gather during this activity.

• Change the heading to "This workshop will be successful if. . . ." Have participants focus on both the product (agenda) and process (guidelines) of the workshop.

Progress Chart

Ready

Purpose:	To guide participants in setting their own training outcomes.
Time:	Approximately ten minutes
Group size:	Up to thirty
Learner risk:	Moderate
Materials:	Copy of progress chart for learner manual flip chart, felt pens

Set

• Prepare a flip chart with a Progress Chart as indicated on the next page. Also include a copy of the Progress Chart in the learner manual.

• On a separate piece of flip chart paper, prepare a completed Progress Chart as an example.

• Note that this activity works best after the workshop outcomes and agenda have been discussed and agreed upon. Learners will have a better idea of what they already know about the topic and where their gaps or needs are.

Go

• Introduce this activity by informing learners that they will be asked to identify their strengths and weaknesses in relation to the workshop topic. Explain that each learner possesses relevant experiences and unique concerns about the training topic. Refer to the flip chart and explain that, in this exercise, relevant experiences will be listed in the chart's "Proud Of" column and that the needs and concerns will be listed in the "Working On" column.

• If it seems the group would benefit from seeing an example, show the completed Progress Chart you've prepared.

• Ask learners to complete the Progress Chart in their learner manual. Advise them that they will not be required to share the data. Indicate that the workshop has been designed to work on both sides of the Progress Chart. Encourage learners to share their "Proud Of" attributes when applicable and to focus on reducing the "Working On" list during the workshop.

• Touch base with the Progress Chart throughout and at the end of the workshop.

Progress Chart

Proud Of . . .   Working On . . .

- •   - •

- •   - •

- •   - •

- •   - •

- •   - •

Rewards

- This technique provides an easy way for participants to set training outcomes. Sometimes learners grapple with goal setting because they find the process too vague. This activity makes goal setting practical and doable.

- Learners identify existing skills and can pinpoint the new skills they need to walk away with. It refines focus for all of the learners.

Risks

- Some participants may view themselves as having no related experiences with the training topic. They have learning needs or gaps but no experience.

Options

- Provide participants with your list of strengths and weaknesses. This reinforces that you, like them, are learning and that you are open to continued development.

- Have participants compare their lists with the session's training outcomes. Are the goals consistent? If not, do you need to take another look at the agenda?

Welcome Letter

Ready

Purpose:	To prepare participants for an upcoming workshop
Time:	Approximately thirty minutes to draft the letter
Group size:	Any size
Learner risk:	Low
Materials:	Personalized or company letterhead

Set

• Create a letter that welcomes participants to an upcoming workshop. As well as outlining workshop specifics, it should explain what will be done to make the workshop a rewarding and positive experience for each trainee.

• Consider the questions in the side box when creating your letter. (See sample letter on next page.)

• You will need to gather the names and addresses of each confirmed participant.

Go

• Sign the letters and mail them approximately three weeks prior to the workshop.

the **Trainer's**
EDGE

What to include in your welcome letter

Include some or all of the following items in your welcome letter:

• Welcome and thanks for selecting/attending the workshop

• Date(s) and time(s) of workshop

• Location of building and room of workshop— provide specific details

• Parking arrangements

• Appropriate dress for the workshop

• Food and refreshment arrangements

• How the room will be arranged

• Some comments about how you will be conducting the workshop

• Expectations for learning and behaviour

• How each person's needs will be addressed

• Breaks and smoking arrangements

• The importance of involvement

• Any pre-workshop assignments (i.e. readings, surveys, questionnaires)

• Your commitment to making this a great learning experience

• Contact information (phone/e-mail/fax) for questions prior to workshop

• If serving lunch, ask if any special dietary requests should be made

Date

Dear *(participant name)*,

Thank you for selecting an HP TrainingWorks Inc. workshop! I hope your expectations will be met and you'll find the workshop valuable.

Workshop details for the Speaking with Class workshop are as follows:

Date: May 7th, 2002
Location: Mayfield Inn at 16615 – 109 Ave. in Edmonton
Room: Ballroom #1
Hours: 8:45 to 4:00
Dress: Casual

Questions: Please call should you have questions about the workshop. I'm here
                to help.

What to expect: A greeting at the door, a spacious room, and continental breakfast at 8:15.

                Round tables for subgroups. Sit where you like. Manuals are provided.

                A hands-on workshop with a wide variety of activities to help you learn
                and remember.

                Ask questions when you have them and/or use the break time to talk
                with me.

Here's to a great workshop for you!

Sincerely,
Hugh Phillips
(780) 444-3420

Rewards

• People are impressed with this personalized approach. It sets up positive expectations.

Risks

• Be sure to proofread the letter carefully. Errors will make you look unprofessional.

• If you mail the letter too early, the impact will be forgotten by the time the session arrives. If it is sent too late, participants may not receive it in time. I suggest mailing it no earlier than three weeks before workshop.

Options

• You may want to e-mail the letters, but this approach is not as personal.

Live Audit

Ready

Purpose:	To gather and share group characteristics such as needs and work experiences
Time:	Approximately ten minutes. Use this activity at the start of a session.
Group size:	Up to thirty
Learner risk:	Low
Materials:	Flip chart, audit template

Set

• Prepare a live audit template on a flip chart as indicated on the following page.

• Choose five or six questions for the audit that are general enough to get quick responses from the participants. Focus on questions that will help members of the group discover relevant information about themselves with respect to the training topic. Use closed questions that require participants to put themselves in one of three categories. (See sample on the next page.)

Go

• Explain to the trainees that it is often useful to find out the relevant background of the group in relation to the workshop topic.

• To conduct the audit, ask participants to respond to each of the questions on the flip chart by a show of hands. Record the number of responses for each category directly onto the flip chart. (See sample on the next page.)

• When the audit is complete, ask the audience for its observations about the characteristics of the group. Be patient with this. The group will need time to survey all of the data. Use open-ended questions to encourage responses. For example, ask, "What observations or conclusions can you make about this group as you review the chart data?"

• Draw some of your own conclusions or reinforce the conclusions of the audience. Link these comments to the workshop agenda to demonstrate that audience needs will be addressed.

Rewards

• Participants will get a very good idea of how they fit in the group. For example, in the sample live audit (next page), seven people know that they are the more expert trainers within the group (first question).

• Most groups I train come with a variety of backgrounds and experiences. I emphasize inclusiveness and balance in the program by stating that there will be something for all levels of experience.

Risks

• Sometimes you get only one person who responds to a particular category. In the sample live audit, for example, only one person trains with groups smaller than five people. Don't isolate this person and, if the person seems uncomfortable, speak to them at the break to help diffuse any concerns.

Options

• Prepare a live audit handout for each learner to complete. Then summarize the responses on one group flip chart.

Sample Live Audit

Train the Trainer			
(Workshop Topic)			
1. Experience	3 <1yr	14 <3yr	7 >3yr
2. Frequency	13 <5/yr	10 <15/yr	1 >15/yr
3. Topics	20 Soft	3 Hard	1 Other
4. Size of Group	1 <5	17 <20	6 >20
5. Other PD	12 1st	10 <3	2 >3

Note: The grey letters on the sample chart refer to the number of responses received for each category.

Trainer Affiliation

Probably the most common way learner–trainer affiliations are developed with the group is through prepared introductions. The trainer shares academic credentials, work experiences related to the topic, and any background information that provides evidence of expertise (such as books written on the topic, articles published, multi-media produced, Web sites developed). In the introduction, you might also refer to people you know who have expertise in the workshop topic.

Many instructors begin this way because this is what they have seen as students and perhaps this is what they are most comfortable with. This method of handling your own introduction also allows you to control the situation. With this approach, however, learners aren't that involved.

While the prepared introduction is a fine way to develop learner-trainer affiliations, you may be interested in some of the following, more creative, ways to conduct trainer introductions. The two techniques I use the most often are:

Gang Up On
Workshop Guidelines

Gang Up On

Ready

Purpose:	To creatively introduce yourself to the group.
Time:	Approximately ten minutes. Wait until learners have introduced themselves.
Group size:	Up to forty
Learner risk:	Low
Materials:	Chair for trainer

Set

• Tell the group that you would like to introduce yourself by responding to questions.

• Position yourself at the front of the room, sitting in a chair. This puts you at the same eye level as the group. It creates a more receptive atmosphere because you are not standing, which is a dominant position. If the group is larger, sit on the edge of a table so everyone can see you.

• Keep your back erect and lean slightly ahead when you sit in the chair. Look at the group with a sense of anticipation. Avoid taking on a closed or avoidance position (arms and legs folded, slumping in a chair, sitting sideways).

Go

• Ask each subgroup to think of two or three questions they would like to ask you about yourself. Indicate that these questions can be about your professional life (background and experience) and/or your personal life (hobbies and home).

• Let the subgroups know they can have a minute or so to prepare their questions.

• Ask a subgroup for its first question. Answer the question and then move to the next subgroup for its first question. (Note: Avoid getting all the questions from one subgroup right away so that each group has a chance to ask you something. Otherwise, by the time you get to the third subgroup most of the questions will probably have been asked.)

• Respond to each question in a concise and clear manner. Brevity will keep the momentum up and the interest high. The entire "interview" shouldn't take more than three to five minutes.

• Repeat this pattern until each subgroup has asked one question.

• Once each subgroup has asked its first questions, repeat the process until all subgroup questions have been answered.

• Conclude by thanking them for such interesting and insightful questions.

Rewards

• Unlike a traditional prepared introduction, participants get to ask the questions they want. In many of my workshops, I am asked personal questions that tie me to the audience. They want to know about my hobbies, if I have kids, my most embarrassing moment, my best training moment, and so on.

• This activity gives you the opportunity to show your humorous side. A great way to begin the workshop!

• Because this activity involves more risk for you than for the learners, it allows you to model risk taking early in the workshop. You set an example that shows that risk taking is a valued and acceptable behaviour.

Risks

• You may be asked a question that you are uncomfortable with. If so, feel free to pass. This models the action that anyone in the workshop can take if asked a question that makes him or her feel uncomfortable.

Options

• Ask the subgroups to write out their questions and put them in the trainer's box. You can answer a few of the questions and save others for later in the day.

• If you're pressed for time, have each subgroup ask fewer questions.

• Change the focus from professional and personal to professional and course related.

Workshop Guidelines

Ready

Purpose:	To provide participants with the opportunity to review, amend, and approve session guidelines and thereby develop an affiliation with the trainer.
Time:	Approximately five to ten minutes. This activity works best with groups that will be with you for longer than one day.
Group size:	Up to forty
Learner risk:	Low
Materials:	Flip chart, name tents

Set

• Plan to use this technique when you are leading a workshop that involves higher risk activities, such as simulations, coaching, and feedback sessions.

• Draft workshop guidelines for your session. (See sample on next page.) Place guidelines on a flip chart or on the back of participant name tents. You may want to start with guidelines that you have found work well with other groups.

Go

• During the opening of the workshop, introduce and review the workshop guidelines. Make sure trainees understand each one.

• Ask the learners to review the workshop guidelines in subgroups. Provide three to five minutes.

• Develop the guidelines, by asking exploratory questions such as, "What other guidelines do we need to help ensure the success of this workshop? Do any of the guidelines suggested need to be revised or deleted?"

• Record the responses on flip chart paper.

• After all ideas have been recorded, seek consensus on the suggestions. Reinforce the importance of adhering to the guidelines.

Rewards

• There is greater ownership and willingness to support the guidelines when learners have made suggestions about adopting them in the first place.

Risks

• You may get a group that finds it difficult to agree on guidelines. If this can be a teaching moment for the group, then work through gaining consensus.

• This activity works best with groups who have some experience in attending training events.

Sample Workshop Guidelines

> • We all have something to learn and something to teach.
> • Understanding, not agreement, is the key.
> • Speak only for yourself, using "I" not "We."
> • Silence is okay.
> • Learning and comfort are related. Do whatever you need to be comfortable.
> • Please turn off your cell phone.
> • There are no dumb questions.
> • Please return promptly after breaks.
> • Listen attentively.

Options

• If you have time, ask participants to generate their own guidelines. Sometimes the workshop topic makes this an excellent introductory exercise. For example, in my Facilitation Skills workshop, the group creates its own guidelines.

• Expand this activity to include standards or qualities for the trainers and trainees. Ask odd-numbered tables to develop guidelines for trainer qualities and the even-numbered tables to develop guidelines for trainee qualities. Review the lists and seek consensus for a course standard of behaviour.

• You may need to revise the guidelines during the course of the workshop. This can be another teaching moment to emphasize the importance of functional standards.

HUGHism

" Preparing learners to learn yields rewards for the entire workshop. "

Chapter 6:
Attention Techniques

A great teacher is not simply one who imparts knowledge to his students, but one who awakens their interest in it and makes them eager to pursue it for themselves. He is a spark plug, not a fuel pipe.

M. J. Berrill

I'm a twin. To be more exact, a fraternal twin. As kids, my brother Hal and I loved joining Dad on fishing trips. The cool, clear, and cozy mountain lakes in Alberta were great places to dip our lines in the hope that a brookie (brook trout) would take the bait!

Dad would say, "To catch a fish, you've got to think like a fish. What does the fish need? What would attract the fish to your line? How could you lure a brookie to take more than a passing glance at your hook? What do you need to get the fish to grab the hook?"

Of course, Hal and I had many theories that Dad encouraged us to try out. We had our own special hooks—the ones that looked great to us but that obviously had little appeal for the brookie. We had our own ideas about live bait, too. Not the ordinary earthworm for us, no way. We insisted on using seafood. All of this experimentation was fun, but, in the end, we'd return to Dad and ask him, "So, just how does a brookie think?"

Dad explained the concept of fish habitat and gave us fascinating information about the brookie. He talked about the insects and creepy crawlies that lived in the brookie's habitat. He also mentioned the daily life patterns of our target fish: the depth they ate at and the time of day they would eat. Dad also told us about how brookie prey moved in the water, and he'd demonstrate how to imitate those movements with the fishing pole. Armed with this intriguing fish lore, Hal and I would head off to fish again. And soon our efforts were rewarded. The sudden bend of the pole, an amazingly strong tug on the line, and we were hooked! What a thrill to pull in a brookie!

So, what does fishing have to do with the attention phase of training? The parallels are clear. The art and skill of getting the learner interested depends on the trainer's ability to think like a learner. It's up to you to grab the learner's attention so he'll find the topic fascinating and worthy of further investigation. In fishing terms, you are guiding learners to search for the food they need to survive—better yet, to thrive—at work.

Metaphorically, fishing principles can teach us much about how to hook the learner and get his attention. That's the goal of the following attention techniques. Try these out to sharpen attention in your workshops:

Story Telling
Mind Mapping
Think • Pair • Square • Share
Quotations
Questions
Prop
Tick Box
Skit
Video
Humour
Gap Analysis
Immersions

Story Telling

Ready

Purpose:	To ignite interest, curiosity, wonderment, intrigue, and fascination, and to set the stage for inquiry and acquisition
Time:	Two to fifteen minutes
Group size:	Any size
Learner risk:	Unknown. A story may resonate with a learner in positive, neutral, or negative ways.
Materials:	Props for story (if required), microphone (if necessary)

inside scoop

I was reminded of the power of a good story several years ago when I was invited to be a keynote speaker at an annual Human Resource Development Canada conference. A forthright gentleman walked up to me while I was at the registration desk. He introduced himself in an enthusiastic fashion and mentioned that he had heard me speak three years ago at another conference. He then said something I'll never forget: "Are your going to tell your spider story? I hope you do, because the conference delegates need that message." He walked away with a smile and an expectant look on his face.

"Wow!" I thought to myself. A seven-minute spider story stayed with that man for three years. He felt strongly enough about it that he has taken the time to remind me of its impact and the benefit it will have for other people. Stories must be powerful! They are! Lesson learned? Don't underestimate the potential of a story. Each of us is a treasure house of unique and wonderful stories. Our responsibility is to mine these stories, to bring them to the surface, and to refine them into well-developed tales with relevant messages for our audiences.

Set

• Construct a story with the usual three parts; beginning, middle, and end.

• Rehearse the story at least a dozen times. Each time you'll find you express things a little differently so that the story becomes more concise and clear. When you rehearse, remember some stories need to be set-up, but others don't.

• Plan the timing of the story carefully; you want to tell it at the appropriate time during the workshop.

• Be sure you link the story to the workshop topic.

Go

• *Don't tell the story—be the story:* When I tell my spider story (see side bar), I take my listeners to the base of a tree. They visualize the spider climbing up the trunk, out onto a branch, and positioning herself on the end of a twig. They see her leap with reckless abandon in her struggle to build a web. Immediately, the audience is plunged into the story. They watch the spider's struggle to succeed.

• *Take the ordinary and make it special; take the "for granted" and make it important:* The spider story is not an extraordinary one, at least not on the surface. It is a story about how the female spider constructs a web. This is a non-event in people's lives. Yet, by telling the intricate and dramatic events that play out in the building of a web, this ordinary story becomes extraordinary. What appears at the surface to be simple and plain becomes significant and timely!

• *Weave universal truths into the story:* There is unexpected drama, excitement, and conflict woven into the spider story. It becomes a compelling event of life and death, success and failure. The story contains some of the cornerstones that shape our lives. As the metaphors are woven into the story, the listeners make connections to their own lives. A simple spider story contains universal messages of hope and triumph!

• *Match the story length with the significance of your point:* The more lengthy the story, the more powerful the point needs to be. Otherwise, you risk developing the craft of storytelling for the sake of art alone and not for achieving training outcomes. So, keep the length of the story proportional to the significance of its point.

• *Details:* Give sufficient detail to create a realistic tale. Too little detail will make the story unbelievable because listeners won't be able to identify with the characters or situation. On the other hand, too much detail bogs down the telling and interferes with understanding. With the spider story, I give just enough detail for participants to see the spider in action.

Rewards

• You become known through your stories. Well-known speakers are often remembered because of their unique and fascinating stories.

• One of the best ways to develop poise in front of a group is to tell a well-rehearsed story. The telling relaxes you and prepares the audience for what is to come.

Risks

- A story may be distracting if learners find themselves reliving their own memories while you tell the story.

- Stories that don't relate to the training topic will not gain the group's attention. You need to link the story with the training event. To help emphasize the purpose of the story, use phrases such as "The point this story illustrates is," or, "The connection between the story and my topic is." Or ask the group, "In your view, what is the point of this story?"

Options

- Split your story into two parts. Tell the first part to get the audience's attention. Stop the story at the point of climax and indicate you'll complete the story later.

Dear Hugh,

I like using stories in my workshops, but I tend to re-tell other people's stories rather than create my own. My own life just doesn't seem exciting enough to talk about. Any suggestions?

Storyless in Saskatoon

Dear Storyless,

I think you probably have lots of stories that have the potential to get a learner's attention. However, most of them will need to be adapted to ensure their relevance for your audience. How can you find good stories? Look in these three areas:

1. Life-altering events: Think through some of the significant events that have altered your life. What stories do you associate with these memorable moments?

2. Passions: What are you passionate about? I love the outdoors—observing and watching nature. So, outdoor stories come "naturally" to me. What is a natural for you?

3. Hobbies: Where do you spend your recreational time? What events can be linked to your training topics?

Hope this helps! Good luck with your next story!

Sincerely,
Hugh

Mind Mapping

Ready

Purpose:	To help learners make intuitive and creative associations with a workshop topic.
Time:	Five to fifteen minutes
Group size:	Six or more
Learner risk:	Low
Materials:	Flip chart, felt pens, tape

Set

• Prepare a sample mind map to show the group.

Go

• Show the sample mind map to the group and explain the thought process that led to its development.

• Begin your current session's mind map by drawing a circle in the middle of a piece of flip chart paper. Then announce your training topic by placing it in the centre of a circle. (See sample A on the next page.)

• Ask learners to think about the topic and share their ideas with the group. As ideas are shared, record them on the chart by drawing a spoke from the outer edge of the circle towards the edge of the paper. Write the idea at the end of the spoke. Draw a circle around the idea. The circle connects to the spoke. As more primary ideas come, write and circle these words at the ends of the new spokes. (See sample B on the next page.)

• Learners will often generate related or secondary ideas, not primary ideas. Record these secondary ideas close to the related primary idea and draw a line from each secondary idea to the primary word. Most primary ideas will have many secondary ideas attached to them. Continue this process until all ideas have been shared. (See sample C on the next page.)

A. Topic

B. Primary Ideas

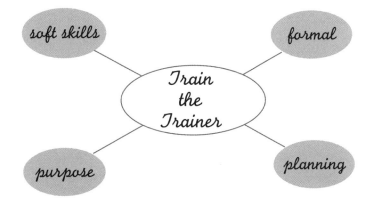

C. Secondary Ideas

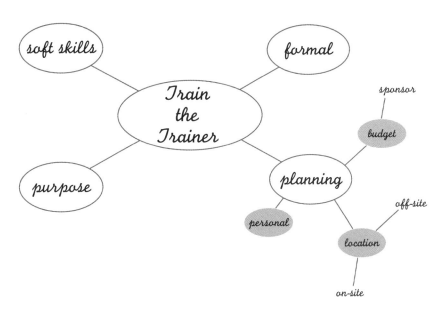

Rewards

• Mind mapping encourages learners to use the spontaneous and intuitive right side of the brain. Later, the left, or logical, side will guide learners as they organize or prioritize the data.

• Mind mapping allows individuals who are visual learners to instantly see connections between ideas.

• Mind mapping is an excellent technique to use when learners already have some knowledge of the topic. It engages the learners immediately and allows them to realize the benefits of using the whole brain.

• The ideas generated allow the trainer to build on the learners' knowledge in a non-threatening way.

Risks

• If the group is not in a relaxed, spontaneous mood, this technique may not work. This type of free association of ideas may seem inferior to a more logical and organized process.

• A few learners don't like mind mapping. Don't force the technique. It will work if people believe in its merits, but the playful side of constructing mind maps is essential to its value.

Options

• I also enjoy using mind mapping with other A's in the training process. For example, at the end of a lecture, in the acquisition phase, I'll ask learners to map what they remember. If learners share their mind maps, learning is reinforced. Mind mapping can also be used to discover ways of adopting new skills in the work place (application phase) or to create work plans (action phase). Obviously, this is a very flexible tool.

• There are many different approaches to mind mapping, which is also referred to as branching or webbing. For other adaptations, consult Joyce Wycoff's book *Mind Mapping*.

Think • Pair • Square • Share

Ready

Purpose:	To immediately involve different types of learners and provide the trainer with quality data in a short period of time.
Time:	Approximately twelve minutes
Group size:	Twelve or more
Learner risk:	Low
Materials:	Flip chart, felt pens

Set

• Print an open-ended question on a flip chart or overhead. Ensure the question is carefully and concisely worded to ensure clarity and relevance. The question must be related to the training topic.

• Be aware of the importance of clear instructions and adherence to time lines for each phase of the activity.

Go

• *Think:* Read the question aloud and ensure everyone understands it. Invite each participant to respond to the question by jotting his ideas down using a bulleted format. Allow ninety seconds for this think phase.

• *Pair:* Ask participants to leave their tables and share their responses with one other person from a different subgroup. This encourages physical movement and gets people thinking beyond their subgroup. Advise learners that they can jot down each other's ideas if they wish. Allow sixty seconds for the pair phase.

• *Square:* Ask participants to return to their subgroups (or to form groups if they have not been developed yet). Ask each subgroup to create a list of seven points from the members' combined data and record the points on a flip chart. Remind them to use large print. Ideas do not need to be ranked or prioritized. Allow five minutes for the square phase.

• *Share:* Display the flip charts side by side. Ask for volunteers to serve as markers, with one marker for every three flip charts. Explain that the entire group is to survey all flip charts and look for similar ideas. As they find similar ideas, they are to voice them so that the markers can check these ideas off on the flip charts using a felt pen. While the markers are checking off the ideas, the instructor creates a summary chart of similar ideas.

You'll notice that some ideas will occur on only one chart. These solo ideas are important. That is why I hang the charts for reference during the workshop.

Solo ideas can be referred in the sharing part of T•P•S•S and throughout the workshop.

• Once the group has found all the similar ideas, the markers are thanked and asked to return to their subgroups. To summarize the activity, the instructor links the summary chart ideas to the workshop program and thanks participants.

Sample Think • Pair • Square • Share

• Open ended question

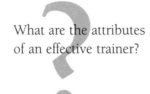

What are the attributes of an effective trainer?

• Group Charts

Effective Trainer
- good listener
- flexible
- knows her topic
- able to manage
- enthusiastic
- orderly
- sense of humour

Effective Trainer
- well organized
- adjustable
- starts/ends on time
- listens well
- paces learning
- can be funny
- knows his stuff

Effective Trainer
- sense of humour
- speaks clearly
- prepared
- really good speaker
- not stuck in his ways
- is knowledgeable

• Summary Chart

Effective Trainer
– Summary
- organized
- good listener
- knowledgeable
- sense of humour

Explanation
The group pointed out these common ideas

• orderly, well organized, and prepared–summarized as organized
• good listener, listens well, and really good listener –summarized as good listener
• knows her topic, knows his stuff, and knowledgeable –summarized as knowledgeable
• can be funny and sense of humour–summarized as sense of humour

Rewards

• One of the greatest rewards of this activity is that it includes many types of learners. In a workshop, you'll have a spectrum of learners. At one end of the spectrum are the quiet, introspective, independent, private learners. They like to think through ideas before responding in a more public way. At the other end of the learning spectrum are the more outgoing, public learners. They like to think out loud or validate their thinking with others. In a workshop, you will have a mix of these private and public learners. The T•P•S•S technique accommodates both ends of the learning spectrum. The Think and Pair tasks will be appreciated by the private learners. The Square and Share activities are more appropriate for the public learners.

• This activity endorses everyone, is easy to conduct, and is non-threatening. And it certainly gets the group's attention!

• This technique fosters a sense of ownership of ideas. The ideas displayed are not the trainer's ideas, but the thoughts of the participants—their words, their stuff! This helps communicate the philosophy that learners' thoughts and opinions will be valued and used in the workshop.

• The trainer's conscious effort to link ideas from the T•P•S•S activity to the workshop is important. Throughout a session, I often find opportunities to refer to the T•P•S•S data to reinforce a point. The teachable moment is much more effective when I refer to their data.

Risks

• Sometimes, markers want to become spokespersons. When you appoint markers, reinforce the limited role you're asking them to play. Markers are not commentators. They simply wait for the group to point out common points identified on the flip charts and then check them off.

• Once in a while, you may get subgroups that have little data in common. When this happens, respond to each flip chart on an individual basis.

Options

• If the group is large, say one hundred people, divide the group into four sections. Then conduct the T•P•S•S technique with each section simultaneously. Give clear instructions at the beginning and appoint a facilitator to coordinate the process for each group. The entire group reviews the four summary charts.

• If the group size is very small, say fewer than ten people, side step the pairing activity.

Quotations

Ready

Purpose:	To engage the audience on a cognitive level.
Time:	Usually under three minutes
Group size:	Any size
Learner risk:	Medium
Materials:	Overhead projector of flip chart to display lengthier quotations, music to add impact

Set

• Choose a quotation (or more than one) that is relevant is to the training topic. You may want to keep a file of interesting quotations.

• Decide on the most appropriate time to use your quotation in the session. Use it at a moment when you most want to gain attention.

• Practice saying your quotation. Polish your delivery to make it sparkle for the audience. Rehearsal maximizes effect and gains audience attention. If possible, you can memorize the quote. This tells the audience that you deem the quotation to be so important it is worth committing to memory.

Go

• Pause before you disclose the quotation. You want to ensure the audience is focused on the words you are about to say.

• Express the quote as if you were the individual who created it. Say it with as much conviction, meaning, and compassion as you can muster. If it is funny, pause before delivering the punch line.

• After you've spoken, wait for your words to settle in with the audience. Let the group reflect on what you've said.

• Acknowledge the source. Decide ahead of time if it would be better to acknowledge the source before or after you've said the quotation. Be flexible with this. Try both ways to see how the audience responds.

Rewards

• A well-positioned, well-rehearsed quote that is relevant to a particular audience gains the group's attention immediately. It can create curiosity, arrest thinking, challenge values, and encourage deeper exploration of assumptions.

• When you quote recognized authorities, you gain credibility as a speaker. Quotations imply that you are well read and know the topic.

• Quotations are a wonderful way to infuse humour into your session.

Risks

• Sometimes participants may not recognize the expert you are quoting or they may take exception to the person quoted. You do not want to risk offending your audience with a quote that is inappropriate. Review the information collected in the audit and you will have a better idea of what constitutes appropriate quotations.

Options

• When using a quote, provide visual back up, either by displaying the quote on a flip chart or screen or by having a visual displayed as you convey the quote.

• With well-known authors or sayings, begin the quote and stop part way through. Can the audience finish the quote?

the Trainer's EDGE

• As I read, I collect worthwhile quotations and categorize them so that they can be easily retrieved. My Web site is a source for quotations. I've organized them under the different training topics.

• Some of the most powerful quotations you can use are the ones you create yourself. I've coined the word "HUGHisms" for the quotes I use in my workshops.

Questions

Ready

Purpose:	To encourage the learners to think more deeply about an issue or topic.
Time:	Five to seven minutes
Group size:	Any size
Learner risk:	Moderate
Materials:	None

Set

• To effectively gain your audience's attention using questions, you need to make sure the questions challenge learners but do not threaten them. If a question is too easy, it will not create curiosity. If it is too difficult, it will confuse and frustrate the group.

• Review Bloom's theories about levels of questioning to ensure the questions you develop are at the right level for your audience. Avoid questions at level one; instead, employ higher-level questions that encourage learners to think more deeply and engage them more thoroughly. (See side bar on next page.)

• Create a well thought out question that is appropriate for the group. Use a visual aid to display the question.

• There is a certain amount of artistry in effectively asking questions. Practice asking questions using pauses, facial expressions, and hand gestures.

Go

• Refer the audience to the question and ask for input. Remember, open-ended questions seek learner opinions. Closed questions seek a yes/no response. Most high-level questions in Bloom's taxonomy are open ended.

• Encourage input from as many participants as possible.

• Record ideas.

Rewards

• Voltaire, the 17th century French philosopher, said, "Know a person by their questions rather than by their answers." His words emphasize the ability of a person to think, to be curious. Questions can captivate an audience.

• You will elicit looks of wonder and delight when you use engaging questions.

Risks

• There are certain risks involved when you decide to ask questions. A question posed to the entire class may receive no response or the same few people may respond each time. (I've heard that, as a rule, 20 percent of the students do 80 percent of the responding.) On the other hand, targeting an individual or subgroup with a question may put them on the spot.

• For a variety of reasons (e.g. cultural, learning styles), some classes are uncomfortable with instructor questions. In these situations, don't give up. Encourage the class and be patient.

Options

• If you have the ability to ask rhetorical questions effectively, do so. With this technique, pose one or more questions to the class, pause for a moment, then move on. You are not expecting an answer but are using questions to focus attention.

• Invite students to generate their own questions. Provide subgroups with index cards and ask them to jot down two to four questions they have about the topic. Respond to their questions as a part of the attention phase of the workshop.

• Place a question box or question envelopes at each table. Invite students to put questions in the box or envelopes at any time. Throughout the session, spontaneously select questions and respond to them.

Making Connections

Bloom's Taxonomy at a Glance

Bloom's taxonomy identifies six different levels of questions. As you move from level one to level six, the questions demand a higher level of thinking. In ascending order, these levels include:

Level	Type	The ability to
1	Knowledge	Recall previously learned material
2	Comprehension	Understand the meaning of what has been taught
3	Application	Use the learned material in new, practical situations
4	Analysis	Break down knowledge into understandable parts
5	Synthesis	Link the parts to form a new whole
6	Evaluation	Judge the value of what has been learned

Prop

Ready

Purpose:	To create curiosity about, concern for, or a comparison with something a learner already knows.
Time:	Two to twenty minutes
Group size:	Any size
Learner risk:	Low
Materials:	The prop itself, equipment to display the prop if necessary

Set

• Use the information gathered in your audit to ensure that the prop you're using is suitable for the group. Remember, the prop is intended to be a visual aid that helps the learner make an association between the trainer's message and the learner's world.

• Place the prop where everyone can see it. If necessary, take a photo of the prop and project the image onto a screen.

• Rehearse your commentary so the connection between the prop and your topic is clear. Be prepared for interruptions and questions and plan how you will deal with them.

Go

• *Timing:* Decide when you will use the prop and keep it out of sight until that moment. Hold it in view for as long as you need to. Then remove it from sight as soon as it is appropriate to do so. You don't want to be upstaged by your prop.

• *Telling:* Use the prop when you tell a story, use statistics, or present research data. Ensure that the prop serves to get the group's attention, not distract it. If the prop is unfamiliar to the group, explain its function or purpose as a part of using it.

• *Translating:* Always link the prop to the workshop topic. Ensure that the prop draws learners into your topic. Use a prop that has significance for the audience.

Rewards

• Some people are abstract learners who prefer to deal with ideas, concepts, and meanings. Others are concrete learners who prefer hands on, visible, and moveable props. The use of props won't appeal to all learners, but you can be assured many will appreciate it.

• Participants remember points that are made with props.

Risks

• There is a risk of being upstaged by your prop. Remember, a prop is supposed to capture the audience's attention, not distract it. When using a prop, think simplicity. You don't need a prop that is difficult to handle, awkward to move, or potentially dangerous to you or the audience. If a prop is used inappropriately, is not suitable for a group, or is not linked with the subject matter, it will upstage the training moment.

• Some learners may interpret the use of a prop as slick or contrived. For whatever reason, they can't get past the prop to its teaching point. For these few, the prop may actually get in the way of learning.

Options

• Provide each table group with a prop. Announce the training topic and have them make connections between the prop and the topic. What could the prop teach us about the topic?

• Bring a prop to class. Cover it. Announce that this prop is directly related to the trainer's topic. Have them guess what the prop might be and why. Use a version of the Twenty Questions game to encourage inductive thinking.

• Reveal part of the prop or put the prop under cover. Learn to milk the moment to maximize interest and intrigue.

• Feel free to combine two attention techniques. In the Milk Carton story (see the *Inside Scoop* on the next page), I combined Props and Questions. It's great fun to combine techniques.

What can you do with a milk carton, a bucket, and measuring spoons?

A parent advisory group in Lethbridge, a city in a semi-arid region of southern Alberta, was holding its monthly meeting. The group was looking for a speaker and someone had recommended moi!

The meeting started at 7:00 pm I knew I had to get the group's attention quickly because I only had half an hour. Besides, this late in the day I knew many of them would be suffering from the saturation factor. They had already absorbed enough information for the day and would be ready for lighter, more entertaining moments. But I had this very important topic to present that could not be taken lightly. What to do? I needed a great opener.

I began the presentation by holding up a milk carton filled with water. The audience could hear the water slosh around as I shook the carton. I posed a question: "Imagine for a moment that this milk container holds all the water on the planet. How much of this water would be safe to drink?" One farmer near the back of the room shouted, "Fifty percent!" Immediately, another person shouted, "A drop!" A few more guesstimates were made that landed somewhere between the proposed 50 percent and the drop.

I then provided some information that would help them frame their estimates. I stated, "Scientists tell us that 97 percent of the earth's water is salt water. So, in this one litre or 1000 millilitre milk container, how much of the earth's water is fresh water?" After some quick figuring, the group said that 30 ml would be fresh water. With that response, I took out my measuring spoons and held up the 30 ml green spoon. "Here is a measuring spoon that holds 30 ml of liquid. Let's fill it and then pour the rest of the water in this milk container into the bucket here on the floor. This bucket will represent salt water and the spoon will represent the fresh water on our planet."

I now focused my attention on the measuring spoon. With one hand cupped under the green spoon, I asked, "If the 30 ml spoon represents the fresh water on our planet, what percentage is safe to drink?" I paused and then responded. "The answer is on the milk container." Pointing to the "one percent" number written on the milk container, I concluded, "One percent of this 30 ml is safe to drink!" The audience became quiet.

And now the punch line: "And to think that Canada is blessed with 18 percent of the world's fresh water and has less than 2 percent of the world's population!"

Props can be a dramatic and effective way to get the audience's attention! I never thought the milk carton would have the impact that it did. It is such a simple and common object. Yet, when used to communicate an environmental message, it became a powerful tool to focus the minds of the audience.

Tick Box

Ready

Purpose:	To bring values and beliefs about the training topic to the surface.
Time:	Twenty to thirty minutes
Group size:	Any size
Learner risk:	Medium
Materials:	Copy of tick box for learner manual, pens or pencils

Set

• Develop a tick box with questions that are appropriate for your audience. To do this, begin by identifying a theme or topic that is pertinent to your trainees. Then identify four to six issues related to this topic. Write opposing points of view for each issue. Ensure that both points of view have merit.

• Arrange this information as indicated in the sample tick box on the next page. A tick box contains two columns (A and B) of numbered statements.

• After developing the tick box, have a colleague edit your work to ensure that the wording of each statement is appropriate and fair. Remember, the tick box is not meant to be a true-false or right-wrong assessment of issues. Rather, it is a way to get learners' attention by sharing views on the issues that will be raised in the training event.

• Include a copy of the tick box in the learner manual.

Go

• Ask learners to read the A and B statements for each issue and then to tick the statement they feel best matches their view. Remind them that neither A nor B is true or false. They are simply two views on an issue.

• After everyone has completed the tick boxes, instruct participants to go back over the ticked items and choose the one that was easiest to tick and the one that was hardest to tick. Then, with an appointed chair at each subgroup, ask participants to explain why the specific items were easy or difficult to tick.

• As participants reveal their responses to the subgroup, monitor the discussion.

• Wrap up the discussion by linking each A and B statement to the course agenda. Indicate that each A and B statement will be discussed in further detail throughout the workshop.

Training Adults

Directions: Read each pair of statements below and then tick the one that is closest to your feelings or opinion.

A

1. A trainer should adjust the course to meet the needs of the learners.

2. Training outcomes should focus on what learners will be able to do.

3. Participation makes learners feel more involved and enhances learning.

4. The best learning takes place when the trainees learn over a few consecutive days so they can focus on the course material.

5. A trainer should make frequent use of a variety of high-tech visual aids.

6. The most effective means of disseminating information is to large groups.

B

1. A trainer should follow a course outline to ensure material is covered.

2. Training outcomes should outline what participants will know and understand.

3. Many individuals feel threatened by speaking out, so lecturing is the best method.

4. A course is most effective if offered for a few hours a week for a number of weeks so the participants can apply the skills between sessions.

5. For many training applications, old technologies such as flip charts are superior to more recent developments.

6. The most effective means to disseminate information is to small groups.

Rewards

• A customized tick box deals with issues the learners are currently grappling with.

• This technique encourages learners to actively listen to a variety of views and bring values and attitudes about the issues to the surface.

• I've seen it happen more than once. One member chooses 2A and gives a cogent reason for their choice. Another member follows with her rationale for selecting item 2B. Both perspectives are valid. The discussion helps each person assess her views. Sometimes, an individual will even change her mind.

• Each of the issues identified on the tick box can become a learning module for training. For example, the sample tick box provides six potential learning modules.

Risks

• You want to ensure that the choices you provide are not extreme. They need to be different, but not so disparate that they set up an all-or-nothing mentality. Even with this precaution, you will sometimes encounter learners who do not like either of the perspectives you provide.

• Even though you take time in your instructions to advise the group that the tick box is not a true-false survey, some learners may still approach it as such. Proper and repeated instructions are essential to ensure success.

Options

• Administer the same tick box at the beginning and end of the workshop. Then, have learners compare their responses. Have points of view or values changed?

• You may find that a scale, from one to five for example, serves your purposes better than tick boxes. Instead of two choices, offer five choices.

Skit

Ready

Purpose:	To have participants make an immediate connection between the workshop topic and their work place or home life.
Time:	Five to fifteen minutes
Group size:	Fifteen to fifty
Learner risk:	Medium
Materials:	Special clothing or props

Set

• Determine some loose parameters for the skit that you will share with the learners.

• Take the time to prepare skit performers. Players should have had the opportunity to rehearse lines as well as to practice gestures and body language.

• Ensure that the skit *sets the stage* for the training topic. Skits are not meant to resolve issues but to present the issues and have participants think about them.

• Prepare questions for the discussion that ensues.

Go

• *Recreate:* Conduct the skit. If required, set the stage by giving needed background information.

• *Respond:* Provide an opportunity for the audience to respond to the skit. Ask questions that will generate discussion.

• *Reinforce:* Ensure that the purpose of the skit is realized. Ask the audience, "What training issue or topic did the skit address?"

• *Relate:* Link the skit to a follow-up learning activity

Rewards

• Drama involves taking a risk, but that in itself is the reward! The instructors at a conflict resolution workshop I participated in knew this (see Making Connections next page).

• Skits arrest our thinking, draw us into the problems presented, and remind us of similar moments in our own lives. The emotion that a skit elicits gets participants thinking and predicting.

• Skits don't usually take long to make their point, and the discussion that ensues helps to focus and formulate thinking about the training issues.

Risks

• Skits involve extra time to coordinate and manage. Trainers may question whether the additional effort will pay off in learning dividends for participants. The key here is to keep it simple.

• Some risk exists around selecting those to be involved in the skit. You want to choose individuals who are comfortable in a performing role.

Options

• Work with prepared skits. Simply assign actors and arrange for rehearsal times. This reduces your efforts significantly.

• Training videos provide professionally acted skits that provide excellent training concepts.

• Start the workshop with the skit—an attention technique—instead of using an affiliation technique. In the side bar story, the instructors started immediately with their skit. The affiliation techniques were used a little later in the workshop. Be flexible and adapt the placement of the A's.

Making Connections

Several years ago I signed up for a conflict resolution workshop. Arriving at 8:45 am, I registered and then walked into the workshop room. I noticed the two instructors doing some last minute preparation. As start time approached, the participants seated themselves in subgroups.

The two instructors continued talking at the front of the room, discussing who was going to start the session. Betty indicated to John that she had started the last three sessions and, in accordance with her e-mail, wanted John to start this session. John indicated that he had not received Betty's e-mail and he was not prepared to begin this session.

We expected the instructors to work this out quickly. Their positions seemed flexible enough. But, to our amazement, John was now insisting that he was not going to start this session. "I hate surprises," he emphatically stated. "I need advance notice. Besides, Betty, you've done the last three course openings and you do a great job!"

Betty began to dig in, too. She wanted a change. She complimented John for the innovative start he had done several weeks ago and suggested he do the same one this morning. What began as a minor tiff between two instructors was now escalating. I was thinking that these out-of-town instructors were a little road weary. Now it was a couple of minutes after 9:00 am and I noticed that the 21 others in the room no longer had expectant looks on their faces. Expressions of interest were supplanted by looks of deep concern.

The situation at the front of the class didn't seem to be improving. Betty started using more emotional words. I remember her saying, "John, things always have to be mapped out for you. Why can't you lighten up and go with it?" Then John accused Betty of being a "disorganized twit." How ironic, I thought. Here we are in a conflict management workshop, and these two experts are sabotaging their own credibility.

At the height of the conflict, the two instructors turned to us in unison. They paused and looked at us with slightly up-turned lips. We'd been had! The loud laughter confirmed it. They had masterfully completed a real life skit. This became a cornerstone for the rest of the session. What a great opener! What an effective attention technique!

The conflict resolution skit lasted three minutes, but its impact lasted for the entire two days of the workshop, and then some!

Video

Ready

Purpose:	To put learners "in the moment" through vicariously experiencing real-life issues, challenges, or conflicts.
Time:	Five to fifteen minutes
Group size:	Any size
Learner risk:	Medium
Materials:	VCR or DVD player, monitor

Set

• Choose a video that is the right length. In the attention stage, the goal is to get learners focused, inquiring, and interested. This means a shorter video is appropriate, say five to ten minutes in length. These videos are designed to intrigue the viewer. (Other videos are much longer and are designed to inform, which is more appropriate during the acquisition phase of training.)

• Preview the video before the class is held and assess its appropriateness for this particular session. (See assessment questions in the Trainer's Edge side bar.)

• Plan follow-up activities such as subgroup discussions that use prepared questions and segue into the acquisition phase of training, a panel discussion, or Q&A time to respond to learner comments and questions.

the Trainer's EDGE

Assessing Video Appropriateness

When you preview a video prior to a session, ask yourself these questions:

• Will the video serve as an effective attention technique and help to bring learning needs to the surface?

• Does the group need to see the entire video?

• Can I ask questions at key points during the video to enhance viewing?

• How will I link the video to the next phase of training?

Go

• Before you show the video, advise the group of the length and suggest tips for effectively viewing the video (such as taking notes, recording questions for later, and refraining from talking).

• Ask opening rhetorical questions and provide interesting background information before you show the video. Mentally engage the learners so they connect with the video's topic or theme as quickly as possible.

• Watch the video.

• Introduce and conduct the planned follow-up activities.

Rewards

• A quality video helps learners think of similar situations at work. I particularly enjoy videos produced by Pfeiffer and Wiley Jossey-Bass. Access their Web site at www.pfeiffer.com/WileyCDA.

Risks

• Sometimes the topic might bring up negative learner luggage.

• The equipment may decide to act up on you. Take the time to practice with the equipment at your venue. How familiar are you with the operating procedures? Do you need back-up equipment? Is an assistant available to help?

• There is often a temptation to overuse or misuse videos. Do not substitute the real thing for the simulated option when the real thing will do. Videos are useful when you cannot replicate a scenario in the classroom.

Options

• Play a video without the sound. Or, stop the video just when the solution seems apparent or the crisis has just been revealed. Get the group to respond and then continue with the video.

• With the advent of camcorders, you may want to produce your own video. For example, with learner permission, I show several clips of participants who have attended my Power Presentation Skills workshop. The clips show speaking snippets from the beginning and the end of the class. It's a motivating way to help trainees see the results they can achieve in training.

Humour

Ready

Purpose:	To create interest, curiosity, and a desire to learn.
Time:	Varies. A few seconds (quip) to several minutes (longer story)
Group size:	Any size
Learner risk:	Low to moderate
Materials:	Varies according to situation. For example, you may need an overhead projector to show a cartoon.

Set

• *Research:* Keep your eyes open for stories, jokes, anecdotes, quotations, puns, clip art, or cartoons that you find funny and that will help you get the attention of the audience. Remember, humour comes from many sources.

• *Relevance:* When you choose a humorous element for your workshop, make sure it is relevant. The humour should draw the learner into the workshop topic. It needs to have a point and a purpose.

• *Rehearse:* Practice your delivery of a quip, story, or pun. Or practice your introduction with the use of humorous slides or cartoons. You want to discover the fastest, cleanest way to get to the punch line.

Go

• *Relax:* Make yourself comfortable when using humour.

• *Risk:* Recognize that there is a reasonable risk in humour. Be willing to take it.

• *Recount:* When telling your story or introducing your cartoon, use a transitional comment. For example, say something like, "Let me illustrate it this way," before you display a cartoon on the overhead or tell your story.

Rewards

• Humour puts learners at ease. They are more attentive and less resistant to learning. They enjoy the workshop experience more fully. Humour increases the energy level in a room and makes for a more conducive learning climate. With humour, the weather forecast for the workshop looks very good!

• When a workshop uses humour, the trainer becomes more spontaneous and dynamic. Authenticity and genuineness are enhanced. You will be seen as a person who can balance the serious and fun sides of training.

Risks

• When you use jokes to get attention, you run the risk that one or more learners may have already heard the jokes or they won't get them. If you do use jokes, personalize them. If the joke is going to be on someone, it should be on you.

• Humour only works in context. When you try to relate a funny event that happened at another workshop, the audience may not get it. Rather than risk recreating a funny moment from the past, work on humour in the moment.

Options

• In this section, I focus on using humour as an attention technique. However, humour reaches far beyond the purpose of creating interest in the training topic. Use it throughout your training session.

• Sometimes you may want to import humour rather than create it yourself. In one of my workshops, I read a funny incident from a novel. The two-paragraph reading is short and always makes my audience laugh!

Humour Essentials

Keep these tidbits in mind when bringing humour to your training topic.

• Humour is a learned skill. I remember talking to Jeannie Robertson, a humorist, who said the hardest thing she does is create humour. She takes humour very seriously and, as a result, is a very funny person, both on and off the stage.

• Forget about humour that deals with the sensitive four: race, religion, sex, and politics. Add to this list humour that uses offensive language. When in doubt, take it out!

• Humour works best if you've established a rapport with the group. Without a good rapport, the group may interpret the humour as making fun of someone, putting someone down, or the trainer simply trying too hard to be funny.

• Read M. Kushner's *The Light Touch: How to Use Humor for Business Success* for ideas on workshop humour. As Kushner suggests, attribute your jokes to Aristotle. That way, even if no one laughs, they will at least think you're smart!

Humour - Attention

Gap Analysis

Ready

Purpose:	To generate awareness of what learners know and what they need to know.
Time:	Ten to twenty minutes
Group size:	Any size
Learner risk:	Medium
Materials:	Gap-analysis tool

Set

• Choose a gap-analysis tool for the training group. Ensure that it measures what it purports to measure by completing one on yourself. Do you feel it is accurate? Does it use plain English? Is it easy to complete? You might even want a colleague to complete the gap analysis or to administer it to you.

Go

• Explain clearly the purpose of the gap-analysis instrument. Remind learners that this is not a test or an evaluation tool. It is given so that each participant will understand what he currently knows and/or believes about the training topic. Give clear and concise instructions. Ensure a quiet atmosphere so learners can concentrate.

• Complete the scoring to help participants reach conclusions about their current knowledge and the knowledge that needs to be learned.

• After the questionnaire scores have been calculated, take the time to interpret the results. What do they mean? Help trainees assess their current abilities and set goals for the day's training session. Point out that specific skills or abilities have been measured and the results relate to the trainee's work and to the purposes and outcomes of the workshop. Do participants need to simply strengthen current abilities or do they need to acquire new skills?

Rewards

•When properly administered and interpreted, a gap-analysis tool can yield accurate and useful insights into the current competency level of each participant. It can provide a non-threatening approach to help participants gain an objective assessment of current skills or attitude states.

• When participants gain a clear view of their deficits with a particular set of skills, they can set realistic training goals.

The Trainer in You

Dear Hugh,

I would like to create my own gap-analysis tool, but I'm not sure where to begin. Could you send some pointers my way?

Gapless in Gimli

Dear Gapless,

As your question suggests, developing a gap-analysis tool is something that needs to be done carefully. Here are a few things to keep in mind when developing a gap-analysis tool.

Don't forget that learners take a certain amount of risk with this activity. After all, they are being asked to recognize and assess gaps in their own knowledge. So, when you develop the tool, keep this personal element in mind. This activity is not intended to embarrass, insult, or de-motivate learners. Rather, the measurement of any learning gap is seen in terms of learning opportunities and options. When learners know they lack a specific skill or a set of skills, they can use the workshop to improve themselves.

When I create gap-analysis tools, I ask myself two main things. What resources, whether work experiences or education, can this tool bring to the forefront to advance the skills participants will be learning in the workshop? And what skills or understandings does each learner need to acquire in order to become more proficient?

Good luck!

Sincerely,
Hugh

Risks

• Poor results from a gap-analysis tool can be discouraging. If you sense that learners are feeling frustrated, deal with the situation up front. Remind learners that no matter what the results of the analysis, the purpose of training is to help raise the bar from where they are to where they would like to be.

• Participants may not be realistic in their own assessment. They may over estimate or under estimate their abilities. In either case, the results are inaccurate and can lead to false conclusions.

Options

• Conduct the same gap analysis near the end of the workshop. This can provide the trainer and learners with a way to assess the value of the workshop. It is also very encouraging for learners to see the difference training has made.

• In order to counter the risk of over- or under-estimation, use two gap-analysis instruments for each person. One instrument can be completed by the learner on himself, and another instrument can be completed by a colleague. This provides two perspectives for each person.

When I completed my post-graduate work at Northern Illinois University, I thought I needed some added adventure before returning home. So, I signed up for a four week Outward Bound course in North Carolina!

The Outward Bound motto is: "To strive and not to yield." When you attend a course, you are usually in a group of fifteen to twenty-four people. For participants to experience their inner capabilities, the facilitators will often put the group in challenging situations without a lot of instruction about how to solve the tasks. The challenge for the group is to figure out a safe solution. It might be how to rappel down the side of a cliff face, find a way through thick bush, spelunk through mysterious caves, or negotiate a ropes course.

In these scenarios, we soon learned to tap into the resources of our group. No one person had all the skills needed to face a challenge, but as a group we could pool our experiences and expertise to help us through. We became good at gap analysis. We had to ask ourselves, "What do we need to solve this task and who has the skill to help us through? If we don't have the skills as a group, then let's develop our problem-solving skills to help us work through the challenge." Time and time again we amazed ourselves with what we were capable of doing as a group and as individuals.

Gap Analysis
Communication Profile

Directions: There are twenty statements on this profile, each one specifying a particular communication skill. Place an "X" on the dotted line to indicate how you would rate yourself on each skill. At the end of this exercise, draw lines between the "X's" so you can see at a glance what communication skills you are good at and what skills you might want to work on today. The intent of this exercise is to help you focus on what you most need from this workshop.

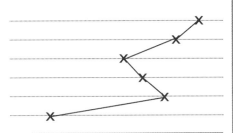

	1 2 3 4 5 6 7 8 9 10
	Low High

Performance Skills

1. I find it easy to express my ideas in front of groups.
2. I am able to deliver a presentation with minimal reliance on notes.
3. I'm comfortable using eye contact to help establish audience rapport.
4. I welcome the opportunity to speak at a meeting.
5. I feel comfortable addressing a large audience.
6. My gestures and body language are congruent with my message.
7. I find it easy to use humour with an audience.

Voice Skills

8. I am able to project my voice—it is easily heard.
9. My voice does not fade at the end of sentences.
10. I avoid using "uh," "um," and other verbal bumpers like this.
11. I use vocal variety to give feeling and meaning to my words.
12. I speak at a rate that is acceptable to the audience.
13. My voice feels good after an hour of public speaking.
14. Hoarseness, nasality, and hesitation are absent from my speaking.

Technical Skills

15. I speak directly and concisely when asked to "say a few words."
16. I use my planning time effectively and efficiently.
17. I use appropriate grammar.
18. I'm good at thinking of appropriate visual aids for my talks.
19. I use anecdotes and stories to support my key ideas.
20. I find out as much as I can about an audience before I speak to it.

Comment:
My greatest strengths are:

#3, 14, 15

My greatest needs are:

#9, 10, 20

Immersions

Ready

Purpose:	To place the trainees in a "challenge situation" in which they may or may not have the skills to perform what is required. From this experience, the participants will identify the skills they need to learn.
Time:	Ten to twenty minutes
Group size:	A maximum of fifteen
Learner risk:	Medium to high
Materials:	Vary according to the challenge situations

Set

• Plan a challenge situation for your learners. Remember that this activity is particularly useful when you are teaching skills. (Revisit my canoe training experience on page 7 for a sample immersion experience.)

• This activity works best with fewer than fifteen participants. This allows time for personalized attention, the maintenance of a safe environment, and the accurate assessment of learner skill levels.

Go

• Explain the challenge situation to the learners and provide them with a recommended time period to complete the task. Let them know that effort, not success, is the goal of this activity. Do not go into detail with your instructions, except where safety is involved.

• Organize the learners into subgroups, as deemed appropriate, and identify safety requirements or conditions. Provide them with the equipment needed to complete the challenge situation. Get them started on the activity.

• Following the immersion experience, provide time to debrief. Use open-ended questions to help learners assess their skill levels and the skills they need to develop to complete the task. Ask them what went well and what did not.

Making Connections

Employees in many corporations are legally required to attend First Aid Training annually. Trainers who conduct these first aid sessions can face a fair amount of resistance because the attendees will claim they know most of their first aid skills and don't need to attend another training session. In working with these trainees, I've devised a number of immersions. Trainees are asked to perform first aid skills without the benefit of any instruction beyond setting up of the activity and identifying the task. In many cases, learners soon appreciate the need for a "refresher" class.

Rewards

- Learners will realize that they need to know more than they do. This discovery is a driving force that "hooks" the learner—the primary purpose of any attention phase technique.

- Learners are usually very eager to engage in the challenge situation and their interest level is maintained throughout the activity. Frustration when they do not know or remember skills creates a stronger desire to want to know more.

Risks

- Some activities involve a certain amount of safety risk. Minimize the risk with due precautions and constant attention when learners are engaged in the challenge situation.

- Some learners may give up in frustration. Instead of turning them on to learning, they resist and want to quit.

Options

- There are many books available on cooperative games. A number of these activities can be adapted as immersion experience techniques.

HUGHism

" The art and skill of creating curiosity depends on the trainer's ability to think like a learner. "

References

Bloom, B. 1956. *Taxonomy of education objectives, handbook I: The cognitive domain.* New York: McKay.

Kloss, R. J. Feb. 1988. *Toward asking the right questions.* The Clearing House: 245–248.

Kushner, Malcolm L. 1990. *The light touch: How to use humor for business success.* New York: Simon and Schuster.

Wycoff, Joyce. 1991. *Mindmapping: Your personal guide to exploring creativity and problem-solving.* New York: Berkley Books.

Chapter 7:
Acquisition Techniques

The aim of education should be to convert the mind into
a living fountain, not a reservoir.
John Mason

For non-trainers, acquisition IS training.

They believe that when a trainer stands in front of a group and imparts knowledge about a subject, that is training. The learners are acquiring information from a subject-matter expert. Nothing more, nothing less.

Managers with this concept of training have pretty simple advice for trainers: "Just pack them in, jam their heads with information, give them a thick manual and tons of notes, leave them overwhelmed (they'll be impressed!), and then send them back to work. Your job is to cover the content. Never mind if you think it is too much. We've got legal obligations for training and we want to ensure that our employees have been told what they need to know."

Perhaps this description is a little tongue in cheek, but in some training situations it's not that far fetched. Fortunately, this view of training is quickly becoming unacceptable. Yes, training is about acquisition, but for learners to acquire knowledge in a meaningful way you have to do much more than "pack them in and jam their heads with information."

For the most part, workshop content is acquired through lectures. It is relatively easy to lecture, especially when you know what you're talking about. Yet, experts estimate that about 90 percent of the information imparted in a "typical" lecture will be forgotten within forty-eight hours. Not great payback for the giver or receiver of the information.

That's why today's trainer does not have to rely on a "typical" lecture to reach his or her audience. We've learned to avoid the "talk and gawk" show. In its place we use interactive lecture techniques (ILT's) that transform traditional lectures into dynamic and stimulating experiences, where long-term benefits are realized for the trainer, the learners, and the organization.

The following ILTs will help you share your knowledge, skills, attitudes, and values in dynamic, interactive, and effective ways. They are easy to implement and require a modest amount of time to integrate. Try out:

Iconing
Five Plus
Full Card
Hot Seat–Hot Tips
Checking In
Checklist
Affinity Diagram
Top Ten
PINing
Banking
Tutoring
Acrostic Challenge

Iconing

Ready

Purpose:	To ensure learners retain knowledge through a combination of fun, competition, and visual icons.
Time:	Adds ten minutes to a lecture
Group size:	Any size
Learner risk:	Moderate
Materials:	Index cards, envelopes, flip chart

Set

• Prepare your lecture explaining a process or procedure. For example, the six steps to building a budget.

• Develop icons (small drawings) that represent each of the key steps in the procedure.

• Draw the icons on a flip chart with each icon inside a box. For example, if you have six steps, draw a square or rectangle frame with six boxes in it; if your lecture has nine key steps, then the square or rectangle frame should have nine boxes in it, etc. Draw an icon in each box.

• Now draw each icon on an index card. You will need one set of icon index cards for each subgroup. Mix up the card sets so the icons are not in the correct order. Put each set in an envelope.

Go

• As you deliver your lecture, refer to the icons on the flip chart. At the end of your lecture, review the process or procedure by highlighting the information associated with each icon.

• Cover the flip chart and distribute the envelopes with the sets of icon cards, one set to each subgroup. Advise the groups to keep the envelopes closed.

• Explain to the learners that when you say "begin" they can take the deck of icon cards from the envelopes and arrange them in the same order as they appeared on the flip chart.

• When subgroups finish arranging the icon cards, they yell "Finished" or give some other indication that the task is done.

• Play the iconing card game a couple of times to maximize the fun and review. Each time they play, have subgroups shuffle their decks of cards and then pass them on to a different subgroup.

• Invite one of the subgroups to walk through its results to provide another review of the steps. Remember, repetition improves retention.

Sample Icon Chart

At a Train the Trainer workshop I conducted for the Canadian Red Cross, participants developed an iconing lecture about how to do the Heimlich Manoeuvre. Nine icons were developed. Here are the icons that were transferred to the flip chart, as well as the written descriptions for each icon.

Step in Process	Explanation of Icons
1	Observation: You see a person choking
2	Inquire: Are your choking? (If person responds "yes," proceed. If "no," stop!)
3	Reassure the victim: I can help you.
4	Make a fist with one of your hands.
5	Stand behind the victim and put both of your arms around him or her.
6	Place your open hand over the hand that forms a fist.
7	Position your hands above the victim's navel and below the rib cage.
8	Apply an upward thrust.
9	Result: You've saved the person's life.

Rewards

• With this activity, participants have a much better chance of remembering a process or procedure. For example, I conducted this technique with a group in Fort McMurray. Ninety days later I returned to conduct an advanced workshop with the same group. I took out the icon chart from the previous session. They recalled the meaning of all the symbols. That's high retention!

• This activity generates a lot of fun for the group. Participants enjoy the game-like atmosphere while they learn the key concepts of the lecture.

Risks

• A few groups may get overly competitive. For them, winning—not reviewing content—becomes the focus. To minimize this aspect, do not choose the winning subgroups to walk through their results at the end of the icon card games. Choose another group.

Options

• Before you lecture, walk through your icon chart to present learners with an overview. This provides learners with a road map that helps them follow the lecture more attentively.

• Instead of suggesting your own icons at the beginning of the lecture, have students create their own icons at the end of the lecture to represent the main ideas. This can be a lot of fun and an excellent way to review.

Five Plus

Ready

Purpose:	To revisit complex and important material five times and still maintain learner interest.
Time:	Adds ten minutes to a lecture
Group size:	Any size
Learner risk:	Moderate
Materials:	5 x 7 inch cards

Set

• Develop tasks that provide different ways of reviewing the material in your lecture. You will need a different task for each subgroup. For example, if there are five subgroups you need five different tasks; if you have six subgroups you need six different tasks, etc. (See the sample tasks on the next page.)

• Print each task on one 5 x 7 inch card.

Go

• Before you start your lecture, let the group know that at the end of the lecture you will be asking the class to participate in a series of review activities about the lecture. Do not expand on these instructions. This is usually enough to set the stage.

• Deliver your lecture. Then, divide the group into subgroups.

• Distribute one task card to each subgroup and give them three to four minutes to prepare a response. (Be sure to wait until after the lecture to distribute the task cards; otherwise, learners may focus on the task instead of the lecture.)

• Pace the activity by periodically announcing how much time remains.

• When the tasks are complete, ask each subgroup in turn to identify its activity and then present the results to the whole group. Subgroups can appoint a spokesperson or everyone from the group can share reporting duties.

• Provide a commentary to follow each subgroup's report. Be brief.

Rewards

• When the subgroups report on their tasks, you will get a very clear idea of whether or not they have understood the lecture and what, if anything, needs to be clarified or revisited. This is a great way to check comprehension in a non-threatening manner.

• Groups retain information longer with Five Plus because they have revisited the material in five different ways. Remember Mehrabian's theory? If you repeat something six times, you increase retention by 90 percent. With this technique, the first time you hear material is in the trainer's lecture. The next five times, though, occur as part of the subgroup tasks. And the trainer's summary is a seventh time!

Sample Five Plus Tasks

Subgroup	Role	Task
1	Illustrators	Provide specific examples or applications of the lecture ideas. How could this apply to your situation? In what way?
2	Investigators	Prepare three questions to ask the presenter about the lecture content. Use open-ended questions that seek more information, clarity, or expansion of ideas.
3	Key Noters	Provide an overview of the key points made in the lecture. Support with examples that may have been provided.
4	Exam Givers	Prepare three questions and accompanying answers to assess participants' understanding of the lecture content.
5	Linkers	How does this lecture link with other material that has been covered? Provide one or two examples.

Risks

• Once in a while, a subgroup will misinterpret the task. Checking in with each group as they work will reduce this risk.

• Sometimes, especially if a subgroup does not work together effectively, this technique can take up too much time. Monitor the subgroups and keep within the timeframe.

Options

• Roles for subgroups other than those included in the sample assignment include "agreers" and "naysayers." The agreers explain which points they agreed with or found helpful; the naysayers comment on which points they disagreed with or don't understand.

Full Card

Ready

Purpose:	To reinforce understanding and retention of technical material (terms, concepts, principles) through fun and repetition.
Time:	Adds ten minutes to a lecture
Group size:	Any size
Learner risk:	Moderate
Materials:	Full card for each participant, markers, prize

Set

• Identify approximately twelve key terms or concepts from your lecture. Ensure that the terms you choose will be mentioned at least two or three times during the lecture. If you only mention a term once, the learners' recall level significantly decreases.

• Make a copy of the Full Card template for each learner. (See sample on the next page.)

• Put eight of the twelve terms on each Full Card, leaving the middle space as a free space. (Alternatively, you may want to put the name of the lecture or topic in the centre square.) Choose different terms for each Full Card and place the words in different spots on the cards.

• Develop definitions for each of the terms or concepts you're using. On a separate piece of paper, make a list of the terms with their definitions.

Go

• Let participants know that, following the lecture, you will be conducting a review activity to ensure retention and understanding of the lesson's terminology.

• After the lecture, distribute one Full Card and a marker to each learner.

• Explain that the Full Card has eight terms that were introduced in the lecture. Let participants know that each learner's Full Card is different. Tell the group that you will read definitions that correspond with the terms on their Full Cards. As you read the definitions, they are to check off the appropriate term on their cards, if they have it.

• Repeat the process with another definition.

• Once a learner checks off all items on the card, she announces, "Full Card!"

• When "Full Card" is announced, stop giving any further definitions. Ask the person with the Full Card to reveal the concepts on her card. If the concepts correspond with the definitions you've given, then the learner has a Full Card and the exercise is over.

- Present the learner with a prize.

Sample Full Card

Coaching Workshop

Closing the Loop	Attending	Planning
Observing Process	*Free Space*	Respecting
Probing	Identifying	Resourcing

the Trainer's EDGE

I tend to avoid using the word "bingo" when using this technique. The purpose of this technique is to revisit the important terms and concepts at the end of a lecture. The fact that this technique resembles bingo is not significant and, if you use the word, it may marginalize the activity in the minds of some learners.

Rewards

• When introducing new concepts and terms to a class, repetition is essential if learners are going to retain the material. There are no short cuts to developing memory, only fun alternatives.

• Speaking of fun, this technique delivers. Participants enjoy playing a version of a game they will undoubtedly know: bingo.

Risks

• Don't go too heavy on the terminology. Select approximately a dozen key concepts or terms that learners must know rather than boggling their minds with a whole bunch of terms. If you have more than a dozen terms to cover, break up the exercise rather than go for broke.

• This technique should only extend the lecture by ten minutes. Resist the temptation to play longer.

Options

• When you check a Full Card, have the winner read the terms and give his own definition for each one.

• Do not stop the exercise after checking a winner's card. Continue to get more Full Cards. After all, the point of this exercise is review, not winners and losers. Those who have a Full Card can work with those who are still working to attain a Full Card.

• Instead of having learners play independently, have them work together in their subgroups. The goal is for all members in the subgroup to get a Full Card before they can win. Encourage members to help each other out.

Hot Seat–Hot Tips

Ready

Purpose:	To encourage learners to ask insightful and penetrating questions.
Time:	Adds ten minutes to a lecture
Group size:	Any size
Learner risk:	Low
Materials:	Index cards

Set

• Prepare examples of appropriate closed and open-ended questions. (See page 105 for ideas.)

Go

• Advise learners that following the lecture they will be allotted time to put the lecturer on the hot seat.

• Deliver the lecture.

• After the lecture, create subgroups with three to six participants in each subgroup. Distribute four index cards to each subgroup.

• Ask the subgroups to take about two minutes to generate three to four questions about the lecture's content and to put one question on each index card. Encourage both closed and open-ended questions. Provide examples of closed and open questions if needed.

• Once the questions have been prepared, sit in the hot seat and invite a subgroup to ask one of its questions. When you respond, keep the answer brief. If a more detailed response is required, provide only a summary and then respond more fully later.

• Ask a different subgroup for one of its questions. Once each subgroup has asked one question, repeat the pattern and ask for a second question from each subgroup, and so on.

• After all questions have been asked and answered, the trainer can have the last word with a few "hot tips" that summarize the lecture.

Rewards

• This activity can be the highlight of a lecture. Your spontaneity and insightfulness reinforce the ideas that need to be remembered. One learner shared with me, "I didn't get your lecture at first, but I did get it when you were in the hot seat."

• You are modeling risk-taking with this technique and setting the stage for ongoing inquiry.

• This technique encourages students to generate thoughtful questions. By limiting the number of questions learners can ask, you are teaching them the art and value of inquiry.

Risks

• Some trainers have not learned to be brief. The Hot Seat session drags on and becomes a lowlight, not a highlight for learners. Make clear, concise, and credible responses your goal. Hot Seat–Hot Tips is the way to practice the three C's!

• Participants may not generate high-quality questions. Come prepared with some of your own "tough" questions to demonstrate just how valuable inquiry can be.

Options

• Conduct Hot Seat–Hot Tips like a press conference. In keeping with that format, prepare an opening statement and then answer questions from "the press."

• This activity works well with guest speakers. Invite other experts to attend the class and take part in the Hot Seat–Hot Tips activity. If more than one expert joins you, then form a subgroup for each guest and rotate so that all have an opportunity to meet each expert.

Checking In

Ready

Purpose:	To reinforce difficult concepts by interacting with the group during the lecture.
Time:	Adds ten minutes to a lecture
Group size:	Any size
Learner risk:	Moderate
Materials:	AV equipment to display the questions, one set of four cards (each a different colour) for each subgroup, index cards

Set

• As you prepare your lecture, develop one question for every seven to ten minutes of lecture time. Use a variety of questions types, such as stem, multiple choice, and open ended. (I find it easy to add an element of humour with the multiple-choice questions.)

• Decide how you will display the questions (overhead, desktop projector, or flip chart).

• Develop a chart that explains the methods you want learners to use when responding to multiple-choice questions. (See sample on the next page.)

Go

• Before starting the lecture, let students know that you will be pausing several times as you speak to "check in" with them by asking a question.

• Explain that the questions you ask will be based on the material that has just been covered in the lecture and that you will be asking them to respond to your questions in two ways: either by writing a response on an index card or, for multiple-choice questions, by holding up a coloured card.

• Distribute the coloured cards and the index cards.

• Refer the learners to the flip chart with the multiple-choice options chart and explain: If you believe the correct answer to your multiple-choice question is "A," then hold up the red card, if you think it is "B," hold up the blue card, for "C," hold up the yellow card, and for "D," hold up the green card. (See sample on the next page.)

• Begin your lecture. At the appropriate time, ask a question. Allow five to thirty seconds for learners to prepare responses.

• If the question was multiple choice, count to three and then have learners display their selected cards. Check the colour of the cards. (Note: I find if I don't synchronize the display of cards, some subgroups will wait for other subgroups to display their cards before showing their own. This means I'm not receiving accurate feedback.) If the question required a written answer, ask for several responses.

• If everyone has the correct answer, congratulate the group and move on. If you receive incorrect responses, ask the learners to briefly discuss their responses. Provide any needed review and then move on.

• Continue with the lecture until the next question. Repeat the process.

Sample Card Colour Chart

Card Colour	Choice	Card Colour	Choice
Red	A	Yellow	C
Blue	B	Green	D

Rewards

• Learners' responses to the questions will give you immediate feedback about whether or not they understand the concepts. This allows you to ensure participant understanding.

• Because reinforcement is frequent, learners stay tuned-in

Risks

• Some students may become embarrassed if they have one or more incorrect responses. To address this situation, see the first adaptation suggestion below.

• It is important to develop questions that are neither too easy nor too difficult. You want learners to think through their answers but avoid too many incorrect responses.

Options

• You can promote a collaborative learning environment by having subgroups, rather than individuals, determine the correct answer. In this case, pass one set of coloured cards and one set of index cards to each subgroup. Explain that when a question comes up each subgroup is to discuss and determine the correct answer. Then after fifteen to thirty seconds, and at the count of three, an appointed person in each subgroup will display the answer card.

• Ask each subgroup to prepare one or two questions at the end of the lecture and then administer the questions to the entire group.

Checklist

Ready

Purpose:	To summarize lecture content and reinforce learning. To review material that a learner is already familiar with.
Time:	Reduces lecture time by at least 50 percent
Group size:	Any size
Learner risk:	Moderate
Materials:	Prepared checklist with optional rating scale

Set

• Create an outline on a lecture topic using a checklist format and determine a rating scale for the checklist. (See sample on the next page.)

• Edit and print the checklist, making a copy for each learner.

• Prepare questions about the items on the checklist.

Go

• Announce the topic that will be covered in the session and distribute the checklist to each learner. Indicate that the checklist contains all the main points of the lecture.

• Instruct participants to review each item on the checklist and respond to the rating scale for each item. Continue until all items have been responded to.

• Remind the learners that the checklist is not a test, but a way to summarize key points about the topic and to ensure understanding.

• When participants have completed the checklist, invite them to ask questions about any of the items on the checklist.

• If learners need prompting, use some of your prepared questions to get the ball rolling.

Rewards

• This technique is a real time saver! A lecture can be shortened by 50 to 75 percent. Through the checklist, you ensure that learners understand the topic content by reviewing information and by hosting a Q&A session.

• The checklist itself is a useful tool after the session is over. I know learners who have made copies for work and used it to brush up on concepts they need to remember. Sometimes, learners will even use the checklist to rate themselves after they've completed a task.

I use the following checklist when I want participants in my Train the Trainer workshops to think about how they a training session.

Climate Building Checklist

In my workshops . . .

	Often	Sometimes	Seldom
1. Seating arrangement encourages interactivity and participation.			
2. AV equipment has been tested and is in the most suitable location.			
3. Workshop supplies are easily accessible.			
4. Music is playing as part of the welcome to participants.			
5. Workshop room is clean and orderly.			
6. Handouts are available for the participants.			
7. Name tents are available with felt pens, pencils, or pens.			
8. Temperature of the room can be adjusted as necessary.			
9. Lighting can be adjusted in the room (e.g. over the screen).			
10. Emergency exits, washroom facilities, and noise levels have been checked.			
11. Parking Lot flip chart is prepared and hung for use by participants.			

As an instructor, I . . .

	Often	Sometimes	Seldom
12. Am available to greet the participants as they arrive.			
13. Have a positive and anticipatory attitude towards participants.			
14. Introduce myself in a creative manner (e.g. Gang Up On).			
15. Eliminate or minimize negative conditions surrounding the subject.			
16. Announce class times, workshop breaks, lunch details, washroom locations, fire escape.			
17. Give rationale for any assignments.			
18. Encourage the learners.			
19. Positively confront erroneous expectations and assumptions from negative learner attitude.			

The activities I choose . . .

	Often	Sometimes	Seldom
20. Promote a learner's personal control of the learning context.			
21. Provide a road map or workshop agenda.			
22. Welcome learners with a displayed message.			
23. Engage the audience early, laying a template for involvement.			
24. Start promptly to reinforce instructor's value of learners' time.			
25. State objectives up front.			
26. Include a live audience audit when appropriate.			
27. Take time to address needs and expectations of the group.			
28. Allow for introductions.			

Risks

• Good reading, comprehension, and critical questioning skills are required for this activity to be most effective.

• Some learners will associate the rating scale with an exam or other type of assessment, even though the Checklist is not intended for this purpose.

• Do not use this technique with learners who do not already have experience with the topic. If you do, it will confuse and confound learners.

Options

• Deliver your lecture, then distribute the checklist for review. Have each participant complete the checklist and conduct a Q&A as in the original format. This is one way to use this technique with students who do not already have a working knowledge of the topic.

• After learners have completed the checklist, have them use the checklist to design their own lecturettes. Have them focus on three to five points. Give them five minutes to prepare. Have them work in pairs or triads to deliver their lecturettes. Relay learners to different subgroups and repeat the process if time is available.

Making Connections

The idea of a checklist came from my flight training. With small aircraft, you are required to complete a "walk about," externally and in the cockpit before every flight. On this walk about, you have a checklist that you use to make sure everything is in working order. It seemed to me that the checklists I used were excellent summaries of my pilot training. Most of the main concepts and key elements to remember were on the two small craft checklists. If a learner has working knowledge of a topic, they don't need to hear another lecture on it. They simply need to do a type of written walk about. Voila, the birth of the checklist technique!

Affinity Diagram

Ready

Purpose:	To generate and incorporate participant data into a lecture.
Time:	Adds ten minutes to the start of the lecture
Group size:	Up to twenty-five people
Learner risk:	Low
Materials:	Two sizes of Post-It Notes: 3 x 3 inch and 3 x 5 inch

Set

• Develop an interesting, relevant, open-ended question that relates to the session topic.

• Record the question on a suitable visual aid (overhead, desktop projector, or flip chart).

• Distribute about a dozen 3 x 3 inch Post-it Notes to each learner.

• Ahead of the session, check to see if the Post-it Notes will stick to the walls. In some cases, they drop off five to fifteen seconds after you post them. If need be, post flip chart pages on the wall so Post-it Notes can be stuck on the paper instead.

Go

• Let the learners know that you would like to hear their ideas about the session's topic and to incorporate these ideas into the lecture.

• Pose the prepared question to the group and refer to it on the visual aid.

• Ask learners to take three to five minutes to respond to the question by recording their ideas on the Post-it Notes at the table. If the learner has more than one idea, ask them to record each idea on a separate Post-it Note. Request that the group be quiet during this part of the activity.

• Collect the Post-it Notes as they are completed and randomly post them on the wall over *a large area*. Later on, when you have twenty learners viewing and grouping the Post-it Notes, you'll realize how essential adequate wall and walking space are.

• When learners have exhausted their responses, invite them to come to the wall and, in silence, take about a minute to scan the various answers.

• Ask the learners to group similar responses together (i.e. ideas that have affinity with each other should be grouped together). Talking is permitted for this part of the activity.

• Once the ideas have been grouped, ask the learners to assign a heading or category to each grouping. Ask them to write the category titles on the larger Post-it Notes and place these above the groupings.

• Provide a quick summary of the learners' work.

• Thank the learners for their input and indicate that you will make an effort to incorporate their data into the lecture.

• Begin lecture. When you use ideas from the Affinity Diagram, ask students to provide examples. This keeps them involved throughout the lecture and helps to ensure relevancy.

Rewards

• Starting with a question is a way to get the learners' attention. With this technique you're combining two A's—attention and acquisition.

• This technique endorses learners' thinking while providing relevant and interesting information that enhances lecture content.

Risks

• Choose your question carefully. Sometimes the question posed doesn't interest the group, or the group has insufficient experience to draw on.

• This technique requires extra effort and spontaneity on the part of the lecturer. If you do not use much of the learner data, the technique loses its value.

Options

• After your lecture, pose the same question again and repeat the affinity diagram technique. You can then compare pre- and post-responses.

• Use the categories to form part (or all) of the lecture outline.

Top Ten

Ready

Purpose:	To generate involvement by starting a lecture with learners' experiences before adding your own knowledge and expertise.
Time:	Adds ten minutes to beginning of lecture
Group size:	Any size
Learner risk:	Low
Materials:	Top Ten response sheet

Set

• Create an open-ended question that relates to your lecture and that will capture the interest of the group. Put the question on an overhead, desktop projector, or flip chart.

• Prepare a Top Ten response sheet for each learner. (See sample on the next page.)

Go

• Distribute a Top Ten response sheet to each learner or, if you've included the response sheet in the learner manual, have learners turn to the appropriate page.

• Pose your question to the group and let learners know they have about one minute to record two or three responses on the response sheet under the Learner's Top Ten column.

• Invite learners to leave their seats and share their ideas with other participants and to add new ideas to their sheets. Instruct them to return to their seats when they have ten ideas. Allow approximately five to seven minutes for this part of the exercise.

• Present your lecture in ten points. Have learners refer to their Top Ten sheet throughout the lecture to see if their ideas coincide with your presentation. Indicate when you'd like learners to add your points to the Trainer Top Ten column.

• At the end of the lecture, invite learners to share ideas from their Top Ten sheets that were used or not used in your lecture. Conduct a Q&A session to clarify points.

Sample Checklist

Note: This response sheet corresponds with the question, "What techniques can improve listening skills?"

Ten Ways to Improve Listening Skills	
Learner Top Ten	Trainer Top Ten
1. _____	1. _____
2. _____	2. _____
3. _____	3. _____
4. _____	4. _____
5. _____	5. _____
6. _____	6. _____
7. _____	7. _____
8. _____	8. _____
9. _____	9. _____
10. _____	10. _____

Rewards

• This is an excellent, collaborative learning exercise. I'm often fascinated watching learners at work on this exercise. They typically begin by touching base one on one. Soon they start grouping into pods of three to five learners. Sometimes the entire group forms a single circle and shares ideas.

• This is a very useful technique during low points of the day, typically between 11:00 am and noon, 1:00 pm and 2:00 pm, or near the end of the training day. Use Top Ten to re-energize the learners!

Risks

• Once in a while, a learner will remain in his seat when invited to share with others. This will not jeopardize the activity or have a negative impact on the lecture. You can choose to ignore the situation or visit the individual and discuss his responses.

Options

• If the planned lecture has more than ten points, modify the response sheet to reflect the number of points you will cover.

• Put learners into subgroups of three to five participants before beginning the activity. Then ask each subgroup to come up with three responses to the opening question or comment. After that, invite learners to leave their chairs and work with other subgroups to complete the response sheet.

• If the group has come up with more than ten points, deliver a short lecturette (ten minutes or less) to cover the additional points.

PINing

Ready

Purpose:	To reinforce the content of a lecture by pairing up learners and having them deliver lecturettes.
Time:	Adds ten minutes at the end of the lecture
Group size:	Any size
Learner risk:	Moderate
Materials:	Post-it Notes (PINs)

Set

• Select key concepts, terms, or quotations from your lecture, one concept per participant (e.g. if there are fifteen learners, generate fifteen concepts or terms).

• Write each concept, term, or quote on a Post-it Note, along with a page number from the learner manual that discusses the point.

• Stick the Post-it Notes (PINs) on one or more flip charts at the front of the room.

Go

• At the start of the lecture explain that a review exercise will be conducted immediately following the presentation.

• As you deliver the lecture, be sure to refer to the concepts that you have recorded on the Post-it Notes.

• After the lecture, reveal the flip chart with the Post-it Notes. Explain that each of the PINs contains a concept, term or quote from the lecture as well as a page number from the learner manual that has more information on the concept.

• Explain that each learner will be given three minutes to prepare a one minute "lecturette" on a PIN concept that they will then deliver to one other participant.

• Invite learners to select one PIN from the flip chart and begin to prepare their lecturettes. Assist them if needed. Pace the activity so the pairs know how much time remains.

• After three minutes, instruct learners to pair up with a learner from another table. Then give each learner in the pair one minute to present the prepared lecturette. (Note: If your group has an uneven number of students, involve yourself. Or, if someone has to leave in the middle of the activity, be ready to team up with the partner.)

• After two minutes, ask learners to find new partners and present the lecturettes again.

- Repeat this process three to four times before having participants return to their seats.

- Provide a summary of the lecture topic (optional).

Sample PIN Topics

In my Speaking with Class workshop, key concepts from one of the lectures included the following:

verbal	vocal	visual	pitch	SAFW
pace	eye contact	gestures	staging	SMART

Rewards

- This activity is a great way to revisit the key concepts and terms of your lecture. The planned repetition is another creative way of using the "repeat-six-times rule."

- This activity gives you the opportunity to learn how well the group understood your lecture. While learners are delivering their lecturettes, walk around the room and listen in on their presentations. Comment as needed.

Risks

- Time can easily get out of hand with this technique. Stick to the time allotments for each part of the activity and remind learners of the time remaining with two-minute and one-minute announcements.

Options

- If you have more students than terms, split the group into two or three subgroups. For example, with thirty students and fifteen terms, have two sets of Post-it Notes. Split the group into two subgroups, each working with one set of notes.

- If your workshop lasts more than one day, begin the second (or third, etc.) morning with this exercise. It combines the affiliation phase with content review.

- Wait until the lecturettes have been prepared before letting the group know that they will be presenting to one other person. Most learners assume that they will be asked to deliver the lecturette to the entire group. This added "pressure" often leads to better lecturettes.

Banking

Ready

Purpose:	To gather and share a group's collective knowledge on a topic. To show the group that you value their knowledge.
Time:	Approximately twenty-five minutes. This technique may replace the formal lecture.
Group size:	Any size
Learner risk:	Low
Materials:	Flip chart (one for each subgroup), markers, index cards, an assistant (optional)

Set

• Divide the lecture topic into sub-topics. You will need one subtopic for each subgroup. For example, if the topic is Types of Visual Aids and there are twenty people in the session, four subgroups (each with five participants) would be given a subtopic. Four possible subgroup topics could be overhead projectors, desktop projectors, flip charts, and manuals.

• Have a flip chart available for each subgroup.

Go

• Once subgroups have been determined, introduce the session topic and subtopics to the entire group. Explain that you will be using the Banking technique to give learners the opportunity to share their wisdom on the topic.

• Assign one subtopic to each subgroup. Provide flip chart paper to each subgroup.

• Ask each subgroup to record as many points as they can about the subtopic. Encourage them to use a bullet format.

• After three or four minutes, ask each subgroup to move to a different table. At the new table, learners read the recorded ideas and, if possible, add other relevant points.

• This process is repeated every three minutes until each subgroup has provided input on each subtopic. (Note: By the time a fourth subgroup visits a flip chart, it may be very difficult to come up with even one or two more points. Watch the subgroups and, if you notice them struggling to come up with new ideas, shorten the timeframe spent at each flip chart.)

• When the subgroups have returned to their original tables, ask them to review their flip charts. Ensure each learner understands all the data, especially the data added by other subgroups.

• Have each subgroup prepare a summary of its subtopic and present the information to the whole group.

Rewards

• Using a learner's experience and knowledge leads to greater buy-in, which means learners are more likely to apply the concepts back at work.

• This activity is a very direct way of showing participants that you value their knowledge.

Risks

• Some subgroups may not express themselves clearly and so their ideas get misinterpreted. Ensure that the home subgroup understands all the data.

• This technique will only be effective if learners work well together in subgroups and if knowledge of the training topic is already in place. Don't use this technique if the material covered in the lecture is new territory for the learners.

Options

• Use index cards instead of flip charts and have subgroups pass the cards from table to table rather than move to each other's flip charts.

• After the exercise, collect the flip charts, enter the information into your computer, and e-mail the data to the participants. Participants appreciate this value-added feature.

Dear Hugh,

It seems to me that a lot of the techniques you use could be used simultaneously. Do you recommend one technique at a time or can I combine them?

Yours,
Combo Gal

Dear Combo Gal,

Absolutely, feel free to combine techniques! Your creativity will make training more fun and rewarding. At the same time, you'll be helping learners retain and understand new or familiar concepts.

For example, I've used the Banking technique to create a Checklist and have combined the Iconing technique with the Affinity lecture. You can even combine an Attention and Acquisition techniques, especially if you have time constraints. This allows both the social needs and the learning requirements to be met at the same time. Or, rotate between Acquisition and Application techniques. For example, provide a lecturette and then use an Application technique to reinforce your lecturette. Then provide another lecturette followed by yet another Application technique. You can repeat the process several times. This will keep the learner involved and reinforces new learning.

Challenge yourself with new and interesting combinations!

Sincerely,
Hugh

Tutoring

Ready

Purpose:	To train technical skills in small groups.
Time:	Depends on topic
Group size:	Individual or small groups (fewer than six)
Learner risk:	Moderate
Materials:	Vary

Set

- Prior to the onset of a tutoring session, participants need to be aware of the time commitment, course requirements, and expectations.

- Think carefully about the concept, skill, or task that you will be explaining to the learner. Rehearse your explanations of each step. Make sure you can break down the skill into simple parts, or at least into manageable parts if it is a more complex skill.

Go

- Explain that you will be using the Whole-Part-Whole tutoring method. This means you will begin by showing the student the whole skill (or process) to be learned, then break down the concept into smaller parts, and end by visiting the entire concept again.

- Demonstrate the whole skill. Do not get bogged down with terminology. Simply show the skill with a modest amount of explanation. This provides the learner with a skill overview. He sees what the whole skill looks like. He has a visual map.

- Break up the skill into manageable learning parts. Show one step at a time. Explain in detail what you are doing and why. Ensure the learner can see every move. Make your motions slow, deliberate, and smooth.

- Encourage questions. As you explain each new step, review the previous steps.

- Provide clear, explicit directions at each step of the tutoring process. Do not assume the learner understands. Insist on frequent feedback from the learner.

- Do one more demonstration of the whole skill, but this time ask the learner to talk you through the skill by telling you the steps to follow. At this stage, the learners do not yet handle the equipment or materials. They focus on explaining the steps.

- When the learner is ready, ask him to demonstrate the skill. Be patient and repeat as needed.

Rewards

- With tutoring you generally see results much sooner than with larger classroom training. Learner potential quickly translates into high-level performance of a new skill.

- When risks are high and performance is crucial, tutoring provides the immediate feedback loops essential to commit a skill to long-term memory.

Risks

- When teaching a dangerous task, the trainer needs to be able to accurately assess the learner's understanding. You need to be sure that the learner is capable of demonstrating the skill before asking him to do so.

Options

- It is better not to use the Whole-Part-Whole method for complex skills. The more complex the skill, the more repetition is required and the more the learner needs to master parts of the process before moving on.

Dear Hugh,

Sometimes it seems to take my learners FOREVER to catch onto a new skill. I'm pretty careful about following the guidelines you've provided with various techniques, so what's up? Am I doing something wrong that is making it difficult for them to learn?

Regards,
Trying to Teach in Toronto

Dear Trying to Teach,

Remember when you were learning a skill for the first time? Chances are you made mistakes. Perhaps you were not sure of yourself. Or maybe you got frustrated or had difficulty remembering all the technical terms. Be patient with new learners. If need be, reinforce and encourage their efforts, and stay calm and collected when giving instructions.

Sincerely,
Hugh

Acrostic Challenge

Ready

Purpose:	To examine a major training concept by summarizing key points of a lecture in an acrostic exercise.
Time:	Adds fifteen minutes to lecture
Group size:	Any size
Learner risk:	Low
Materials:	Copy of acrostic grid in learner manual

Set

• Create an Acrostic Challenge page that coincides with a lecture topic. Put the Acrostic Challenge in the learner manual. (See sample on the next page.)

Go

• Advise learners that they will be asked to complete a review exercise following the lecture.

• After the lecture, ask learners to turn to the appropriate page in their learner manuals. The Acrostic Challenge page will have a key phrase relevant to the topic written down the side of the page. For example, in a Train the Trainer workshop, the key phrase may be "effective trainer." (See sample on the next page.)

• Ask the learners to summarize key points of the lecture by thinking of words that begin with the letters of the phrase. Use the words to create an acrostic. (See sample on the next page.)

• Encourage learners to come up with ideas first and then make these fit with the letters provided. For example, in the sample acrostic, the word *outcomes* comes to mind for effective training. But since none of the words can start with the letter *o*, the word *expectations* was used to mean the same thing.

• Once the acrostic has been created, explain how participants can use the rating grid to evaluate their own performance in the areas identified. (For example, the learner who completed the grid on the next page rated her enthusiasm as a trainer at sixty out of one hundred, her flexibility at seventy out of one hundred, and her fun factor at about forty out of one hundred.)

• Once the rating grid is complete, ask learners to identify their three greatest strengths as well as three areas to work on.

Effective Trainer Grid

	20	40	60	80	100
Enthusiastic					
Flexible					
Fun					
Excellence					
Caring					
Technical (competent)					
Inviting					
Visual aids (uses them)					
Examples (many)					
Terrific (excel)					
Ready (present)					
Artistic (creative)					
Intentional (prepared)					
Natural (warm)					
Expectations (outcomes)					
Responsive (follows-up)					

Three strengths	Three areas to work on
excellence	*fun*
technical	*example*
artistic	*intentional*

Rewards
• Because the grid is developed, and therefore owned, by the group, it usually gets used.

Risks
• Some learners do not like word-based activities.

Options
• Use the Acrostic Challenge technique to develop a self-evaluation tool either for the workshop or for your own performance.

HUGHism

"Education makes us competent trainers.
Experience makes us credible trainers.
Expertise makes us confident trainers."

References

Brandt, Richard C. 1986. *Flip charts: How to draw them and how to use them.* San Diego, CA: Pfeiffer & Company.

Jolles, Robert L. 1993. *How to run seminars and workshops: Presentation skills for consultants, trainers, and teachers.* New York: John Wiley & Sons.

Mehrabian, Albert. 1981. *Silent messages: Implicit communication of emotions and attitudes.* 2nd ed. Belmont, CA: Wadsworth Publishing Co.

Nierenberg, Gerard I. 1973. *Fundamentals of negotiating.* New York: Hawthorne Books.

Chapter 8:
Application Techniques

A wise teacher does not explain what he sees. A wise teacher brings
the student to the window so that he can see for himself.

Anonymous

Carol was competent, but not confident.

Early on, in my Coaching for Peak Performance workshop, she displayed the ability to master information about coaching skills. Her questions were insightful and thought provoking. Her ability to synthesize information and evaluate the relevance of ideas helped others in their learning quests.

To my surprise, however, during the first afternoon role-play, she hesitated in her role as a coach working through a mentoring scenario. She seemed to have trouble articulating her thoughts and lacked the original enthusiasm she had with the group.

To her credit, she received collegial feedback on her lacklustre performance with grace and a stronger determination to do better the next time. And she did! By the time Carol had played the role of coach three more times over the two-day workshop, she had developed a high level of poise in her coaching abilities. At the end of the workshop, she shared how her greatest growth occurred during the practice time provided in the workshop. It allowed her to internalize and own what she had learned. She left feeling very confident!

Acquisition develops competence; application fosters confidence.

Dear Hugh,

I really enjoy the learner interaction that comes with subgroup work. But I'm never quite certain how diligent to be when I monitor subgroup work.
Any thoughts on this?

Yours truly,
Monitor Wary

Dear Monitor Wary,

It's tricky, isn't it, knowing how closely to monitor a subgroup's work? Yes, we need to provide guidance and ensure proper understanding of concepts, but we don't want to be too pushy. If at all possible, observe from a distance. You want to monitor a subgroup, not manipulate it. If a subgroup seems unfocused, walk closer to them. Check to see if members understand the purpose and procedures. If they still need assistance, encourage them with some ideas or questions.

Hope this helps.

Sincerely,
Hugh

That is largely because application is the hands-on phase of training. The trainer attempts to "bring learners to the window" by giving them the opportunity to use the skills they have learned during acquisition. Application encourages the learner to "own" the knowledge they have gained in the workshop.

In this chapter, I introduce you to hands-on moments in training, moments that will help you make the application stage dynamic and memorable for your learners. I divide these techniques into four categories: *Subgroup Activities, Simulations, Supervised Practice,* and *Assessments.*

Subgroup Activities

I find that many application techniques are most effective if conducted with smaller subgroups rather than with the whole group. In general, individuals share stories and insights more readily within smaller groups, which means subgroup members can benefit from each other's wealth of experiences.

Many of the techniques described in this book are meant to be conducted in subgroups. When it comes to the application stage, I frequently employ two subgroup techniques:

> Diad Hum
> The Jigsaw

the Trainer's
EDGE

What Size is the Best Size for a Subgroup?

In my experience, the ideal size for a subgroup discussion is four to five people. With this size, I've observed maximum involvement with lots of ideas generated in a relatively short period of time. With subgroups of six or more, it's easier for one or more people to opt out of the discussion. Participants will also find it easier to engage in side conversations.

In general, I consider triads or trios to be the minimum size for a subgroup. If the participants are comfortable with one another these smaller subgroups can work well. I often use the triad when working with groups of fewer than twenty. However the risk here is that it only takes one person to make a group malfunction. Diads or pairs can work only if you've got considerable trust and comfort.

Diad Hum

Ready

Purpose:	Discussion of issues, questions, and/or ideas to help learners apply them in the work place.
Time:	Approximately ten to twenty minutes
Group size:	Any size
Learner risk:	Moderate
Materials:	Flip charts, markers, and index cards

Set

• Prepare a question that relates to the material covered in the acquisition phase and that will encourage learners to examine new knowledge and skills more fully. Remember, open-ended questions work best. Write the question on a flip chart.

• On a second flip chart, write the heading Summary Chart.

Go

• Explain to learners that they will have the opportunity to dig deeper into the new knowledge they've acquired.

• Invite the learners to divide themselves into pairs (or diads) and decide who will record responses to the posted question.

• Provide each diad with a felt pen and several index cards.

• Reveal the prepared question and instruct the pairs to jot down responses to the question. Give them about five minutes.

• During this "five-minute hum," monitor interactions and prompt diads that need help.

• Pace the learners by announcing when they have two minutes and one minute remaining.

• After the five minutes have passed, ask each diad to summarize a point in one to four words. Record the responses on the summary chart.

• As you record responses, write down the exact wording you receive from the diad to ensure you are capturing the pair's ideas, not your own. Do not ask for discussion.

• Once you have received one response from each diad, go back to the first diad and ask if it has another idea to share that has not yet been mentioned. If so, record the point using a different coloured marker from that used for the first series of responses. Record the second response under or near the diad's first response. This will personalize the summary chart and create a feeling of ownership of ideas within the diads.

• Repeat this process with all diads until all ideas have been shared.

• Select a point and ask for clarification or expansion (either from the diad that came up with the idea or from other learners). Ask for examples. When the point has been explored sufficiently, summarize the input briefly and move to another point.

• At the end of the discussion, link the ideas shared with the next learning module.

Rewards

• Working through an exercise in subgroups helps to create teamwork and synergy. Learners are more apt to admit they don't understand at the subgroup level than at the group level. Struggling with ideas brings them closer as they learn to learn from each other.

• Valuable information, insights, and further questions come during the debriefing session. This stage is often identified as the highlight of the activity because learners are able to validate their contributions and learn from other subgroups.

Risks

• If you use subgroup techniques too frequently, participants soon use them as gab sessions rather than learning opportunities.

• Without clear directions and monitoring, subgroup discussions can get off track.

Options

• Instead of the Diad Hum try the Triad Buzz. This adaptation uses groups of three instead of two, and triads are asked to record ideas on flip charts instead of index cards. Then the flip charts are grouped together for examination. One or two participants flag the common ideas and the trainer then records them on the summary chart. The debriefing session follows.

• The Pyramid technique follows a similar pattern. You start by having individuals work on a question or issue. Then have learners divide into pairs to develop the issue further (maybe you'll have them define priorities or set a goal). Then have each pair join another pair to form a "quad" to take the problem to a solution stage. In conclusion, join quads together to appraise the drafted solutions.

The Jigsaw

Ready

Purpose:	To develop subject-matter experts (SMEs).
Time:	Approximately twenty to forty minutes
Group size:	Up to one hundred
Learner risk:	Moderate
Materials:	Flip charts and markers

Set

• Divide the workshop content into several topics. For example, a lecture on visual aid equipment could be divided into four topics: overheads, flip charts, desktop projectors, and white boards.

• Decide on a specific task to accompany each topic and an adequate time frame for completing the task.

Go

• Divide the class into subgroups based on the number of topics. For example, with four topics and twenty in the group, divide the class into four subgroups of five learners.

• Ask each subgroup to appoint a recorder. Supply the group with a flip chart and a marker.

• Assign a topic and specific directions to each subgroup. Ask the recorder to jot down any ideas generated by the subgroup onto the flip chart. (For example, if assigned the visual aid topic suggested above, the subgroup could be asked to chart the pros and cons of usage.) Depending on the nature of the task, this part of the jigsaw technique may take up to half an hour.

• As the subgroups work on the task, monitor their interactions and guide those that seem to need assistance to generate ideas.

• Pace the learners by announcing when they have ten minutes remaining. With five minutes remaining, ask subgroups to review and edit their compiled information and provide one copy to each subgroup member.

• Once the groups have completed the summary flip charts, have the members of each subgroup number off. For example, if there are five people in each subgroup, each member will be assigned a number between one and five.

• Guide the "ones" in each subgroup to form a new subgroup and to bring the compiled notes on their topic to this new subgroup. Repeat this process with the "twos," the "threes," and so on. (Note: The numbering off in subgroups and the regrouping can be a little tricky, so ensure you understand the process and practice before using it.)

• Once the new subgroups have been formed, explain that each member will serve as a subject-matter expert (SME) on the topic discussed in their initial subgroup. Each SME will give a one- to two-minute report on her topic.

• Pace the reporting by letting groups know when the two minutes is up and it's time for another report to begin. Encourage subgroups to manage their time well.

• Once all of the SMEs have had the opportunity to share their wisdom it is time to debrief. Ask the subgroups to return to one large group and summarize the learning that took place.

Rewards

• For adult learners to benefit from training, exercises need to be participant centred and instructor driven. The Jigsaw technique qualifies admirably, as it puts the onus on adult learners to apply what they've learned from the acquisition phase.

• By asking learners to report on their subgroups' findings, you are asking them to be trainers. In the reporting stage, learners do more than simply summarize knowledge: they think through an issue.

Risks

• Because this is a self- and subgroup-directed activity, learners need to be responsible and mature; otherwise the reporting process will break down.

• This technique depends on careful pacing. If you don't keep a tight rein on time lines, subgroups will lose focus.

Options

• Sometimes, subgroups won't all have the same number of participants. In these situations, you will need to do some on-the-spot adjustments by joining the subgroup that is short a member.

• In groups larger than fifty, modify the technique by dividing the entire group into sections. For example, four subgroups will make up one section. Then employ the technique with each section simultaneously. The process remains the same; you just subdivide first.

Simulations

Simulations link learning with reality, theory with practice. Whatever the training topic, these techniques transport learners to possible real-life scenarios. The benefits are clear. Simulations bridge the gap between the classroom and the office, they lead to focused and practical discussions, they encourage learners to ask questions before making decisions, and they help learners face decisions more confidently back at work.

In this chapter, I will introduce you to two simulation categories:

Work place simulations People simulations
Case Study Role Play
Project Games

I avoided role plays.

Both as a participant and as a trainer, I used to stay away from anything that smelled like a role play. I viewed them as time wasters. And besides, the outcomes were hard to predict and it all depended on the openness and willingness of all participants to make it work. The role play, for me, was too much of a risk to take.

Now I'm a fan of role plays.

Both as a participant at workshops and as a trainer, I thoroughly enjoy participating in and conducting role plays. Role plays provide opportunities to immediately apply what you've learned. They develop both competence and confidence in learners because they foster instantaneous response and feedback. They simulate, as closely as possible, what a real-life situation could be like. They occur under the control and guidance of a skilled trainer so that you get the opportunity to practice and hone a skill before you actually have to use it back at work.

What prompted my shift in attitude?

The opportunity several years ago to develop a coaching skills workshop. Can you imagine training others on how to coach without giving each learner the opportunity to actually coach? I mean, coaching videos are okay to watch and learn from, but coaching skills come so much more readily and permanently from doing. And the doing is often best facilitated in training with the role play.

Simulations provide the opportunity for first-hand experiences and move you just one step away from the real thing.

Case Study

Ready

Purpose:	To apply new knowledge and skills to a work-related problem or case.
Time:	Thirty to forty-five minutes
Group size:	Any size
Learner risk:	Moderate
Materials:	Learner manual with case study

Set

• Using your audit as a guide, prepare a relevant, non-biased case study that relates to the material covered in the session and to the work responsibilities of the participants. Essentially, the case study is a workplace-based story with a complication that can be resolved with the new knowledge or skills learned in the workshop. (Note: Case studies can also be purchased from training supply houses.)

• Develop questions to accompany the case study. Use Bloom's levels of cognitive thinking to devise questions that progressively test a learner's understanding of the material covered in the acquisition phase. (See a summary of Bloom's theories on page 105.)

• Include a copy of the case study in the learner manual. (See sample on the next page.)

• Decide if you want to assign the case study task on an individual or subgroup basis. (The implementation steps below explain how to use this technique with a subgroup; see the adaptations section for other ideas.)

Go

• After the acquisition phase of the session is complete, explain to the group that they will be asked to review a case study. Let them know that case studies are an excellent way to apply new knowledge to relevant, problem-focused events. Use this time to create an interest in the case study topic.

• Divide the larger group into subgroups. Explain to the subgroups that they will have about thirty minutes to read the case study and to respond to the questions about the scenario described.

• Ask learners to turn to the appropriate page in their learner manuals. Advise them to read the case study twice and to review the attached questions as they read. One member of the subgroup can read the case study aloud, or each member can read it independently. Once the case study has been read, a recorder can jot down ideas for resolving the conflict/problem described in the study.

• As subgroups work through the issue, monitor their progress and provide guidance or input when necessary. As you monitor the subgroups, remember that learners may become intellectually and emotionally linked with the case study. If so, you may need to intervene. Acknowledge that the case study is a "slice of life" and individuals need to be able to acknowledge and address emotional connections should they occur.

• Pace the subgroups by letting them know when they have fifteen minutes remaining, ten minutes remaining, and five minutes remaining.

• When the allotted time has passed. Ask various subgroups for their input and relate their ideas to the session's training outcomes. As well, comment on the variety of workable solutions the subgroups have come up with.

Sample Case Study

Team Building

Bill wants to become better at working with people. As a team leader for more than a year he has found himself continually frustrated with a lack of cooperation. Bill remarks, "I know we could be accomplishing more. Sometimes it takes hours just to make basic decisions. A perfect example is last week's planning meeting—each person was arguing and attacking each other's perspective. How can we start working together?" To find an answer, Bill began to analyze each of the four members of his management team.

First of all there is Bob. Bob is one of the most creative people on the management team; he always contributes new ideas and loves working with people. He is outgoing and very friendly. So much so that it is hard to get work done. When I am really pressed to a deadline, I almost have to lock the door so Bob won't keep coming into my office. One of my challenges with Bob is that many of his new ideas never result in anything. Also, Bob tends to want to take action first and think about it later.

Next there is Susan. Susan has an unbelievable ability to develop rapport and respect with other people. She is one of the most conscientious members of the team and does an excellent job in the personnel area. But when I try to involve Susan in some of the broader issues, she seems to lose interest. If we suggest making a major change that might affect her schedule and her objectives, it takes Susan a long time to accept that.

Tim is the third member of the management team. Tim always has a detailed explanation, even when you sometimes don't want to hear it. Bill is bothered that over the last several weeks he has continued to receive reports from colleagues of Tim's increasing insensitivity to the people problems in his department. Again, it seems that Tim is more concerned with being perfectly right than with doing the right thing. Concerning time, Tim has a continual problem motivating his staff to meet some of the deadlines.

The last member of the team is Fran. Fran came on staff eighteen months ago. Her initial challenge was to install a new evaluation system that would meet the needs of the expanding program. Fran gets so excited about the project I literally have to send her home at night. She did an excellent job and got the new evaluation system up and running in record time. My problem now is that Fran seems to have lost interest in the day-to-day running of the new evaluation system. In fact, I've even heard she's been looking around at some other jobs.

Bill sat back and looked at his list. It became obvious that each member of his management team had some very definite strengths, but that each also had weaknesses. Bill asked himself, "How can I take the members of my team and get them to work together? Where do I begin? How do I move in the right direction?"

Discussion questions

1. In light of the styles lecture you received prior to this case study, analyze each team member and determine his or her temperament style. Comment on the team members' natural strengths and weaknesses and what might be done to manage their weaknesses.

2. What advice would you give to Bill about managing the conflict between Bob and Tim?

Rewards

• Case studies help learners connect theory with practice. They provide a way for learners to take the knowledge of the instructor (theory) and relate it to a current work event.

• The case study involves learners because the subject matter is relevant and learners can vicariously experience the thoughts and actions of case study characters.

• Pat answers rarely work for a case study. Learners are challenged to think through the case using new knowledge and information. Often, a number of actions or solutions arise that provide options rather than final answers. Which, of course, is what real life is all about.

Risks

• You can't rush a case study. The discussions often bring about a learner's "ah-ha!" And that is what trainers want to achieve. Time is needed for learners to uncover assumptions, biases, and knowledge that shape the case.

• It is easy to focus on abstract notions rather than concrete elements in a case study. Groups get caught up on ideal resolutions that may not be very realistic.

Be alert to this pitfall and guide your learners to link theory with practice.

Options

• Have learners read the case study and respond to the questions individually. Then bring them together for a large group debriefing.

• Have different subgroups respond to different questions.

• Use the case study as the basis for a role-play, with individuals performing specified parts. (See role-play technique on page 168.)

• Address the needs of different learners' styles by using case-study videos. Some training videos do a good job of putting case studies in a visual mode.

• Start your training session with a case study. Use a technique that is typically in the application phase to gain attention.

Project

Ready

Purpose:	To apply new knowledge by having learners complete a specific task or project that relates directly to the workplace.
Time:	Varies
Group size:	Any size
Learner risk:	Moderate
Materials:	Vary according to project expectations

Set

• Determine whether or not the workshop topic lends itself best to individual or team-based projects. Your decision will depend partly on the workshop's training outcomes. For example, in my Power Presentations Skills workshop, participants are introduced to a twelve-step planning tool called the SMARTpad. In the application phase of the training, I use the project technique to have each learner use the SMARTpad to design and deliver a seven- to ten-minute presentation. If possible, this presentation should be one that can be used back at work.

• Use the information gathered in the audit and outlined in your training outcomes to develop a relevant project for each learner or team. Usually, the project sets up a problem that the learner or team has to investigate and resolve.

• Prepare a handout or a page in the learner manual that explains the project in detail. The explanatory material needs to clearly define the problem, outline the tasks to be completed, and include a reporting mechanism. Sometimes, projects are completed outside the workshop. Be sure to include as much detail and context as you can. (See sample on the next page.)

Go

• Introduce the project to the learners. Explain that the project will give learners the opportunity to apply new skills and knowledge to a relevant workplace problem or situation.

• Refer the group to the page in the learner manual that describes the project in detail, or distribute a handout with a detailed explanation.

• Review the components of the project (tasks, time frame, reporting mechanism) and answer any questions.

• If the project includes in-class work time, learners can begin work immediately. As they work through the project, either individually or in their learning teams, monitor their progress and offer guidance as necessary. Pace the task by announcing when ten minutes and five minutes remain.

• Upon completion of the projects, ask teams or individuals to present their undertakings. Have a Q&A session so learners and the trainer can ask the project authors about

the Trainer's EDGE

When developing project parameters, make sure your expectations can be met in the time available and that they reflect the group's capacity. By considering these factors, your expectations remain realistic and the learners are more likely to enjoy the process and results of the project

the procedures, results, and conclusions they came up with. Relate the results to the training topic.

Sample Project

In my Power Presentations Skills workshop, I spend the first morning working through the SMARTpad, a design tool that teaches the twelve steps of creating a presentation. The students are then given a project in the afternoon to create a seven- to ten-minute presentation using the SMARTpad. Following their completion of this project, which usually requires between forty-five minutes and one hour, learners then practice their presentations once or twice before delivering them to the whole group. Constructive feedback and suggestions for modification are then given.

Rewards

• Whether done individually or in learning teams, projects foster the opportunity for each learner to reflect on, relate to, and re-connect with work. Learners often make use of this time to ask relevant questions and search for the plausible answers to a work issue.

• The challenge of a relevant project gives learners the confidence to use new learning on the job.

• A well-structured reporting period increases a learner's sense of responsibility for the project and emphasizes the importance of the project.

Risks

• Projects mean extra work for the trainer. Sometimes you have to spread yourself pretty thin in order to help learners manage their projects effectively.

• Projects work best with individuals or groups who can work well independently. If you're not sure of a group's capacity, you may need to reassess using this technique.

Options

• Assign a project that will be completed between training sessions—for example, a team-based project that includes conducting research and writing a summary.

• Invite learners to keep a journal of their thoughts and feelings as they work through the project. Prepare questions or leading statements to guide their journal entries (structured journals) or encourage them to take time, without any prepared questions, to reflect upon their work (unstructured journals).

Role Play

Ready

Purpose:	To apply skills learned in the workshop to simulate workplace scenarios.
Time:	Twenty to forty minutes
Group size:	Any size
Learner risk:	Moderate to high
Materials:	Possible props for scenarios

Set

• Decide on the most appropriate place to use the role-play technique. I've found it works best following a lecture, a video, or a discussion. It can be used to bring theoretical concepts to life.

• Choose a scenario that is closely linked to the session's topic and the learner's work situation and decide on the performance format. Here I describe how to set up the multiple role-play format. (See the role-play format chart for other options.)

• Develop the role-play script. You may want to supply learners with a general scenario and ask them to fill in the details through the performance. Or you can provide them with a well-prepared script that

the Trainer's EDGE

Role-play Formats

This technique can be set up in several ways. I tend to use one of the following three formats.

• Single Role Play: Assign the role-play scenario to a pair or trio of learners. Have them perform the role play for the rest of the class.

• Multiple Role Plays: Divide the entire group into trios. Two learners will perform the scenario for the third learner. Use break-out rooms so that these subgroups can simultaneously perform their role plays. Each group can be given the same role play or they can be different.

• Modeling: Model your expectations of the role play by taking part in an initial scenario. Then have learners use the single or multiple role-play techniques.

includes background summaries and problem situations. (This type of script involves less risk for the learner.)

• Prepare the script as a handout or a page in the learner manual. Include notes on the reporting process so the performer knows what to expect after the role play is over.

• Prepare an observer's record sheet as a handout or a page in the learner manual. The reporting sheet needs to reflect the content covered in the session and clearly outline the types of feedback required. (See sample on page 171.)

Go

• At the appropriate time in the session, explain that you will be inviting learners to participate in a role play in order to apply the new skills and knowledge they've learned. Let the group know that the role-play technique will benefit them by bringing together the cognitive, affective, and psychomotor dimensions of learning.

• Divide the group into trios and distribute the role-play scenario handout or refer them to the appropriate page in the learner manual.

• Explain that two learners will perform the scenario while a third observes the situation and takes notes on the ways that the performers implement the knowledge and skills covered in the session to solve the problem presented in the role play. The observer will report back to the performers at the end of the role play. Once the trios are in their break-out rooms, they can determine among themselves who will perform and who will observe.

• Remind the learners that this technique is about using learned skills, not winning an Academy Award.

• Explain the importance of the observer role. The observers need to ascertain whether or not the information learned in the session is applied appropriately to the scenario.

• Distribute the observer's reporting sheet or refer to the appropriate page in the learner manual. The observer's reporting sheet should provide clear instructions and identify the skills and behaviours to look for.

• Spend a bit of time reviewing the guidelines for giving effective feedback, which are provided on the reporting sheet. This will help ensure that the performers receive quality feedback.

• Answer any questions about the scenarios or the observer's role and then direct the trios to break-out rooms. Let them know the timeframe to plan, perform, and respond to the scenarios.

• You will need to visit the various break-out rooms to monitor this technique. When doing so, let the players work out their own roles. Intervene only if players seem really stuck. When you intervene, you may want to ask performers to switch roles or simply move them in the right direction by having them take a breather and reminding them of concepts covered in the acquisition phase.

• The observer's report to the role players constitutes the debriefing or reporting component of this technique. During this process, the performer is asked to refrain from talking unless the observer asks him or her a question. Role players are asked to receive the observer's comments without trying to explain their own intents or justify their actions.

• Once the observer has finished commenting, the performer is given the opportunity to provide feedback on their role—what they thought and felt about it. This allows the performers to shed the role and get back into their own comfort zone.

• When the multiple role plays are complete, invite the group to come back together. Provide some general ideas about ways the role-play topic integrates with the training topic—that is, what has been learned, what can be applied at work. Affirm the work done by the performers and observers. Their risks have led to important learning for all.

Sample Role-play

In my Coaching for Peak Performance workshop, I use the role-play technique following the acquisition session on coaching skills. Learners are divided into triads and engage in multiple role plays. Each triad is given three role plays so that every learner in a triad has an opportunity to be a coach, to be coached, and to be an observer. To facilitate the multiple role plays, break-out rooms are made available for each triad.

During the multiple role plays, I rotate between break-out rooms, observe the process, and intervene only when necessary. At the end of the multiple role plays, all triads return to the main workshop room where I provide an overview and summary of coaching performances.

Observer Record Sheet

Instructions

1. Your task is to be the best observer you can be. You will assist the performing learners to learn about themselves and the skills they are using. A role play often provides performers and observers with insights into the course content and into themselves as well.

2. While two of your classmates are taking part in the role play, you only need to observe the learner who will be playing the role of _____.

3. This sheet is provided so you can record your observations and thoughts about what you see.

4. Use the 3-2-1 format to report back to the role player. Tell the learner the following:

     Three things they did well—based on the skills you were watching for

     Two things they need to work on—again, based on the skills you observed

     The one best thing they did during the role play

5. After the role play is finished, you will be given five minutes to prepare your thoughts before reporting back to the performer.

6. Your goal is not to record everything you see. Focus on the aspects of the role play that you think are important. Give specific details about a few events rather than a few details on many events. Quality is more important than quantity.

7. If you are one of two observers watching the same performer, you'll have the opportunity to exchange notes during your preparation time. This is optional.

Skills Observation

Please look for the following skills in the role player:

(Trainers develop this section based on the workshop topic.)

Please look for the following values exhibited:

(Trainers develop this section based on the workshop topic.)

Rewards

• The role-play technique brings together the cognitive, affective, and psychomotor dimensions of learning. Learners are given the opportunity to practice the skills they learned during the acquisition phase (cognitive), to learn how they feel when they try out the learned skills (affective), and to be physically involved in the drama that unfolds during the role play (psychomotor).

• A good role play is engaging, energizing, and enlightening. It can be the highlight of the workshop because of its strong link to work situations and the opportunity it provides to try out new skills that are directly applicable to the work place.

• This technique provides an opportunity to receive immediate, constructive feedback. Learning is reinforced soon after the event.

• Role play helps participants build confidence. A successful role play reaffirms the learner's knowledge of new skills, and learners believe if they can do it at the workshop they can do it at work.

Risks

• Some learners are more interested in leaving an acting legacy than focusing on learning outcomes.

• You need to have adequate space and time for this technique to work. If you don't have access to break-out rooms, or if you think you will be pressed for time, don't use this technique.

• All role plays have an emotional component. Your role is to keep the emotions in balance so that players aren't blindsided or sabotaged by their affective level. Sometimes players need to be reminded that this is a role play meant to *simulate*—not *duplicate*—work. Sometimes a learner will really get into the role play and find it difficult to disconnect from the role.

• Role play is a comparatively high-risk technique. Learners may resist, especially if they are not comfortable within the group. Respect and acknowledge the resistance and attempt to move on.

Options

• During the reporting stage, have the performers provide their perspective first and then have the observers give their feedback.

• Have the learners create their own role-play scenario without any guidance from you.

Games

Ready

Purpose:	To reinforce newly acquired skills and values through a mixture of fun, competition, and cooperation.
Time:	Fifteen to sixty minutes
Group size:	Three to forty
Learner risk:	Low to moderate
Materials:	As required by the game

Set

• Choose a game that will reinforce the skills, knowledge, or values covered in the session. (See side bar on next page.) When you choose, you will want to consider how inclusive the game is. Does it involve everyone in some way, or does a select group play while others look on? Can it be modified to include the whole group?

• Play the game yourself to be sure you're familiar with it. By playing the game, you will experience its merits and drawbacks first hand. You will be able to modify the game for your particular group.

Go

• Explain that you will be using a game to reinforce the skills, knowledge, or values covered in the session. Explain that games help us learn in several ways: by compelling us to think about our values, by offering a different way to think about ideas, and by allowing us to assess our skills in a non-threatening environment.

• Introduce the group to the particular game you have chosen. Explain the process and guidelines clearly and concisely.

• If the game requires the group to be divided into subgroups, do so.

• Answer any questions the various subgroups may have. Then let them know how much time they have to play the game.

• As the subgroups play the game, monitor progress by circulating through the room. Provide guidance and clarification as needed. Pace the game by letting learners know how much time remains.

• After the game has been played, bring the group back together for a debriefing/reporting session. Ask each subgroup to report on the game: Did individuals learn anything? How did the game reinforce values, knowledge, or skills? Did the game lead participants to any self-revelations?

Rewards

- Games offer a fun way to accomplish Mehrabian's repeat-something-six-times rule.

- Losers benefit as much as winners. Losing is a form of winning when insights and awareness come during the game. Ensure this is the case with your game.

Risks

- It's amazing how time can fly when you're having fun. Ensure the time you've allotted to the game gives the training benefits you want.

- It may seem odd to debrief after a game. But if you don't, learners will enjoy the game without applying it to the workshop topic.

Options

- You may discover a game that meets some of your needs but not all of them. Feel free to modify games to suit your particular group and topic.

Many games lend themselves to the training arena and many others have been developed specifically for training. A couple of my favourites are these:

Prisoner's Dilemma:

Helps players think about values. Throughout the game, participants decide whether to cooperate or compete. The impact of these choices becomes evident later in the game.

Bafa Bafa:

Helps learners experience the barriers imposed by stereotypes. In the game, two subgroups become members of an assigned, unique culture. Each subgroup is then instructed in the ways of their culture. Next, they send an ambassador to the other culture. It's not long before stereotypes emerge about the "other" group.

Some excellent learning games sources are Wiley Jossey-Bass, University Associates (the source for Prisoner's Dilemma and Bafa Bafa), *Games that Teach*, and Creative Training Techniques International. See the works cited at the end of this chapter for publication details.

the Trainer's EDGE

Supervised Practice

The techniques in this section give learners the opportunity to practice a new skill in a hands-on environment. Kinesthetic or hands-on learners, who find that practice is the best way to learn, will find these techniques particularly useful. Whether you're training a soft skill (like learning to be more assertive) or a hard skill (like figuring out the sequential steps to change a logic computer board), these techniques provide learners with practical, manipulative experiences. The techniques in this section include:

Behaviour Modeling
Drills

Behavior Modeling

Ready

Purpose:	To observe a skill being performed and then to practice that skill.
Time:	Fifteen to forty-five minutes
Group size:	Up to twenty
Learner risk:	Moderate
Materials:	As required for the demonstration and practice

Set

• Choose the skill that you will model to the learners. (Note: I've used this technique to model how to design a PowerPoint presentation, how to listen effectively, and how to give and receive feedback.)

• As the trainer, ensure you have practiced the skill or procedure that you are about to model for learners. You're not striving for perfection (unless safety is involved), but you do need to be comfortable and confident so that learners observe a doable skill.

• Ensure all necessary equipment or practice materials are available.

Go

• In the application phase of the workshop, explain to the group that you will be demonstrating a skill and that you will ask learners to repeat the demonstration once you've modeled the expected steps. Let them know that this technique, known as Behaviour Modeling, allows them to practice new learning in a hands-on environment with immediate feedback.

• Begin by giving a verbal explanation of the skill. This explanation paints the big picture and allows the trainer to establish a common language by introducing terminology and format.

• After the verbal explanation, demonstrate the skill or procedure. Explain how the skill or procedure works, but do not go into a lot of detail yet.

• Now break the skill down into logical steps or parts. Show the first step and give a detailed explanation.

• Invite the learners to practice this first step. All learners need to verbally explain the step as they practice it. When learners have successfully demonstrated step one, introduce the next part of the procedure. If errors are made, provide helpful feedback immediately. Then have them repeat the step.

• Now demonstrate the second step and give a detailed explanation. Link step two to step one.

• Have the learners repeat step one and practice step two. By linking the steps, the learners begin to sense the flow and pattern of the skill.

• Continue to explain and show the steps of the skill or procedure, interspersed with practice sessions for the learner. Ensure you link the steps as you train.

• Provide feedback at each practice. Be patient. (See the Trainer's Edge on the next page.)

• As part of the debriefing/reporting session, you may decide to give comments on the behaviour the learner modeled. (See sample feedback form on page 179.)

Rewards

• The Behaviour Modeling technique provides immediate and on-going instructor responses. This is a wonderful way to learn a new skill because the reinforcement affirms or alters behaviour.

• Many learners prefer experiential learning. Behaviour Modeling is made to order!

Risks

• Not all conditions or situations can be addressed through the Behaviour Modeling process. Be sure the skill you choose to model fits the technique.

• Sometimes learners can model the action without really understanding the in and outs of a process.

Options

• You may find that kinesthetic learners will have more success if they can experience the skill as soon as possible, rather than wait for the first practice session. Be prepared to adjust the Behaviour Modeling process.

• Use a video rather than yourself as a model. This frees you to be a more objective commentator. Consistency is a major advantage of video. Ensure you view the video before using it in training.

the Trainer's EDGE

Giving Effective and Appropriate Feedback

In this workshop, you will have the opportunity to give and receive feedback. Here are a few tips to keep in mind when giving feedback to your colleagues.

Be Specific

Don't just say "good job" or "that's not right." Be specific about the behaviour that was performed properly or that you'd like to see eliminated. Don't beat around the bush.

Immediate

As soon as you are ready to give constructive feedback, ask the performing learner to return to the subgroup. The closer to the performance the feedback is received, the more impact it will have.

Earned

False praise will have a negative effect on the performing learner. It can also cause resentment or concern among other learners who may get feedback later in the exercise. When giving corrective feedback, be sure you have your facts straight and talk directly to the learner.

Practical

Provide insights and suggestions that can be used by the person receiving the feedback. Be down to earth.

Individualized

Use the learner's name. The personal touch is especially important when giving positive feedback because learners like to hear their names associated with good work.

Consider the 3–2–1 method

This process starts and ends on positive notes. Choose six points to comment on:

Three things the performing learner did well

Two things they need to work on as they continue to advance their skills

The **one** thing they did the best

This method works well because it does not overwhelm the performing learner, yet the learner is given substantive and qualitative feedback.

Feedback Form

Learner: _____   Trainer: _____

Observer: _____   Skill Practiced: _____

Step One
Task:

Level of Performance: Very good   Satisfactory   Needs Practice

Comments:

Step Two
Task:

Level of Performance: Very good   Satisfactory   Needs Practice

Comments:

Step Three
Task:

Level of Performance: Very good   Satisfactory   Needs Practice

Comments:

Drills

Ready

Purpose:	To reinforce learning through repetition.
Time:	Five to fifteen minutes
Group size:	Any size
Learner risk:	Low
Materials:	As required by the exercise

Set

• A number of useful drills exist. Decide which drill is best for your group.

• Try out the drill yourself. Look for ways to economize on time and provide adequate challenge for participants. Ensure success is achievable.

• Prepare instruction pages for each subgroup.

• Set up the materials for the drill ahead of time.

Go

• Explain that you will be using a drill to reinforce the new skill or knowledge. Explain that this technique reinforces learning through repetition.

• Distribute instruction pages and review them with the group. Answer all questions.

• Divide the learners into subgroups and let them know how much time they have to complete the drill.

• As the subgroups work on the drill exercise, monitor their progress. If a particular subgroup is having difficulty, intervene to ensure they understand the directions.

• Pace the learners with two-minute and one-minute warnings. Keep the drill moving along. Don't deliberate or get side tracked. This technique is meant to reinforce content, not foster analysis.

• Once everyone has completed the drill, provide answers or have the group give the answers they came up with. Discuss errors and ensure learners understand the correct answer.

the Trainer's **EDGE**

Many drill exercises have been developed for training seminars, and it's not that difficult to create your own. Here are a few of my favourites:

Coaching Card Game:

Subgroups are each given a deck of twenty-eight cards, divided in half by a Post-it Note. Each subgroup matches the coaching skills named in the top fourteen cards with the definitions included on the bottom fourteen cards. I use this card game following a walk-through and demonstration of coaching skills.

Crossword Puzzle:

At the opening of an afternoon session, I like to give subgroups a crossword puzzle. Answers are based on the concepts and terms covered in the morning session.

Temperament Card Game:

Each subgroup receives a deck of twenty cards with words that describe the four temperaments. They sort the cards into four groups of five cards each, representing the four temperaments.

Rewards

• Drill exercises aid retention. People become more and more familiar with the terms or concepts that you are drilling.

Risks

• To downplay individual competition, conduct drill exercises with subgroups. This fosters a more collaborative atmosphere and makes any failures during the drill less threatening for individuals.

• Generally, drill exercises focus on recall, not on higher levels of thinking such as analysis or synthesis. But participants may get bored with simple recall exercises. Keep your drill exercises as challenging as possible.

Options

• Because drill exercises can be quite redundant, it is important to vary the pace, content, and approach. This keeps the exercise fresh for you and interesting for the learners.

Assessments

I believe the greatest honour bestowed on a trainer is the opportunity to assess learner performance. We assess performance not because we're better, know more, or have an experience edge, but because we care. We want to know that the training we've provided has contributed to a learner's growth. If you don't care, why would you even conduct an assessment?

Early on in my training career, I recognized this role as both a privilege and an opportunity: a privilege because, by accepting my assessments, learners grant me a place in their ongoing learning; an opportunity because assessments move learners along their educational path by affirming or modifying learner behaviour.

When I assess performance, I supply a learner with feedback—one of the core components in the learning loop. Without it, learners don't know whether the skills and knowledge they've learned are valid, workable, or meet expectations. Feedback enables learners to close the learning loop knowing that they have understood a concept and are ready to move on. Alternatively, it helps them acknowledge that they still need to practice more to meet an expected standard.

The challenge in many training situations is finding the time to give feedback. Sometimes, especially with large groups, it feels like there is barely enough time to cover the content, let alone grant learners the time to practice and provide feedback. But we know feedback presents invaluable information, insights, and support for the learner. What are we to do?

One option is to allow learners to play a role in assessing one another. Some trainers may find it difficult to share this role with learners. After all, aren't you the expert? Nevertheless, transferring responsibility for assessment to the learners enhances learning and increases learner ownership of new knowledge and skills.

In the application phase of training, feedback usually occurs as learners practice and apply new learning. In this section, I outline:

Learner-directed assessment techniques
What's in a Number
Learner Feedback
Trainer-directed assessment techniques
Quizzes
Video Analysis

the Trainer's EDGE

I've talked about the feedback I receive from learners and how I try to view their comments, both positive and negative, as a gift. I know wisdom can be found in their feedback. And so it should be with your assessments of learners. Take the time to provide insightful, intelligent, and intuitive assessments that will endure like a treasured gift.

What's in a Number

Ready

Purpose:	To practice new skills or apply new knowledge through written assessment.
Time:	Thirty to forty-five minutes
Group size:	Any size
Learner risk:	Moderate
Materials:	Flip chart for each subgroup, writing pads for each learner, assessment forms

Set

• Prepare a What's in a Number assessment form that outlines several concepts covered in the acquisition phase of the training. Make the assessment as relevant as possible to the learners' situations. This link will help learners see the relevance of the activity and create interest in the debriefing discussions. (See sample on the next page.) The form can be prepared as a handout, or as a page in the learning manual.

• Develop a Summary Chart. (See sample on page 185.)

Go

• Explain to the group that you will be using an assessment technique to guide them in the application of the new skills or knowledge that they've learned in the session.

• Distribute the assessment form, or refer to the proper page in the learner manual.

• Review the directions and the items on the form and respond to any questions.

• Let the learners know how much time they have to complete the assessment form. Remind them that they are not to consult with one another at this stage but are to complete the assessments on their own. This will lead to a wider range of scores and therefore a more profitable discussion.

• As learners work on the assessment form, monitor their progress. Encourage them to include comments for the values they assign. Pace them by letting them know how much time they have left to complete the exercise.

• Once the allotted time has passed, quickly collect individual scores and record them on the Summary Chart.

• Use the scores to prompt a discussion. Invite learners to elaborate on the rankings, especially for those items with widely differing scores. You will want to keep this part of the debriefing session moving along. Seek out no more than three to five comments for each point, unless there is an expressed need to go further.

- Do a final summary to link the discussion with the overall course outcomes.

Sample What's in a Number Assessment Form

How Does Our Training Room Measure Up?

Name: Bob

Directions: Examine each of the following aspects of the training room we are in right now. Rate the appropriateness/effectiveness of the elements listed below on a scale of 1–10 (1 is poor and 10 is excellent). Be prepared to comment on each item.

	1–10	Comment *(sample comments provided)*
Lighting	7	Lighting is good, but the two south facing windows with no blinds allow the sun to come into the room. Of note is that the sun will hit the screen in the pm.
Tables	6	Round tables are preferred to the rectangular tables provided. Tables are old and not that steady. Lots of previous student deposits (gum) under the table.
Chairs	5	Chairs not that comfortable for a workshop longer than two hours. Need to be replaced ASAP.
Temperature and Ventilation	8	Temperature can be controlled with an easy-to-use thermo control. Air conditioning is very good and can be shut off as needed.
Electrical Outlets	4	Very poorly placed electrical outlets. Only two provided and those are at the sides of the room. Extension cords are required and there is a safety concern with the running of these around the room.
Decor	8	Very pleasant. Neutral colors and not distracting. Appropriate for learning.
Acoustics	9	Excellent. The best feature of this room. Instructor and participant voices can be heard easily.
Visual Presentation Aids (white board, flip charts, desktop projectors)	8	Very well supplied room. Two permanent flip charts available. Storage place for flip chart pads. Desktop projector mounted in ceiling with easy access to hook up at front of room. Room can be darkened easily as required. White boards placed on the east wall for group work and overhead projectors (2) are in the adjacent storage room. There needs to be a contact number provided in case of any AV breakdown.

Training Room Qualities Group Summary					
Participants	Bob	Susan	Betty	Phil	Rita
Lighting	7	6	4	9	5
Tables	6	5	5	4	3
Chairs	5	5	8	5	6
Temperature and Ventilation	8	9	8	8	10
Electrical Outlets	4	4	3	3	3
Decor	8	5	3	8	2
Acoustics	9	8	9	9	10
Visual Presentation Aids (white board, flip charts, DTPs)	8	6	7	5	8

Rewards

• The results of this technique can be very practical. For example, in my Train the Trainer workshops, I often use the sample form provided here to assess the training room. I then forward the summary score sheets and comments to the training coordinator. In several cases, this has led to improvements in training facilities.

• By generating scores independently and placing them on a summary sheet, each learner takes responsibility for his or her own application of knowledge.

Risks

• Learners may not feel that the concept/scenario they're evaluating has any significance to them or to the course. Be sure to make the rating system meaningful and the subject matter relevant.

Options

• If you have more than twenty participants, divide the group into subgroups of five to seven. Have each subgroup create its own summary sheet and host its own discussion. If you choose this approach, model the technique with one subgroup first. Monitor subgroups during the discussions.

• This can be a low-risk or high-risk activity depending on the assessment scenario. The sample assessment of a training room is low risk, but assessing one another's presentation skills would be a high-risk variation. The feedback from a high-risk scenario can be very useful, but the learners need to be prepared for it. Often a higher degree of risk generates greater reward.

Learner Feedback

Ready

Purpose:	To have learners assess other learner's skill performance.
Time:	Thirty to forty minutes
Group size:	Up to forty
Learner risk:	Moderate
Materials:	Feedback Tip Sheet and Feedback Form

Set

• Decide which skills best lend themselves to being performed and evaluated.

• Develop a Feedback Tip Sheet that gives guidance about providing feedback. (See sample Tip Sheet on page 178.)

• Develop a Feedback Form for recording the written assessment. (See sample on page 189.)

Go

• Indicate that learners will be asked to provide feedback to co-learners as they perform skills learned in the workshop. Explain that both the learner performing the skill and the observers assessing the performance will learn the skill more thoroughly with this technique.

• Explain that subgroups will compile comments on a standardized, easy-to-use form.

• Distribute the Tip Sheet on giving feedback. Review the Tip Sheet to ensure observers know how to provide quality feedback. It is very important that observers realize how critical their role is to the success of this activity.

• Divide the group into subgroups of three to five. Ask for a volunteer to be the performing learner.

• Let the performing learner know that she has a certain amount of time to demonstrate knowledge of the new skill. Let the observing learners know that they should take notes throughout the performance so they can provide a meaningful assessment. Remind the observers how important their roles are. (See the Trainer's Edge on page 189.)

• When the practice session is complete, invite the performing learner to take a break. She may want to leave the room or just leave the subgroup.

• Then let the observers know they have three to five minutes to compile feedback. (I like referring to this stage as the huddle!) Provide the subgroup members with feedback forms or refer them to the appropriate page in their learner manuals.

- Monitor the subgroups as they compile feedback. Keep your ears open for feedback that may be too critical. Advise as necessary.

- Invite the performing learner to return to the subgroup. Have a spokesperson for the observers share the feedback they've compiled. Ask the performing learner to give her input. Then ask her to respond to the observers' feedback.

Rewards

- Learners tend to listen to their co-learners. They value objective and accurate observations from colleagues who, like them, want quality and practical feedback.

- Many of the debriefing forms that I use ask observes to look for the skills that were taught and modeled earlier in the workshop. The repeated use of the debriefing forms helps learners to incorporate learned skills into long-term memory.

- When working with larger training groups, it is not possible for the trainer to give individualized and customized feedback. Learner feedback is an expedient and effective method.

Risks

- If learners do not know each other before the workshop, then the risk they take is not as great as with learners who are colleagues and who live with what they say to each other. Take this into consideration when working with collegial participants.

- Some learners fear giving feedback because they figure what they say will come back to them in their feedback sessions. This does not generally happen; nevertheless, the fear can be real.

Options

- The trainer should serve as a model in observing and giving feedback. This gives observers a higher level of confidence to perform their role to their satisfaction and in the best interests of the receiving learner.

the Trainer's EDGE

The Important Role of the Observer

The success of this technique relies on the observers. Effective observers will encourage performing learners to improve; ineffective observers will make performing learners feel like they will never improve. Here are three points I keep in mind when preparing observers for this technique.

1. Learners who serve as observers need to be focussed in their role and realize that their assessment can be of great value to the performing learner and have a lasting positive impact.

2. Coach observers to observe astutely, to record thoughts precisely, and to organize the summary during the huddle.

3. I find that one to three observers make for a productive and insightful subgroup. Any more, and the performing learner can feel like he's being fed to the wolves.

Sample Feedback Form

Note: A variation of this feedback form can be found on page 179.

Presentation Skills Feedback

Directions: Be specific and descriptive when completing this feedback form.

Name of performing learner:_____

Skill assessed:_____

The three presentation skills you performed that we found particularly effective were:

The two things that would have made this presentation more effective are:

The best thing we noticed about this presenter was:

Quizzes

Ready

Purpose:	To assess learner understanding of workshop content.
Time:	Usually fifteen to thirty minutes
Group size:	Any size
Learner risk:	Moderate
Materials:	Pens and pencils, quiz

Set

• Choose a concept or idea from the course content that lends itself to a quiz format of assessment.

• Decide on the type of quiz that you will use. There are a variety of formats to consider; be innovative.

• Prepare the quiz and make enough copies for each learner or include it in the learner manual.

Go

• Explain to the group that you will be assessing their knowledge of the material covered in the acquisition phase through a quiz. (You may even want to let the group know this at the outset of the acquisition phase.) Let them know that these quizzes focus on helping the learner to learn, not on asking them to recall content.

• Distribute the quiz for this session or refer learners to the appropriate page in the learner manual.

• Together, review the directions. Ask if anyone has any questions.

• Let the learners know how much time they have to complete the quiz. As they work through the quiz, pace their work by letting them know how much time they have remaining.

• When the allotted time has passed, ask learners to share their answers with the group. Use responses as a way to generate discussion about workshop content.

Sample Quizzes

Some of the techniques discussed in the book are in a quiz format. Try the following:

Rewards

- The types of quizzes you give can vary immensely. The opportunity to be innovative with quizzes encourages learners to be creative and caring in their responses.

- Quizzes help learners evaluate competency levels. By combining quizzes with affirmation and encouragement you will motivate your learners.

Risks

- Learners inevitably start to compare their grades or comments with those of others. The comparison is often unfair since learners come to the session with various degrees of experience. Someone who is new to the company will likely not perform as well as a more senior staff member.

Options

- Instead of administering the quiz at a set point in the application phase of the workshop, intersperse questions throughout the acquisition and application phases.

Dear Hugh,

Sometimes I train for organizations that want me to submit actual grades at the end of a training event. Any suggestions about how I should meet the management's need for grades and the learners' needs for a supportive learning environment?

Take care,
Quizzy in Quebec City

Dear Quizzy Quebec City,

For the most part, the quizzes I use do not rely on grades but on corrective individual or group feedback to a series of questions or activities. Like you, though, I have run into training scenarios where grades are required at the end of the course. Here are two quiz options I use when I'm expected to assign grades.

1. The exam-discussion

Last year, when I was taking my advanced sailing exam, the course included a two-hour written exam, followed by a discussion of the exam answers with the instructor. This proved to be a valuable learning experience. The exam became the basis of a discussion and a great way to confirm my learning as I strove to become a competent sailor! I now use this technique when I have to give and grade exams.

2. Student-directed exams

During the latter half of a course, I have students submit potential exam questions. Then I select and edit some of the questions to form the basis of the final exam. Students mark their own papers as the answers are discussed.

I think these options should work for you!

Sincerely,
Hugh

Video Analysis

Ready

Purpose:	To assess by analyzing videotaped performances of learners.
Time:	Fifteen to thirty minutes per learner
Group size:	Up to twelve
Learner risk:	Moderate
Materials:	Video recorder, tapes, tripod, playback monitor, extension cords, flip chart

Set

• If possible, let learners know before the workshop that there will be a video component.

• Set up the video equipment. Attach your camcorder to a tripod. Do not try to video tape without a tripod. Plug in your camcorder unless you've already charged the batteries. The camcorder should have a zoom lens so that it can be placed at the back of the room, out of the way.

• Ensure adequate room for the video performance.

• On a flip chart, outline the three-part process for each video analysis: performance by learner, review of video by class, and feedback to the performing learner.

• Prepare an observer feedback form to guide the trainer and the observers to look for specific training concepts and skills during the performance. (See sample on the next page.)

Go

• Explain to the learners that you will be using video analysis to assess their ability to apply the new knowledge and skills learned in the workshop. For example, during the second day of the Power Presentation Skills workshop, each learner has the opportunity to have his five- to seven-minute speech recorded on video and played back for review.

• Refer learners to the flip chart that outlines the performance, review, and feedback processes for the technique. Explain that the individual being videotaped is called the performing learner. Other roles include observers, a timekeeper, and a technical assistant. Often the instructor does the video recording.

• Inform the class of the hand signals that will be used during recording. For example, use one signal to indicate the performing learner and instructor are ready to record, another signal to indicate a pause in recording, and a third signal to halt recording.

• Distribute the observer feedback form to the observers and the performing learner. Give them the opportunity to review the form and ask any questions. (See feedback tips outlined on page 178.) Ask observers to take notes during the performance.

• Once the performing learner and observers are ready, give the signal to begin the video session.

• When the time allotted for the video session has passed (or when the performing learner indicates he has finished), give the signal to stop the recording.

• Show the video of the performing learner. While it is playing through, the trainer and the performing learner can compile their comments for the feedback session. Observers can add to their own notes as the video plays.

• Ask observers to give their feedback to the performing learner. They can use the 3–2–1 method (page 178). Before the trainer provides feedback, ask the performing learner to provide his reaction to the performance and to the observer's comments. Then the trainer provides feedback.

• As the trainer, use the video to provide feedback and highlight the points you want to emphasize with the performing learner, the observers, and to the group. Use the 3–2–1 method (page 178).

Sample Observer Feedback Form (excerpt)

Observer Feedback Form
Power Presentation Skills Workshop

Verbal Skills   Comments

1. Found it easy to express ideas in front of a group
2. Read the group and adjusted the pace accordingly
3. Was able to deliver with a minimal reliance on notes

4. Well organized and prepared
5. Used anecdotes and stories to support key ideas
6. Was aware of audience needs and interests

7. Delivered a good opening using the START model
8. Displayed a sense of humour when appropriate
9. Made effective use of visual aids

10. Delivered a powerful closing using the STOP model
11. Answered questions with conciseness and skill
12. The person had a theme that was evident

Other comments...

Rewards

- The main benefit of this technique is the opportunity to see yourself "live." The performing images make a mark in the learner's mind and help to reinforce or eliminate behaviours.

the **Trainer's EDGE**

When giving feedback, shape your comments into trainable moments. Catch the performing learner doing something you want to highlight. Trainable moments give concrete and easy-to-understand feedback that the entire group can benefit from.

Risks

- Some learners get stage fright when they see a video camera.

- This technique requires lots of time. Class sizes need to be small in order for everyone to have a chance to perform.

Options

- Provide students with an instructor's critique, based on the video performance, on the last day of class.

- Make two recordings of each performing learner. One near the beginning of the workshop and one near the end. At the end of the workshop, compare the two performances.

HUGHism

"Tell me … and I'll remember for 48 hours.
Show me … and I'll remember for a week.
Involve me … and I'll walk away with skills to last a lifetime."

References

Bloom, B. 1956. *Taxonomy of Education Objectives.* New York: D. MacKay Publisher.

Creative Training Techniques International, 7620 West 78th Street, Edina, MN 55439; http://www.creativetrainingtech.com.

Jossey-Bass Publishers, 989 Market St. San Francisco, CA 94103 - 1741; http://www.josseybass.com

Mehrabian, Albert. 1981. *Silent messages: Implicit communication of emotions and attitudes.* 2nd ed. Belmont, CA: Wadsworth Publishing Co.

Sugar, Steve. 1998. *Games that teach.* San Francisco: Jossey-Bass Publishers.

University Associates, 3505 North Campbell Ave., Suite 505, Tucson, Arizona 85719; http://www.universityassociates.com

Chapter 9:
Action Techniques

I don't know what your destiny will be, but one thing
I do know: The only ones among you who will be really happy are those
who have sought and found how to serve.
Albert Schweitzer

Dan was a prisoner.

And he was attending my Proactive People Skills workshop in Toronto. His prisoner status was spawned by the initiative of his boss, who had signed Dan up for the workshop without seeking his consent. As a result, Dan was at the workshop against his will. He was convinced this event would waste his time and he soon let me know about it.

Part way through the first day of the workshop, we began to discuss the idea of opposite temperaments. When you have a temperament opposite that of another person, you frame your motives very differently than your opposite. You live in contrasting worlds, so to speak. Your strengths are the other's weaknesses, and visa versa. As this was being discussed, Dan privately made a connection between himself and his 17-year-old son, a person he had not had a civilized conversation with in the past two years. He soon began to see how he had been trying for seventeen years to make his son become more like him, instead of recognizing the uniqueness of his son, and that indeed his son had strengths that were of value to all. At the end of the first day, Dan stayed behind and shared with me what he had discovered.

The next day he sat up front and took many notes. Near the end of the workshop, when we focused on action, Dan made some well-thought-out commitments to work more proactively with his son to restore their relationship.

Two months later, I got an e-mail from Dan confirming significant improvements in his relationship with his son. Actions do speak louder than words, and in Dan's case they made a lifetime difference.

The action phase is a very exciting one for learners. Finally, they can move from testing and validating information for themselves to planning how the information will be applied at work and, perhaps, even at home.

The techniques that follow will guide learners to turn their learning into well-planned and successful actions that make a difference.

I divide the techniques I use in this Action chapter into two parts: planned action and on-site action.

Planned Action

Planned action techniques are completed in the workshop and help learners to think and plan how they will use what they've learned back at the office or elsewhere. I divide my planned action techniques into three categories: review techniques, commitment techniques, and job aids.

Review techniques are designed to revisit the main ideas of the workshop. Taking time to refresh and reinforce what has been learned sets the stage for learners to consider what ideas and skills they want to take away and use. It's amazing just how much can be covered in a workshop. Learners need to be discerning and realistic in determining what they will use after the workshop. It's all too easy to get overwhelmed and even discouraged with the vast array of ideas and skills that were acquired and "need" to be applied back at work. By highlighting the key learnings and skills of the workshop, learners can take the time to assess where they want to put their time and just how much they can transfer back at work. By doing so, learners can leave with well-articulated and realistic actions. Three techniques are used to help review the workshop. These techniques include:

Icon Summary
Looking Back
Then and Now

Commitment techniques help learners think through the specific actions they will take as a result of the workshop. Two techniques are used here:

Action Plan
Buddies

Job aids provide another level of support to make it easier for learners to act upon what they want to do as a result of their new learning at the workshop. the job aid I use frequently is:

Skill Tool

These three levels of planned action will enable learners to make simple, effective, and lasting changes and will bestow upon the trainer the satisfaction that they have indeed helped learners to make a difference.

Icon Summary

Ready

Purpose:	To summarize and synthesize workshop content and process with icons.
Time:	Twenty to thirty-five minutes
Group size:	Twelve to thirty-six
Learner risk:	Moderate
Materials:	Flip chart paper, markers, masking tape

Set

• If available, have a sample icon summary chart available to use as a sample. If not available, the technique will still work very well for you.

Go

• Explain to the group that this technique involves creating icons to represent major workshop concepts, ideas, or processes. Icons are visual symbols or pictographs.

• (Optional) If you think the group would benefit from seeing a sample icon summary chart, show it now. Emphasize the thinking involved in developing the icons or pictographs.

• Ask learners to refer to their learner manuals and to any notes they've taken throughout the session. (You may want to briefly walk through the learner manual, drawing attention to the major concepts and exercises.)

• Provide a piece of flip chart paper and four to six markers of different colours to each subgroup. Explain that they will have about fifteen minutes to develop icons to represent the various workshop highlights. Suggest the subgroups spend the first three to five minutes brainstorming approaches and ideas before drawing their icons.

• Pace the activity by letting them know when ten, five, and three minutes remain.

• Monitor progress by moving between the subgroups, offering guidance as necessary. Remind them that artwork isn't as important as the expression of the idea.

• Once the allotted time has passed, ask members of each subgroup to number off. For example, if there are five people in each subgroup, each will be assigned a number from one to five.

• Appoint the "ones" to go to one of the icon summary charts, the "twos" to go to another icon summary chart, and so on. These new subgroups have an interpreter for each of the icon summary charts.

- Invite each subgroup to view its chart. Encourage them to figure out each summary icon chart without the aid of the interpreter. If a subgroup needs assistance, then the interpreter for that chart can assist.

- Rotate subgroups through each of the icon summary charts, allowing two minutes at each one.

Sample Icon Summary Chart

Participant/Passive/Prisoner

Brainstorming

Brushfire Event

3 x 3 Audio Visual Rule

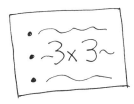

Rewards

• Creative juices really flow with this activity. By the time the charts are done, learners will have summarized the workshop more effectively than if they had to create a verbal summary report. And they'll have fun doing it!

• When subgroups visit each others' charts, they not only remind themselves of workshop content, they see these concepts interpreted in different ways. This adds to the retention and adaptability of ideas.

• This activity usually generates lots of laughter, bonding, and high energy. That's because this technique combines an action technique with the human interaction of an affirmation technique.

Risks

• If no one in a subgroup likes to draw, the technique can stall. Encourage the group and stress that interpretation of ideas, not artwork, is the main thrust of this activity.

• Creativity takes time! You can't rush this technique.

Options

• When you combine this technique with the Iconing technique (page 125) found in the Acquisition Techniques chapter, you'll find that learners excel at this activity.

Looking Back

Ready

Purpose:	To review key course ideas, concepts, activities and skills. Prepares learners to take advantage of on-site action techniques.
Time:	Fifteen to thirty minutes
Group size:	Any size
Learner risk:	Low
Materials:	Varies according to activity

Set

• Decide on a review activity that reinforces the product of the workshop, that is, the concepts, ideas, and skills. (See the Sample Activities below for suggestions.)

• Review the preparation and implementation strategies for the activity you choose.

Go

• Explain to the group that you will be using a review technique as a way to clarify, solidify, and verify the learning of key course concepts and ideas. In turn, this will prepare them to get the full benefit of any on-site action plans they initiate.

• Ask the group to take a few minutes to review learner manuals, tip sheets, notes, and handouts.

• Begin the review activity.

• As learners engage in looking back, circulate amongst the tables. Listen to the subgroup discussions to ascertain their level of understanding of course ideas and concepts. Add to or clarify subgroup discussion as needed.

Sample Activities

Activities to use for Looking Back can be drawn and adapted from the techniques used in the Attention and Acquisition chapters. Simply modify the techniques for review. Some of the techniques that I use for review include:

Mind Mapping	page 96
Think-Pair-Square-Share	page 99
Affinity Diagram	page 140
PINing	page 144
Banking	page 146
Acrostic Challenge	page 150

Rewards

• Looking Back helps learners move ideas and concepts from short-term to long-term memory and it helps them to think more deeply about concepts, and may even reveal new thinking! The three R's are achieved: increased retention, reinforcement, revelation!

Risks

• If this activity is used as a simple recall exercise with no challenge to it, learners will find it boring.

• When using any of these review techniques, ensure that you don't add any new information. Review is a time to revisit what has already been taught, not to add on more course concepts.

Options

• If time is available, combine several of the above techniques. For example, I'll use Mind Mapping to generate review ideas and then use the Acrostic Challenge to summarize these ideas.

• Use the Looking Back technique between learning modules as a way to reinforce concepts and build greater retention.

• Enrich this technique by integrating the process side of learning along with the product review. That is, focus on what was learned (product), how it was presented (process), and how learners reacted (process).

Then and Now

Ready

Purpose:	To compare workshop entry and exit skill or attitude levels.
Time:	Depends on type of inventory
Group size:	Any size
Learner risk:	Moderate
Materials:	Inventory instrument as developed by instructor or purchased through commercial vendors

Set

• Develop an inventory instrument that measures the skill level or attitudes of learners with respect to the workshop topic. (See example on page 205.) An option would be to purchase such an instrument from a commercial vendor.

• In order to become familiar with the instrument, administer it to yourself. You may find you have to adapt the instrument for your workshop purposes.

• Rehearse instructions to ensure you are comfortable with administering the instrument.

Go

• Early in the session, explain to the group that they will be asked to complete a skills or attitude inventory. Let them know that this instrument will help them to assess their entry skill or attitude level.

• Administer the inventory. Give clear, concise, and complete instructions. Encourage participants to be realistic, rather than pessimistic or optimistic, as they complete the inventory. Pace the timing by indicating remaining time.

• After the inventory has been completed and scored, interpret the results with the group. Some learners will be impressed with their entry-level skill or attitude, while others may be disappointed with their results. Indicate that the inventory measures each person *at this time* and that the purpose of the workshop is to advance skill or attitude levels.

• Inform learners that you will administer the inventory again near the end of the workshop to give each learner a comparison between their entry and exit skill or attitude levels in the workshop.

• During the action phase of the workshop, administer the same inventory a second time. When it is completed and scored, invite learners to compare results from the first and second inventories.

• Host a class discussion to examine learner responses to the inventories. Where improvements have been noted, affirm learners. Where there is no improvement or even a lower score on the second inventory, suggest that this may be an opportunity to make some decisions about actions that can be taken to improve the score. Indicate that on-site action techniques will be used to help each learner advance their skill or attitude levels.

Rewards

• Learners like to compare charts, graphs, or tables that show where they were with how far they've come. The measurable "then and now" can motivate and inspire the learner.

• Positive results from the Then and Now inventories reinforce the desire to follow through with action plans.

Risks

• The reliability of the inventory can be limited by the objectivity of the learner.

• Some learners doubt the validity of tests and inventories.

Options

• To increase objectivity, have a colleague complete the inventory on his fellow learner, too. This provides two perspectives for each person, which can lead to more comprehensive assessments.

• Use the Checklist technique (page 137) as a Then and Now inventory.

Dear Hugh,

I'm planning to use the Then and Now technique in my next training session. Should I be administering the inventory during the training event itself or before it begins and after it is over?

Wanting to do it right in Wawa

Dear Wanting,

Good question, but there's no pat answer. Inventories can be effectively administered during the workshop or they can be completed prior to the workshop date and one to three weeks after. Conducting the technique during the workshop eases administration and allows you to respond to learner inquiries. Conducting the technique before and after the workshop helps prepare the learner and provides follow-up.

You get to weigh the advantages and disadvantages on this one!

Sincerely,
Hugh

Public Speaking Inventory

Directions: Throughout this workshop, I will cover seven presentation skill topics, each with three subtopics. Right now, I'd like you to assess your current knowledge/competency with these concepts by completing the pre-session column below. Later in the workshop, I'll ask you to complete the post-session column.

To complete the pre-session column, colour along each line using the coloured pens provided. Determine how far along the line to colour by using the numbers at the top of the column to guide you. The "1" indicates a high degree of difficulty with the concept (i.e. you do not understand it or you feel it is an area you need to improve) and "10" indicates a high degree of competence or understanding of the concept. Once you complete the pre-session column, you'll be able to see at a glance which areas you need to work on during the workshop and what areas you can already perform competently.

		Pre-session 1 2 3 4 5 6 7 8 9 10	Post-session 1 2 3 4 5 6 7 8 9 10
Speaker	Ability	_____	_____
	Confidence	_____	_____
	Comfort	_____	_____
Situation	Formal	_____	_____
	Meetings	_____	_____
	Impromptu	_____	_____
Preparation	Clarity	_____	_____
	Creative	_____	_____
	Organization	_____	_____
At the Time	Memory	_____	_____
	Physical	_____	_____
	Acceptance	_____	_____
Delivery	Voice	_____	_____
	Body	_____	_____
	Style	_____	_____
Difficulties	Time allotted	_____	_____
	Individuals	_____	_____
	Physical space	_____	_____
Audience	Participation	_____	_____
	Disposition	_____	_____
	Consequences	_____	_____

Action Plan

Ready

Purpose:	To list specific actions that will be completed after the workshop as a result of newly acquired skills and attitudes.
Time:	Fifteen minutes
Group size:	Any size
Learner risk:	Low
Materials:	Action plan printed in learner manual or provided as a separate handout

Set

• Draft an action plan template for the learner manual or as a separate handout. (See sample on the next page.)

• Prepare a sample completed action plan for demonstration purposes. This can be prepared as a visual aid.

Go

• During the affiliation stage, inform the group that you will be asking them to develop an action plan near the end of the workshop. (Wait until learning outcomes have been agreed upon before giving this announcement.)

• Explain that, as a way to maximize on the time invested in this workshop, each learner will be asked to develop an action plan that outlines how their new skills and abilities will be incorporated back at the workplace.

• Indicate that time will be given throughout the workshop to complete the action plan.

• Refer learners to the action plan template in their learner manuals. Show them the sample completed action plan. Use the sample to stimulate thinking.

• At the end of each learning module, ask learners to refer to their action plans. Give learners two to five minutes to generate and record action ideas. Each time learners visit their action plans, provide encouragement by reminding them of its significance in helping to advance their professional development.

• In the action phase of the workshop, bring closure to this technique by having learners review the listed actions. If other ideas come to mind, that's a bonus!

Action Plan
Train the Trainer Workshop

Comment: You have invested valuable time in this workshop. What ideas do you want to use when you deliver your own workshops? Time will be given throughout this session for you to note action ideas that you want to use. You are encouraged but not required to share your ideas with others!

The Actions I'll Take	I'll Get Started By
Purchase the training book *The Trainer in You*	Aug. 1
Develop and submit a lesson plan using the 8 A's	Sept. 15
Observe two trainers training in my core group	Oct. 15
Use two new techniques in each of my next four workshops	Sept. to Dec.
Enroll in a university program for advanced training courses	Jan. to Mar.

Rewards

• A written commitment to use new skills and knowledge helps build a sense of achievement for the learner.

• By introducing the technique near the beginning of the workshop, you are emphasizing personal accountability and responsibility for learning.

Risks

• Some learners see the Action Plan as one more task in their already busy lives.

Options

• To reinforce learner action plans, provide workshop mementos such as bookmarks, a tip sheet (laminated, credit-card size), checklists, or certificates.

• Search the web for sites that compliment your workshop topic. Provide web site addresses for participants to use in their action plans.

• When you're working with teams or work groups, have each team draft a group action plan.

Buddies

Ready

Purpose:	Pair up learners who agree to stay in contact and support one another after the workshop.
Time:	Thirty to forty-five minutes
Group size:	Any size
Learner risk:	Moderate
Materials:	No special considerations

Set

• Draft buddy guidelines handout (see next page) and a sample contract (see page 210).

• Contact former workshop participants who have successfully used the Buddies technique (or who currently are Buddies). Ask them if they would be willing to provide the group with a testimonial about their experiences with this technique. If so, discuss the role they would play in the session and make necessary arrangements.

Go

• Early in the workshop, let the group know that you will be using the Buddies technique later in the session. Explain that this technique involves two participants teaming up and agreeing to support each other after training. Advise them to start thinking of who they might like to partner with.

• At different times throughout the workshop, take time to talk about the Buddies technique. Refer them to the guidelines in the learner manual. Let them know they should have a partner chosen before the action phase begins.

• During the action phase of the workshop, have learners identify their buddies. If you are using testimonials, introduce the experienced buddies at this time. Have them describe their encounters and respond to questions. Participants will get motivated more quickly when they hear how other buddies have benefited each other's professional careers!

• Have the buddies get together to draft a contract that contains contact information, guidelines, purpose, and commitments. Essentially, the buddies are meant to assist each other to attain the goals they've set during the workshop. Refer them to the sample contract in their learner manuals.

Rewards

• "Two heads are better than one," goes the saying. And Buddies is a fine example. When the two are well matched and committed, learners help each other to advance their professional development in lasting and memorable ways!

Risks

• Sometimes it's difficult to find compatible buddies. This is especially true with in-house sessions that partner up fellow employees. During the audit, inquire about staff morale and find out about the techniques employees are currently using to support one other. In some cases, the risk will be too high for Buddies to work.

• If the activity becomes one-sided, buddies tend to drift apart.

Options

• It may be appropriate, especially with teams, to consider adapting this technique to include three to four workers under one Buddies contract. The purpose remains the same—helping and supporting each other after the workshop.

• In some company-based workshops, where the range of work experience is broad, I like to pair senior or experienced workers with novice or newly hired employees. This kind of professional relationship is not based as much on reciprocity as on providing an opportunity for the more advanced worker to mentor a co-worker.

Buddies: As Easy As 1–2–3–4!

When you are developing a contract to share with your buddy, consider the following:

1. Time frame:

Buddies are expected to support one another for one to three months.

2. Boundaries:

Buddies need to determine the ways they will keep in touch (phone, e-mail, in-person meetings) and when the best times to consult are.

3. Reciprocity:

Both buddies will support each other. You both need to do your part for the commitment to sustain itself to the end of the contract.

4. Purpose:

Together, buddies will decide what they will do to support and encourage each other. Mutual agreement is required.

Note: In most cases, buddies should select each other. However, if participants have a wide range of experience, education, or compatibility, you may want to assist in the selection.

Buddy System Contract

Training Event: Power Presentation Skills
Training Date: February 11, 2002
Training Location: Renaissance Hotel, Regina, SK
Instructor: Hugh Phillips

Buddy Name:	Judy Deane	Buddy Name:	Jeff Simpson
Position:	HR Supervisor	Position:	Manager
Company:	Saskatchewan Mattress	Company:	Saskatchewan Agriculture
E-mail:	deanej@abc.com	E-mail:	simpsonj@xyz.com
Phone:	306-489-0000 Ext.123	Phone:	306-244-3333 Ext. 33
Fax:	306-444-1234	Fax:	306-234-4321

Pledge

We agree to

• Provide professional assistance to each other on matters that pertain to the outcomes of the Power Presentations Skills workshop
• Respect the time and professional commitments of each other
• Be Buddies for the next three months, then review the need for future mutual professional support

Activities

• Watch each other give at least one presentation within the next month and offer feedback using the feedback sheets provided at the Power Presentations workshop

• Read one book listed in the Power Presentations bibliography and provide a working verbal summary for my Buddy

• Help each other with the SMARTpad presentation planner, as deemed appropriate

_____   _____
Signature   Signature
Buddy A: Judy Deane   Buddy B: Jeff Simpson

Skill Tool

Ready

Purpose:	To introduce and use a skill tool that can be used to simplify tasks at work.
Time:	Thirty minutes to three hours
Group size:	Any size
Learner risk:	Low to moderate
Materials:	The skill tool

Set

• Select or develop a skill tool that assists learners to complete tasks at work in a more efficient and effective manner.

• Develop a demonstration of the skill tool. If possible, use an actual work assignment. This will increase the probability that the learner will use the skill tool after the workshop.

• Rehearse the instructions about how to use the skill tool.

Go

• Explain to the group that you will be introducing them to a skill tool that will assist them in applying their new skills. Let them know that you will be working through a relevant example with the tool so they will be familiar with it when they return to work.

• Present a work task to the group and demonstrate how the skill tool would be used. Demonstrate the whole process from start to finish.

• Now repeat the process one step at a time. Present each step in a logical sequence and give a detailed explanation of each step.

• If the process is complex, invite the learners to practice each step before going on to the next one.

• Encourage learners to ask questions and welcome suggestions for creative uses of the tool. (Who knows, you may have a very versatile tool that can be used for other learner tasks!)

• Don't rush the demonstration/explanation. Let learners explore, ask questions, and ponder its usefulness. Learners will need time to become familiar and confident with using the new skill tool.

• Review one more time, highlighting the main points of using the skill tool. Ensure understanding by having learners take the lead in talking through the process.

Dear Hugh,

I've used both your POWERtool and your SMARTpad with great success. Now I feel I'm ready to develop a skill tool of my own. What types of things should I be thinking about as I get ready to develop it?

Yours truly,
Toolie

Dear Toolie,

I'm glad to hear you've enjoyed my POWERtool and SMART pad! When I was designing these tools, and when I recommend other tools to my learners, I keep this following checklist in mind. A good skill tool should satisfy the following objectives:

- Save time
- Simplify a task
- Be user friendly
- Look professional
- Work well in its intended environment

I look forward to using your skill tool some day!

Sincerely,
Hugh

- If time permits, let learners apply the tool to another work-related task. This provides additional testing of the tool and validates the tool's usefulness.

Sample Skill Tools

I have developed three skill tools that I use in my workshops:

1. The SMARTpad: A presentation planning tool that outlines how to design a talk in twelve easy steps.

2. The C•O•A•C•Hpad: A tool used to prepare for coaching appointments. Especially useful for mentoring, confrontation, and counselling.

3. The POWERtool: A tool that guides a trainer in workshop design and delivery. Chapter 18 provides full details on the use of this tool.

Rewards

- Skill tools save time, make work easier, and help to ensure outstanding performance.

- Skill tools employ the KISSS principle—keep it simple, straightforward, and smooth. They make complex tasks more doable.

Risks

- Some will reject the tool because they didn't find they had enough time in class to become proficient users.

Options

- Convert the skill tool into an electronic format for use on the Internet or as a software program.

On-Site Action

Planned action techniques take place in the workshop and aim to motivate learners to implement new knowledge and skills when they return to work. On-site action techniques involve the learner (and sometimes the trainer) at the worksite itself. While an idea may be planted or a technique outlined at the workshop, the action takes place at the learner's work place. I divide on-site action techniques into two categories: Networking and Professional Support.

The network that develops during a workshop enriches the training experience and is a wellspring of potential support for learners when they return to work. By supporting the development of these networks you are setting the groundwork for collegial, professional learner relationships. The techniques I've used with excellent results are:

Puts and Calls
Care Groups

Professional support is often needed for action plans to take flight. As we all know, creating an action plan at a workshop is an entirely different task than actually fulfilling the goals in a busy workplace. Learners often need support in order to complete an action plan, and managers are often willing to provide that support.

If the manager is unable to make this commitment, however, a coach or mentor may be able to provide professional support. More and more frequently, I hear about organizations that provide mentors or coaches to support learners when they return to the work place. These coaches—sometimes the trainers themselves—offer the follow-up encouragement and assistance that employees need to implement activity plans. The professional support technique that I use is:

Management Follow Up

Dear Hugh,

The training market is so competitive these days. What can I do to give myself an edge?

Yours truly,
Looking Ahead in
Lethbridge

Dear Looking Ahead,

I like Harvey MacKay's take on this question. He says, "In today's world, talent alone will not save you. Genius will not. Experience will not. Guts and hard work will not. If you need a job, money, advice, help, or hope, there's only one sure-fire, fail-safe place to find it—your network."

For trainers, networking will not only enhance your impact as a trainer, it will sustain your career and keep you fresh and vibrant before your audiences.

Sincerely,
Hugh

Puts and Calls

Ready

Purpose:	To link and support learners with similar interests, challenges or goals.
Time:	Fifteen to thirty minutes in class
Group size:	Up to forty
Learner risk:	Moderate
Materials:	Flip chart, Post-it Notes, markers

Set

• Prepare four to six Puts and Calls flip chart pages. (See sample on page 216.) Tape the charts on the wall.

• Above the charts, put the title "_____ Stock Exchange." Insert the host organization's name in the blank.

Go

• During the affiliation stage of training, distribute Post-it Notes to the group. Refer learners to the flip charts and advise them that a Stock Exchange will be operating during training hours.

• Explain to the group that the point of this technique is to link learners with similar interests and to encourage learners to support one another when the workshop is over.

• Indicate to participants that they are stock exchange brokers. In this role, they need to post their contact information in the Broker column on the charts.

• Ask each participant to write down his or her name, business e-mail address (and fax, phone, and mailing address information if each likes) on a Post-it Note and to place the Post-it Note in the Broker column.

• Explain that throughout the training event learners are encouraged to place their puts and calls on the charts. A "put" is an idea, resource, or the name of a technique that a learner is willing to share with other learners. To "place a put," a learner simply writes the idea, resource, or technique on a Post-it Note, signs it, and places it in the Put column of the stock exchange. (See sample on the page 216.)

Making Connections

This idea came from linking the stock market to training! When you get involved with stock options, you have the choice of placing a "call" or a "put." Both involve setting prearranged dates for either purchasing or selling stocks. By adapting this template to training, Puts and Calls came to be!

- When participants use the Call column, they are asking for assistance. If they'd like help with a certain skill or technique (like managing time or learning more affirmation techniques), they indicate this need on a Post-it Note, sign the note, and place it in the Call column. (See sample on the next page.)

- Inform learners that this technique is voluntary. No pressure or persuasion should be applied to learners who decide not to participate.

- At the conclusion of the training event, close the stock exchange. Let the group know that you will compile the information into a Puts and Calls document and e-mail it to each learner as soon as possible.

- In the letter accompanying the information, remind learners that they are now connected to each other by their willingness to provide value-added ideas and resources to each other, or to seek specified help from others with their particular challenges. All it takes is a phone call or e-mail to access assistance or give help.

Rewards

- Learners leave not only with the trainer's ideas and knowledge but also with a network of professionals they can call on for solutions to work challenges.

- This idea sometimes extends the exchange of ideas and techniques. Learners who are professionally connected begin to network for other job-related purposes.

Risks

- For follow-though to occur with this technique, a group needs to have a strong foundation and work well together.

the Trainer's EDGE

Several years ago, I received a phone call from a long-term client. He began not with "Hello," as one would expect, but with, "What did you do?" His tone of voice was quite positive, so I relaxed and replied, "I don't know, but it sounds like it must be working."

He laughed and then explained the impact of the Puts and Calls technique on his staff. He indicated that they were "networking like crazy." This was a company that developed its own trainers and outsourced professional consultants and trainers to help them. Recently I had been hired to do an advanced Train the Trainer course for them. As part of the workshop, I used the Puts and Calls technique. With it, participants created a network to access the wide range of training abilities in the company. The give and take within the group was tremendous and the end result was a group of trainers who discovered an untapped resource—themselves!

Options

- Create a Learner's List, which includes learner names (first and last), e-mail addresses, and/or phone numbers, and distribute it to the group. Again, participants should not feel pressured to add their names to the list.

Sample Puts and Calls Chart

Note: This partial puts and calls chart was obtained during a three-day Train the Trainer workshop. The names and contact information are fictitious.

ABC Inc. Stock Exchange

Puts and Calls

Brokers	Puts	Calls
Carmen Jones cjones@shaw.com	• Resources/games in leadership and team building (David S.)	• Interactive ice-breakers e-mail: (Terry)
David Smith e-mail: dsmith@getter.com	• Developing self-directed teams (John W.)	• Tips to deal with difficult people (Barb)
Kristin Webster e-mail: webk@flow.en	• Expertise and information on skills standards development (Carmen)	• Ideas—introducing new products in 20 minutes—make it stick! (Carmen)
Barb Marshall e-mail: bcm@hotwave.org	• Have Survival Guide book (delivering United Way session) (Joan)	• Volunteers to form a committee to provide training/mentoring (David S.)
John Wesley e-mail: jcw@gogetter.com	• Prochaska's Model of Change (Terry)	• How to do a Web homepage (Barb)

Manager Follow Up

Ready

Purpose:	To involve managers in training follow up.
Time:	Approximately one hour. Determined by manager and learners/employees
Group size:	Any size
Learner risk:	Moderate
Materials:	Determined by manager and learners/employees

Set

• Prior to the training event, meet with the manager (or another contact person) to discuss training goals and to set up a post-training meeting to discuss training follow through.

Go

• Either prior to the session (in your welcome letter) or early in the session, let learners know that management has agreed to support their learning through involvement in a follow-up plan.

• Explain that the details of the plan have not yet been developed, and that the learner will help determine the particulars of this professional support.

• When training is complete, schedule a meeting with the manager (or another contact person) to provide a brief summary of the workshop and to discuss the action plan created by the learners in the workshop. (See sample meeting agendas below.)

• At this meeting, emphasize the value of manager support for maximizing the return on the training dollars invested. Explain that the details of the Management Follow-up Plan will be determined together by the manager and the learners to ensure expectations are mutually acceptable.

• Let the manager know that the learners will be in touch to schedule the first meeting.

Sample Meeting Agendas

If at all possible, I meet with managers both before and after the training session. In the meeting that takes place prior to the training event, I provide the manager with a snapshot of the workshop and gain buy-in to post-training support. At the post-training meeting, I deal more specifically with the follow-up plan.

The agendas I use to guide these meetings look something like this:

Pre-training event meeting (conducted during the audit stage)

1. Provide a synopsis of the training program and review its learning outcomes

2. Introduce the idea of the importance of pre- and post-workshop support for the learners

3. Suggest realistic ways to involve management in the support of learners after the training event is finished

4. Together with the manager, discuss ways to ensure efficient and effective use of the manager's time in post-training support

5. Set a date and time for a post-training meeting to talk more specifically about follow-up support

Post-training event meeting (conducted as part of the action phase)

1. Inform the manager of the workshop highlights and note significant learning

2. Discuss the learners' action plan. Be specific and indicate the time frames the learners have set for themselves. Ask for management response and input to the plan.

3. Discuss ways that the manager can assist in the completion of the action plan, but indicate that details need to be ironed out with the learners

4. Thank the manager for her time, interest, and support

5. Provide the manager with my contact information in case further questions arise

Rewards

• By presenting a draft of a Manager's Follow-up Plan in a post-training meeting, you are helping to ensure that training dollars have been well spent.

• When managers agree to support learners, this creates a win-win situation: learners value the manager's support; managers value the employee's follow-through.

Risks

• Despite all your efforts to get support for the learners, the manager involved may be unwilling or unable to help out.

• Sometimes it's the learners, not the manager, who derail the process. The effort to follow through must be mutual.

Options

• The manager may or may not be the most appropriate person to provide post-training support. Consult with your contact person or another reliable source to assess the best person.

- Encourage attendees to establish a care group. This is a small group of workshop attendees and others who have a common area of interest and who will agree to meet periodically after the workshop to support each other in their professional development.

Sample Manager Follow-up Plan

Power Presentation Skills Workshop

Training Date:	December 13, 2002
Trainer:	Hugh Phillips
Participants' profiles:	Fifteen participants from five internal departments
Name of Manager:	Roberta Jones
Name of Learner:	Jeff Smith

Personal Action Plan:

Actions	Date completed by
1. Give two presentations in next month to front-line staff	Jan. 31
2. Read the book "You've Got to Be Believed to Be Heard"	Feb. 15
3. Design one presentation for a colleague using the SMARTpad	Mar. 15

How I would like my manager to assist me

1. Agree to a Manager's Follow-up plan

2. Attend one of my presentations in the next month

3. Provide ten minutes of feedback on the presentation she saw me do

Actions agreed to by my manager	Date completed by
1. Establish Manager's Follow-up Plan	Dec. 15
2. Agree to help with actions 1, 2 and 3 as noted above	Feb. 15
3. I will explore other training opportunities with Jeff	Mar. 15

HUGHism

"The transfer of ownership from the trainer to learner is one of the most exciting phenomena of training."

Chapter 10:
Affirmation Techniques

*The source of all energy, passion, motivation, and an internally generated
desire to do good work is our own feeling about what we are doing.*

Peter Block

When I began training, I spent little time on the affirmation phase. I tended to max out on the knowledge and skills aspect of the workshop and let the people dimension take care of itself. But the more I trained, the more I began to realize that training is primarily a human event, secondarily a learning opportunity. I discovered the value in well-planned, thoughtful affirmation exercises. Affirmation benefits the trainer in three ways:

1. Whether learners use the ideas and insights you've shared has to do with them, not you. By affirming learners, you put the focus where it should be—on their intelligence, intuition, and integrity.

2. The ultimate aim of your workshop is not to have learners leave and be impressed with you, but to have them leave impressed with themselves. Affirmation helps you achieve this goal.

3. Affirmation helps ensure that participants leave the workshop knowing and feeling they are valued, which in turn accentuates the merits of newly acquired skills.

I divide the techniques in the affirmation phase into three areas: *topic affirmation, learner affirmation,* and *trainer affirmation.*

Topic Affirmation

Sometimes motivational speakers get a bad rap. They excite audiences with visionary messages, techno graphics, powerful stories and quotations, and an enthusiastic, inviting, and flowing speaking style. Then the speaker leaves and within a matter of a few hours or perhaps by the next day, participants are back where they started. The excitement is gone. Day-to-day realities replace the inspirational world conveyed by the speaker.

But I'm not convinced this bad rap is deserved. These speakers know, as we sometimes need to be reminded, that motivation is the key to human action. In our regular workaday worlds, we often look inward. We may gather useful insights about ourselves, learn valuable lessons, and develop greater awareness of others. We focus on events that have already occurred and ponder their significance. When we're "up" or motivated, though, we look ahead with hope and anticipation. Motivational speakers take this hope and use the magic of the moment to inspire and encourage the listener. Ultimately, what we do with the words we hear depends on intrinsic motivation, the internal drive that sustains each person.

As a trainer, you play an important role in motivating your audience to follow through on planned action. So, near the end of a workshop you want to inspire and energize your learners. Take the time to wrap up or summarize the event. Motivate learners by affirming their abilities, remarking on their progress, and inspiring them to achieve even greater heights. The techniques you choose to accomplish this have to be congruent with your character and experience and, of course, be appropriate to the topic.

The two techniques that work for me are:

Motivational Stories/Quotations
Visualization

Dear Hugh,

I know you coach us to include the affirmation phase in our training. But isn't a quick thank you at the end of the event good enough? I barely have time to cover content, let alone take time to tell learners how good they are.

Yours truly,
Content Guy

Dear Content Guy,

Affirmation is just like any other phase of training. It will not happen unless you plan it. And don't underestimate the importance of this phase. It cannot be marginalized as a simple two-second thank you at the end of the day. Affirmation gives balance and perspective. Remember when you affirm and acknowledge people, they in turn will be inspired to intellectually and emotionally accept their responsibility to apply the content you so carefully taught.

That said, the length of the affirmation phase depends on the length of the workshop itself. You may not need more than a few minutes at the end of a half-day workshop, while a five-day event will require an hour or more. In the end, the amount of time you invest in the affirmation phase will depend on the training topic, the maturity level of the group, and your assessment of how best to help the learners disconnect from the group.

Hope this helps!

Sincerely,
Hugh

Motivational Stories/Quotations

Ready

Purpose:	To inspire and energize learners by highlighting goals they can achieve as a result of training.
Time:	Five to fifteen minutes
Group size:	Any size
Learner risk:	Low
Materials:	As required

Set

• Choose a motivational story or quote that relates to the session topic and is appropriate for your group of learners. You want to choose a story/quotation that captures the theme of the session while it entertains or motivates your audience. You can use a personal story, adapt a story that has already been published, or retell a story that you've heard from someone else.

• As you decide on a quote or story, keep in mind that the purpose of motivational stories is to identify what is taken for granted and make it important. The story can be about something that could happen to any of us, but you make it important by telling what had to be done to overcome internal and/or external barriers.

• Take the time to become familiar with and rehearse the story or quotation. If you can, memorize the quotation. The more familiar you are with the quotation or story, the more expressive and dynamic you'll be.

Go

• Near the end of the session, tell the story or recite the quote. If you have planned on telling several stories throughout the session, save the most powerful one for last.

Rewards

• As you develop your story telling skills, you will become known and remembered. If you're thinking of repeat business, these signature stories may lead to other invitations.

• Audiences love stories, and when you end with a good one the group leaves feeling encouraged, hopeful, and optimistic.

Dear Hugh,

I've started to develop a file of motivational stories and was wondering: What are signature stories and should I add them to my file?

Sincerely,
Storytelling in Saskatoon

Dear Storytelling,

A signature story is a story that you tell so well that people come to associate it with you. For example, past president of the National Speakers Association, Jim Cathcart, tells a simple story about the growth of an acorn. But the unique spin he puts on the story makes it memorable and enlightening. He's even written a book, *The Acorn Principle*. The acorn story has become his signature story.

I strongly encourage you to develop your own signature stories for your file. Turn some of your ordinary experiences into extraordinary events—not necessarily because of what happened, but because of what you learned. Practice enough and soon you'll generate your own signature story!

You can develop your own signature quotations too.

All the best,
Hugh

Risks

• Always identify the source of your story or quotation. You want to leave the audience with an authentic signature, not a forged one!

• Remember, the story must link with the workshop event. If the story misses its mark, it is probably because it didn't relate to the workshop theme.

Options

• Display a visual backup to accompany a motivational story or quotation.

Visualization

Ready

Purpose:	Using visualization to help learners exceed their own expectations.
Time:	Ten to fifteen minutes
Group size:	Up to fifty
Learner risk:	Low
Materials:	A marker in the room, such as a clock, painting, etc.

Set

• Prior to the training event, practice the visualization technique in the training room. Choose a marker (an object to point to) and practice the steps described below.

Go

• Ask the participants to stand and position themselves at least two arm lengths apart from each other. Now ask them to focus on the marker that you've chosen, for example, a clock hanging on the wall.

• Explain that you will demonstrate the motion you'd like the learners to perform, but ask them not to participate until the demo is complete.

• Raise your right arm and point it towards the marker (e.g. the clock). Then turn your arm to the right around your body *as far as you can comfortably go* and point to a second marker in the room, for example a picture. Announce that second marker. Bring your right arm back and lower it to your side.

• Invite learners to do the same and to choose a second marker that they can comfortably point to. Ask learners to make a mental note of the second marker's location. Emphasize that the movement is not hurried. Arm movements need to be slow and gentle. Do not push or force the arm to go past a comfortable position.

• Now ask learners to close their eyes. Have them imagine raising their right hands, pointing to the first marker (e.g. the clock), and then swinging their arms around to the right and visualizing going past the second marker. Ask them to imagine returning their arms back to the first marker and then to their sides. Repeat this mental rehearsal two more times, step by step. Each time they are to imagine themselves going past the previously imagined marker.

• Ask learners to open their eyes. Have them raise their hands and point to the clock. Have them slowly swing their arms around to the right and encourage them to move it as far as comfortably possible. In most cases, people will be able to move their arms beyond the original second marker.

• Point out to the learners that visualization can be a powerful force to help them achieve their goals. Relate the activity directly to the action technique you've employed and link the activity to the workshop goals and training outcomes.

Rewards

• Many learners will be amazed by just how far they can go past that original second marker. They really impress themselves!

• This activity is powerful because participants actually see and feel their hands going past the original second marker. I've seen this technique create incredible awe and energy in a group.

Risks

• Some learners may feel uncomfortable with visualization activities.

• Sometimes, a few learners will experience no difference through visualization.

Options

• Have learners move from the physical experience of exceeding their marker to the mental challenge of seeing themselves succeed at work. For example, have them successfully visualize working through a conflict situation at work using the skills they learned in the workshop.

Learner Affirmation

Each training moment is unique.

The same people, in the same room, with the same purpose, at the same time of year—the exclusive nature of your group deserves special recognition. And the learners in your group need to play a role in that recognition.

Affirmation helps the group recognize the merits—and magic—of the training event. It is important to acknowledge the sharing that has taken place, the relationships that have developed, the risks that the group has faced together. By helping learners acknowledge these connections, you ensure the breaking up of the group is a pleasant experience.

Learner affirmation techniques endorse the group's powerful interactions and recognize that all have played a vital role in establishing the group's identity. You give learners the opportunity to thank and acknowledge one another. And you take the opportunity to acknowledge them yourself. The type of learner affirmation technique you choose (and the amount of time you spend on it) depends on the length of time a group has spent together and the degree of connectedness you sense within the group. As a general rule, the longer a group has been together, the more significant the planning for a disconnecting event should be.

The affirmation techniques described here can be adapted to your training session. They are:

What I Remember About You
Sharing Circle
Awards
Learner Letters

the Trainer's EDGE

In the 1980s, I was involved with organizing the award-winning, month-long Shell Merit Fellowship Institute with thirty Canadian teachers. The closeness and camaraderie that developed within the group were truly astounding. Life-long professional relationships were established. Because of this bonding, we needed a full-day celebration to help us disconnect! Together, trainer and learners planned an end-of-training event that commemorated our accomplishments and rejoiced in our growth.

What I Remember About You

Ready

Purpose:	To share personalized and positive feedback with fellow participants.
Time:	Fifteen minutes
Group size:	Eight or more
Learner risk:	Moderate
Materials:	What I Remember About You sheet, pen or pencil

Set

• Prepare a What I Remember About You handout for each participant. (See sample on the next page.) Use coloured paper or parchment to make the handout special. Believe it or not, some people will keep these sheets for years to come! (I still have one from 1989!)

• Spend some time thinking about the unique nature of this particular group. Use these thoughts when you compliment the group at the end of the session.

Go

• Near the end of the session, compliment the group members for the work they've done throughout the session. Make this a personal thank you and use the opportunity to express your feelings about this particular group.

• Indicate that you will be using the What I Remember About You exercise to give learners the opportunity to acknowledge the contributions of their classmates to the success of the workshop. Let them know the activity is optional. Ensure that everyone knows each other's names.

• Ask the group members to move their chairs into a circle. Pass out a copy of the What I Remember About You sheet to each participant. Ask them to fill out the name, date, and course title blanks on the sheet. Now ask the learners to pass their sheets to the person on the right.

• Explain that the person who receives the sheet will take about half a minute or so to write a short, positive phrase (one to five words) about the person whose name appears at the top of the sheet. Once everyone has done so, ask the papers to be passed to the right again.

• Have participants take a few seconds to focus on the person's name at the top of the sheet. Again, invite them to write a short, complimentary phrase about that person. Continue to circulate the sheets until everyone has his or her own paper. (Note: Keep the activity moving at a steady pace. Don't let quick responders or reflective thinkers drive the task.)

• Provide time at the end for each learner to read his or her sheet.

Sample What I Remember About You Sheet

<table>
<tr><td colspan="2" style="text-align:center">What I Remember About You</td></tr>
<tr><td>Name:_____</td><td>Date:_____</td></tr>
<tr><td>Course: _____</td><td>Location: _____</td></tr>
<tr><td>
• _____
• _____
_____
• _____
• _____
</td><td>
• _____
• _____
_____
• _____
• _____
</td></tr>
</table>

Rewards

• The What I Remember About You sheets are a wonderful source of encouragement for learners.

• This is a very personal activity. Learners will remember the words of their colleagues for years to come.

Risks

• This activity works best with a group that has developed an open and authentic relationship. If this has not happened, you may want to choose a less risky technique.

• Some participants may simply race through this exercise and give little thought to their responses. For them, the technique is just another workshop exercise.

Options

• If the group is large, over fifteen or twenty, only pass the sheet part way around the circle before returning it to its owner. Or, divide the group into subgroups for the activity.

Sharing Circle

Ready

Purpose:	To highlight fellow participants' positive attributes.
Time:	Fifteen minutes
Group size:	From eight to twenty-five
Learner risk:	Moderate
Materials:	Flip chart and marker

Set

• Prepare a flip chart with three questions to guide the sharing circle. Some possible leading questions are: What have I enjoyed about this group of learners? What has someone else taught me? What will I remember about this group?

• Choose questions that are suitable and applicable for the group. Appropriate questions are key to the success of this exercise.

Go

• Near the end of the session, invite the class to form a circle with their chairs. Compliment them on their ability to work well as a group (or on a different strength you observed).

• Explain that each member will have an opportunity to say a few closing words about a particular learner or the group as a whole. Let them know the activity is optional and anyone who does not wish to participate can indicate so by saying pass.

• Refer the group to the three items listed on the flip chart. Indicate they will be given about thirty seconds (or whatever amount of time you determine) to share. Let them know that, to help keep the activity moving, you'll raise your hand when the time limit is up for each person. The person speaking will need to wind-up at that point.

• Randomly select learners to share their impressions. (I've found that the spontaneity of randomly choosing participants provides greater participation and exerts less pressure on learners.) You may want to start this activity yourself before choosing a learner. This way you can model the task and the time frame.

• When the last person has participated, thank the group.

Rewards

- With so much time committed to content and tasks in a workshop, this exercise provides a breath of fresh air and allows learners to experience the bond they share in their quest for learning.

- This activity is a little riskier because it is so people-focused. But the rewards are greater, too. Trust comes from having survived a risk.

Risks

- The emphasis on people may distance the task masters of the group. They may feel uncomfortable with such a touchy-feely exercise. These learners will appreciate the option to not participate.

- The thirty-second timeframe may be very difficult for some learners to stick to, especially if the training experience has been a profound one. Play this by ear, but do your best to keep the activity moving.

Options

- Make this into a Topic Affirmation exercise by changing the focus of the questions from the people to the task. For example, you could ask the following questions: What do I plan to do as a result of this workshop? What are the three most valuable things I learned? What do I wish we'd talked about more?

Awards

Ready

Purpose:	To recognize the contribution of each learner with a take-home award.
Time:	Five to fifteen minutes
Group size:	Any size
Learner risk:	Low
Materials:	The awards

Set

• Decide on the type of award you'd like to present. (See the sample list of award ideas below.)

• When you choose the award that is best for this group, consider the types of awards the group has received in the past and how you can make your award appreciated and valued. Whenever possible, use an award that is appropriate to the group. For example, when I'm working with gas company field employees, I use work site gifts like safety glasses or a marker pen. Either of these gifts will get used on the job.

• Plan an event for presenting the award. This might be ten minutes at the end of a one-day workshop or a full-day celebration at the end of a longer, more in-depth training session.

Go

• Near the end of the workshop, put your award event plan into action.

• Make sure the award presentation has plenty of flare. For example, if you are awarding certificates of completion, give each person a certificate that is not theirs. Have learners find the person who owns the certificate. Then have them ask their colleagues to describe one action they will take as a result of the workshop and congratulate them on their success.

Sample Award Ideas

Type of Award	*Considerations*
Certificate of Completion	Include name of workshop, date(s) of workshop, your name, and the participant's name. Make sure the participant's name is spelled correctly. (See sample on page 234.)
Participant Ribbon	If distributed before the end of the session, these can be worn throughout the training event.

Workshop Prizes	Recognize individuals, subgroups, and the larger group throughout the session with prizes (instead of waiting until the end). Pens, calendars, day timers, and mini-calculators are all examples of useful, relevant prizes. Have fun awarding workshop prizes. Don't make them too expensive, or those who don't receive a prize will feel left out. Don't make them too cheap, or those who receive them will see them as a mere token.
Group Photo	This is a good idea for longer workshops. Organize carefully so no one is left out. Advance notice and dress instructions need to be provided. Frame and mail out the photo ASAP after the workshop.
Group Sweatshirt or T-shirt	Again this is more suitable for longer workshops. Give the group time to participate in the design of the clothing. Note size requirements carefully.
Group Icon or Product	Use your imagination—or the group's—for this. Anything from a coffee mug to a workshop collage will work. At one session I attended, we created a branding board. Each subgroup created their own brand, which was burnt onto a piece of timber and hung in the training room!

Rewards

- People enjoy receiving a tangible object that they can display on the office wall, wear with pride, or use in their work. For example, I regularly receive thank you letters from learners who comment on the positive impact their certificates of completion have on their supervisors, managers, or CEOs.

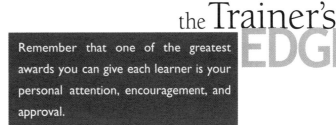

the Trainer's EDGE

Remember that one of the greatest awards you can give each learner is your personal attention, encouragement, and approval.

Risks

- Spelling counts! Take extra care to ensure the correct spelling of learners' names. Spelling can always be corrected, but the impression left with a learner may be that the trainer didn't care to get it right the first time.

Options

- Present awards at points throughout the session instead of just at the end.

HP TrainingWorks
Seminars

achievement
through
learning

Certificate of Completion

Awarded to

_____

For Attending and Participating in

_____

_____   _____
Signature of Participant   Date

_____   _____
Location   Hugh Phillips, President

Learner Letter

Ready

Purpose:	To affirm learners by having them write letters to themselves.
Time:	Fifteen to twenty minutes
Group size:	Under thirty
Learner risk:	Low
Materials:	Stationery, envelopes, stamps, and pens

Set

- Decide on an appropriate time for learners to write a letter to themselves.

Go

- Early on or midway through the training session, explain that you will be asking learners to write a letter to themselves as part of a closing activity. Together you can brainstorm ideas to include in the letter.

- Near the end of the session, revisit the brainstorming you did earlier and have learners add to or reconsider the brainstormed ideas. Some ideas to discuss include: what they've learned during the workshop, feelings/impressions about the workshop and the people who attended, people they want to contact, books or Web sites they plan to access, learning highlights they want to remember, how this training might benefit colleagues.

- Encourage learners to go beyond thinking of this technique as a shopping list of things to do before the letter arrives. Inspire them to think of ways to alter behaviour, take on new challenges, or to help others advance themselves.

- Distribute stationery and envelopes to participants. Let them know they will be given ten to fifteen minutes to compose a letter to themselves.

- As they finish the letters, invite learners to place them in the stamped envelopes and seal them. Ask them to put their mailing address on the envelopes and to use your address as the return address.

- Let them know that you will mail the letters within one month's time. Indicate that all letters are confidential.

Rewards

- This technique often leads to ongoing professional development.

Risks

- A few learners may be concerned with confidentiality issues. They will worry that someone will read the letter while it waits to be mailed.

Options

• Use a postcard instead of the letter. Store the completed postcards in a large sealed envelope and give them to a trusted third party to mail. If you are holding the workshop at a particular hotel or resort site, local postcards can be used. Templates for postcards also exist on a number of desktop publishing software programs and can be customized to suit your event.

• If you've done a lot of subgroup activity in the workshop, it may be appropriate for members to be accountable to each other. In this case, the subgroup drafts a letter that will be sent to all members. The trainer still mails it out at the specified time.

• If appropriate, have learners share letters with one another or within a subgroup. This increases accountability and may inspire some participants to expand their letters. If you choose this adaptation, ask learners *before* they start writing if they are comfortable sharing them.

• Expand the Learner Letter technique by having learners focus on the impact their absence has had on the workplace. The letter could consider questions like: How has my time away affected my co-workers? How has my time away affect my loved ones? Should I be doing anything prior to my return to work? How will I thank those who enabled me to attend the workshop?

Trainer Affirmation

In topic affirmation, learners celebrate what they have learned. In learner affirmation, participants encourage one another. With trainer affirmation, the instructor takes the time to recognize significant others who helped make the workshop a success.

In the Learner Affirmation section, I talked about the full-day celebration that took place at the end of the month-long Shell Merit Fellowship Institute I was involved with (see page 227). Part of the celebration included extending written and personal thanks to the many people who worked to make the institute such a memorable event. Extensive efforts were made to find out the names of everyone who helped us succeed, whether they were audio-visual personnel, administrative assistants, technical support workers . . . and the list went on and on!

This experience taught me just how important it is to recognize people who contribute to a training event's success. It's important not only to the individual's who are thanked, but also to me as I take steps to ensure a satisfying closure to a training event. The techniques I've used with great success are:

Recognition Letters
Significant Others

Recognition Letter

Ready

Purpose:	To endorse participant involvement in the training session by sending letters of recognition on behalf of those who supported/organized the training event.
Time:	Fifteen minutes
Group size:	Any size group
Learner risk:	Low
Materials:	Letterhead, envelope, stamps

Set

• Prepare a sample recognition letter that you will be able to personalize for each participant. (See sample on the next page.)

• Prepare a recognition letter form for gathering details from each participant.

Go

• In the early to middle part of the workshop, let participants know that you are prepared to write a recognition letter on their behalf to the individuals who supported their training. This will give each participant time to decide who the letter should be sent to and ensure they have contact information. Advise learners that this offer is optional.

• As the workshop draws to a close, remind the learners of the recognition letter you'd like to write. Read a sample letter so the learners know the type of information you will include. Indicate that you will be using your company letterhead for the letter.

• If learners agree to have you send a recognition letter on their behalf, give them the recognition letter form. Ask them to complete it and return it to you. Indicate that you will not be using the names given to you for any reason except this one-time letter of recognition.

• Write letters about the participants and send them to the individuals identified on the form.

Sample Recognition Letter Form

Recognition Letter Form

You've worked hard and contributed to the success of this workshop. I would like to recognize your efforts and involvement by sending a letter to the individual(s) from your work place who supported your decision to take part in training.

By completing this form, you are granting me permission to write a letter of thanks to one or more people who supported your attendance at this training event.

Name of Learner:

People to send recognition letter to:

Name: _____   Name: _____

Position: _____   Position: _____

Address: _____   Address: _____

City: _____   City _____

Prov/PC: _____   Prov/PC: _____

Sample Recognition Letter

Dr. David Smith, President
Home Oil & Gas Production
1111 11
Calgary AB T6T 6T6

Dear Dr. Smith:

Re: Recognition of Kathy Jones

HP TrainingWorks Inc. is a professional training and development company that conducts workshops across Canada. Our latest national workshop was conducted in April and was entitled WOW (Workshop On Workshops).

On April 15th and 16th, Kathy Jones attended the Calgary WOW event. Her keen insights, active involvement, and willingness to try new ideas in training were a model to other learners and strongly encouraged me as the facilitator.

Kathy has an obvious desire to raise the bar on her training skills. She wants to apply the learnings of WOW into her workshops back at Home Oil & Gas Production.

I commend Kathy's competent and capable efforts to advance herself. She recognizes the importance of continuing education and values her clients enough to invest the time to make the difference in the services she provides at Home Oil & Gas Production.

Thank you for your interest in and support of Kathy, and in the value you place on professional development.

Sincerely,

Hugh Phillips
President

Rewards

• These letters build good will. For every one hundred letters I send out, I get about five to ten spontaneous responses, thanking me for my thoughtfulness and interest in recognizing a staff member.

• It is personally and professionally rewarding to let others know just how much you've enjoyed working with enthusiastic learners and to express the hope that training will help advance the learning goals of the organization.

Risks

• Some learners will think you're simply trying to get more contacts for your database and invading the privacy of managers and CEOs to promote your own ends. Let them know your intent right away to avoid this misinterpretation.

• Ensure you have the correct spelling of the contact person's name. Some learners may not print neatly. If needed, contact the learner to confirm the name, position, and address.

Options

• Send letters via e-mail instead of regular mail.

• Use a commercially prepared or company thank you card and hand write your note to the contact person.

Significant Others

Ready

Purpose:	To acknowledge those who have supported the training event.
Time:	Fifteen minutes to identify individuals
Group size:	Any size
Learner risk:	Low
Materials:	Letterhead, envelopes, stamps

Set

• In sessions that are five days or longer, identify the individuals who contributed to the success of the training event. Make sure to include those whose behind-the-scenes work is often overlooked. Some significant others to consider include managers, supervisors, the cafeteria manager, office administrator, head of maintenance, technical support workers, director of training, and audio-visual personnel.

• Write a separate letter to each significant person you identify. Avoid the temptation to write one "cookie cutter" letter for all. The personalized approach will be appreciated. (See sample letter on the next page.)

• Identify personal as well as professional efforts that were taken to ensure the success of the workshop.

Go

• Send the letters of thanks/appreciation to the individuals you identified.

Rewards

• This technique builds rapport and maintains sound working relationships. The goodwill built with this technique will benefit you in many ways and for a long time.

• This technique conveys the message that, as a trainer, you value an attitude of gratitude.

Risks

• Ensure you spell names correctly. If needed, contact the individuals to confirm names, position titles, and addresses. Find out the ways in which the people contributed to the success of the event.

Options

• Attach digital photos of the workshop to e-mail messages and send these to the behind-the-scenes workers.

Dear Lois,

On September 17-21, the High Impact Training workshop was conducted at your training site. I want to thank you for your cooperation, support, and involvement in this workshop. Here are some of the actions you took that I noticed and am grateful for:

- E-mailed questionnaires to assess learner needs

- Confirmed the training room and all the required AV equipment

- Arranged for refreshments and lunches. Your thoughtful attention to the special needs was great

- Touched base with me each morning of training to ensure all was in place

- Coordinated the evaluation forms

- Forwarded a follow-up questionnaire to the training director and managers

What a difference your efforts made in the training event. Our achievements came in good measure because of your enthusiastic and professional support.

Sincerely,

Hugh Phillips
President

HUGHism

"Take time to affirm,
And you endorse the investment of people and time!"

Chapter 11:
The Fifth Dimension

Things which matter most must never be at the mercy
of things which matter least.
Goethe

Several years ago, I was closing a workshop with a one-page evaluation form. After the session, I sat down to review the feedback I had received. One form had a "PS" at the bottom of the page; it read:

P.S. Hugh, you covered a lot but didn't uncover much.

My first reaction was to think, "Same to you lady." My defensive reaction was due, in part, to the fact that this was my eighth straight day of training. I was tired and not ready to receive what I viewed as criticism. Of course, I missed the profound meaning of this comment.

After a two-day break, I was training again. In a more rested, relaxed, and receptive mood, I found myself repeating, "You covered a lot but you didn't uncover much." Like a lightening bolt, right in the middle of a workshop, I got the message.

My insight? Product is the covering, process is the uncovering.

As a trainer, I was an expert at filling up the learner's mind with lots of information and skills. I was in love with my content, and with great enthusiasm I would give each learner a banquet table of knowledge, skills, attitudes, and values. I excelled at product, but boy-oh-boy I had a lot of work to do on process. What a wonderful gift from this participant.

I set to work on improving the process aspect of my workshops. I had no idea that training was about to become much more exciting and fulfilling for me.

Defining Product and Process

Novice trainers focus on product. They feel responsible for teaching ideas, passing on information, and helping learners practice skills. They spend so much time getting to know the content that they have little time to pay attention to process. But as novice trainers mature, content becomes more familiar. Time is freed up to create better ways of training. The idea starts to grow that perhaps there is more to training than giving out information. Process is just as important as product.

Product is what you do in training. It includes things like content, discussions, techniques used, work to be done, decisions made, and goals achieved.

Process is how you train. It includes things like the approaches you take, the procedures you adopt, the guidelines you establish, the group interactions you encourage, and the level of participation you achieve.

In other words, product is the substance of the workshop; process is the style. I like to use a metaphor that describes product as the words to a song and process as the music.

The Five Dimensions of Training

It's true: training is not rocket science. You don't have to have multiple degrees and years and years of experience to be a trainer. But I believe you do need to be aware of and competent in five different areas in order to anticipate a high degree of success. The first four areas, or dimensions, all relate to product, but the fifth dimension—the one I feel most trainers need in order to grow in their profession—focuses on process. Let me briefly reiterate the first four dimensions. These are all concepts that have been touched on elsewhere in this book. Then I'd like to focus more time on the fifth dimension, and see what we can find out about process.

The First Dimension: Knowledge

We know that learners attend workshops to increase their knowledge. They expect the trainer to be a subject-matter expert and that the content covered will be relevant and current. A trainer enhances his knowledge of a subject through education, experience, and expertise—the three E's we talked about in Chapter 1. A well-equipped trainer combines practical experiences with lasting expertise and wisdom.

The Second Dimension: Skills

A successful training event translates knowledge into action through the learning of new skills. This is often what separates education from training. The primary focus of education is to *know*. The primary focus of training is to *do*.

Some of the skills a learner acquires in training are "hard" or technical skills. In computer training, for example, learners become familiar with a program package by using a variety of technical skills. Repeated and reinforced practice of technical skills enables learners to walk away from the workshop able to use the computer program adeptly.

Other skills acquired in training are "soft" skills. Learning how to listen attentively, resolve conflict, work on teams, and deliver high-impact presentations all involve these soft, people-focused skills. Trainees return to work with increased ability to collaborate, cooperate, and communicate.

The Third Dimension: A Positive Attitude

Training is much more than sharing knowledge and acquiring skills. As we train, learners pick up a myriad of signals about a trainer's attitudes. If our training style and our attitude are consistent, then learners find us credible. Sometimes the instructor's attitude will influence the learner's attitude. This leads to a challenging question for trainers: Is our attitude worth catching? Do we "walk our talk"? Are the soft skills we teach congruent with the soft skills we use in the training event? Any manager will tell you that they don't simply want a more educated employee returning from training; they want a person with a positive attitude.

The Fourth Dimension: Values

Attitudes do not exist in a vacuum. They are shaped and supported by a higher dimension: values. Your values shape your interactions with learners and with the content you are training. Do you know what your training values are?

Whatever values you hold, be assured they are important. Bob Pike, a well-known trainer in the United States, advocates that trainers "Teach from a prepared lesson as well as from a prepared life." What I take from this is that the trainer's values are as important as their training topic. You cannot separate the two. One supports the other.

The Fifth Dimension: Process

The fifth dimension drives the first four dimensions. *Process* supports the *product*; it makes the product come alive! The more attuned you are to process, the more likely you are to achieve your product goals.

Once process was brought to my attention, I began to look for ways to "uncover" workshop material, not just "cover" it. I examined *how* I trained and started to vary my approach to workshop content. For example, my

Making Connections

I recall very clearly the impact that Norman Vincent Peale, author of The Power of Positive Thinking, *had on me when I heard him speak at a National Speakers Association convention. Dr. Peale, then 92 years of age, spoke in front of fifteen hundred people. His bright mind and quick wit made him a hit with the audience. His commonsense thinking, combined with astute observations, challenged us all. But clearly, for many, what impressed us most was Dr. Peale's positive attitude. The man walked his talk. There was congruency between what he said and what he did.*

lectures became much more interactive. I began to infuse my lectures with simple techniques (many of them included in the techniques sections of this book) that paced learners, challenged the class, and created greater interest and attentiveness. Lecturing was much more interesting and fun now. The class connected more with the content because the process was so much more alive.

For example, Q&A sessions took on a new twist. Instead of asking lots of closed questions, a habit I picked up somewhere along the way, I began to ask many more open-ended questions. As well, I resisted the impulse to answer everything that came my way and began to use other methods of handling questions, like relaying the question over to the class, bouncing it back to the inquirer, or parking the question for later, more thorough examination.

As I became more adept at process, I found that the interactive learning environment now allowed learners to internalize the product more thoroughly.

Tasking and Maintenance Skills

When you begin to focus on process, you'll find the most useful strategies can be divided into two camps: tasking skills and maintenance skills.

Tasking skills are used as you figure out *how to get the work done*. These include things like setting agendas, regulating time frames, and developing decision-making methods.

Maintenance skills are used as you figure out *how to develop healthy group interactions*. These include things like ensuring members feel included, dealing with difficult learners, establishing levels of influence, and making sure members are satisfied.

Finding the Right Balance

Every group, every situation, and every training topic influences the balance between product and process. For example, if you have a limited amount of time and a large group, you pretty much have to emphasize product. On the other hand, if you've been given adequate time and your topic focuses on a higher dimension of training, such as attitudes and values, you will be able to concentrate on process. Obviously, the balance between process and product is not set in stone. For each training scenario you'll need to ask yourself, "What is right at this time, for this group, on this topic, and at this place?"

Let's take a look at a few of the different situations you may find yourself in.

Scenarios

In the following four hypothetical scenarios, I use percentages to indicate the amount of time given to product or process in a workshop. The first number refers to the percentage of time given to the four dimensions that make up product: knowledge, skills, attitude, and values. The second and third numbers indicate the percentage of time given to process, that is, tasking and maintenance respectively. (For example, if a scenario had the numbers 60–30–10, 60 percent of the time in a workshop would be invested in product, 30 percent in tasking, and 10 percent in maintenance.)

Then I examine the scenario in terms of its strengths and limitations. By looking at the percentages I can predict possible workshop conditions and identify the possible strengths and limitations of the situation. I'll suggest why the weighting of these particular percentages may or may not work for a particular group.

I'll conclude this section by looking at the way you spend time on product and process in your own training!

the Trainer's EDGE

The scenarios suggested here are by no means the only ways of balancing product and process. Although you can go into a workshop with an idea of how you'll balance the two, the percentages may shift throughout the session based on its needs, circumstances, and conditions. Still, you'll be able to ascertain an average rating that you can then use to assess workshop delivery.

Scenario ONE: **75–20–5**

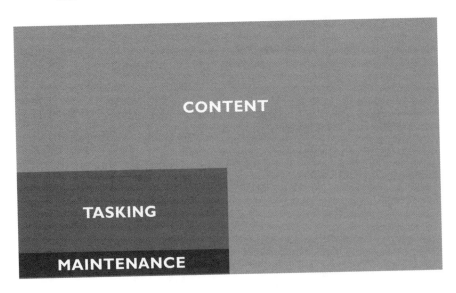

Possible strengths

- With three-quarters of workshop time spent on content, learners will get a good dose of knowledge and skills. Most, if not all, trainees will be happy with this emphasis, especially if the workshop is information and skill based.

- With one-fifth of workshop time spent on tasking matters, learners will understand what is expected of them. The trainer provides a good amount of learning structure.

- Some subject areas lend themselves particularly well to an emphasis on product and tasking. For example, workshops with a heavy emphasis on content and/or technical material will work well with this scenario.

- If group rapport already exists, maintenance activities will take place prior to and following the workshop, so the trainer does not need to focus on maintenance during the workshop.

Possible limitations

- The small amount of time spent on maintenance may indicate the trainer is not skilled in this area or downplays the human needs in the workshop.

- These percentages suggest a high-control trainer who prefers a top-down approach to running a session. Learners play by the trainer's rules and regulations—no consensus decision making, just following the leader.

- Perhaps the larger amount of time spent on tasking is a direct result of the small amount of time spent on maintenance. The trainer has to keep the group under control because learners are not encouraged and their feedback isn't sought.

Scenario TWO: **90–5–5**

Possible strengths

- This scenario suggests that a very large group is receiving training and these are the only conditions under which it can run. Tasking expectations would be provided in handouts, and the trainer-student ratio would be too high to spend much time on maintenance.

- An intense transfer of knowledge happens in this scenario. Perhaps a well-known instructor has been invited in to share her expertise. With little time for questions or personal responses, learners attend to take in the wisdom of the instructor. (Let's hope the trainer is blessed with a sense of humour!)

- If a trainer hasn't been given a lot of time to conduct a session, this scenario uses the time given to get content across.

- When training a group of experienced learners, it's okay to focus content as much as possible.

Possible limitations

- The trainer thinks that his only job is to inform. All that matters is what he knows and what the learners need to know. This is a classic example of the "talk and gawk" show.

- By supplying excessive information and not providing the opportunity for interaction, the material is not internalized. Learners have less chance of retaining what they've learned.

- No time is given to resolve instructor-learner tensions that may surface.

- These are the percentages that characterized my workshops when I was told I "covered a lot but didn't uncover much."

Scenario THREE: **75–5–20**

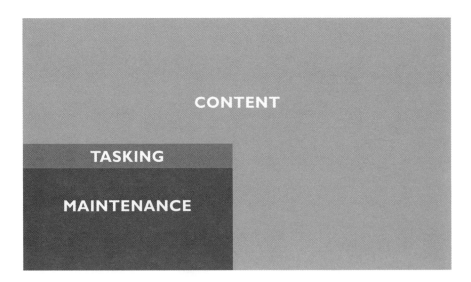

Possible strengths

• Like the first two scenarios, this one focuses on content. If the learners are information driven, they'll be pleased.

• The time spent on maintenance suggests this may be a group with high maintenance individuals. Or maybe the whole group comes from a work environment characterized by low trust or respect. Participants come to the workshop needing some affirmation since they get little at work. You are able to cover a fair amount of information because you are sensitive to learners' needs.

• This scenario works well for groups of self-directed learners with positive attitudes about trainers. They take responsibility for training and need little guidance in their work habits. They come to training on a regular basis and know the ropes.

Possible limitations

• The low emphasis on tasking may mean that time is not well managed. The trainer may love interacting with others but not be great at spelling out the guidelines and structures needed for an efficiently run classroom.

• With few tasking instructions provided by the trainer, learners may be confused about expectations. This leads to greater learner frustration and more time spent on maintenance. Sometimes low tasking leads to high maintenance.

• If a trainer is not confident with his tasking skills, he may hesitate to impose any restraints on the class. In this case, he overcompensates on the people side, even if results are sacrificed.

Scenario FOUR: **20–40–40**

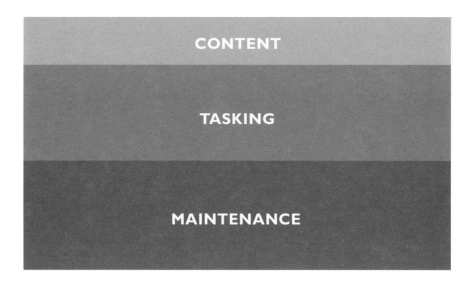

Possible strengths

• A new team often needs to pay greater attention to process than product. When a team is functioning well (i.e. the process is well grounded and well utilized), it is in a position to deal with the product matters, like issues and decisions. Team building usually has to precede team working.

• This scenario works well for soft-skill workshops that emphasize participant interaction. The process generates and validates the product.

• Due to the diversity of the group, learners learn as much from one another as they do from the trainer. The group looks inward for information, not outward.

• To keep a group functioning with such high process numbers requires strong facilitation skills. The trainer will be well versed in and proficient with tasking and maintenance.

Possible limitations

• Trainees who come to gain new information will be disappointed. The focus is on the group, not on the transfer of knowledge. Some learners will feel they are wasting their time.

• The reason for the emphasis on maintenance may be that the group has a lot of unresolved conflict and this hinders the trainer's goal to share information and expertise. Sarcasm and hostility may dominate this type of group.

• This scenario could suggest learner frustration with a trainer who lacks process skills. Therefore, a lot of time is spent clarifying working conditions and trying to meet the needs of frustrated learners.

YOUR Scenario: _____-_____-_____

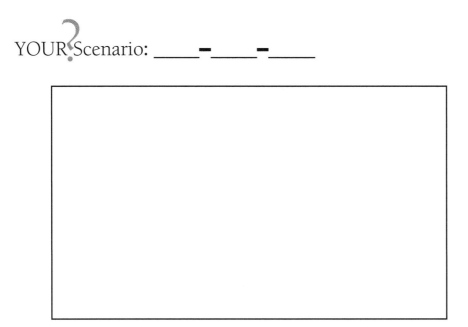

So what about you? How much time do you spend on product? On process? Complete two scenario charts: one indicating your ratings now and one indicating where you would like to see yourself down the road. Take some time to examine the strengths or limitations of your current ratings.

My Scenario

When I talk about the product/process balance in my workshops, I often complete two charts: one indicates my percentages when I first started training and another, more recent, version reflects my growing emphasis on process. Typically, the compliments and concerns I received about my workshops early in my career went something like this:

Compliments	*Concerns*
Well organized	Not enough time for questions
You stayed focused	Have the group introduce themselves
You kept us working all the time	Breaks were too short
Time really flew by	Would be good to have lunch together
Excellent manual—full of ideas	Get to know our names—show you care

Quite clearly, these comments reflected my emphasis on product. Now I strive to change the balance and include more process skills. I've taken my audiences' frequent and consistent feedback to heart and now emphasize maintenance and tasking skills, too. I ensure strong interaction not only for activity's sake but also for the benefit of networking, affirming, and communicating with each learner.

Individual Versus Group Needs

When you assess the balance between product and process, you are, of course, considering the entire group. But don't forget that every group is made up of individuals. Not everyone will fit the scenario. Some trainees need more structure; others want only to take in new knowledge. While you need to be

insidescoop

I remember working with a learner who didn't seem to connect very well with the group. He was aloof and distant and seemed focused on other things. During the first break, we had a chance to chat. We started off talking about the weekend football game, but after a while I asked him how the workshop was going for him. He said, "To be honest, I'm not really here right now. It's not your fault. It's just that at breakfast this morning my teenage daughter and I had quite an argument. It's an issue that's been festering with us and we still haven't managed to resolve it. I've been re-living our argument all morning, trying to work out in my mind what I can do." I then asked him if he had come up with any options. He said that he had, and we chatted further about them.

This learner was in need of considerable maintenance early in the workshop; his percentages would have been something like 25–25–50. Just having the opportunity to chat with him at the break helped to meet some of those maintenance needs. In fact, as he was leaving for lunch he commented how much he appreciated having some time to vent with me at the first break!

aware of individual needs, remember your primary focus is on the group. If you strive to find the correct balance for every individual, you will no longer be running one workshop, you will be running a whole bunch of one-on-one sessions in one place, at the same time!

You cannot be all things to all people all of the time. If you try to, you'll lose sight of the workshop's purpose and you'll be physically and emotionally drained. Don't worry, though; most adults will ensure that their tasking and maintenance needs are met. Also, by using affiliation and affirmation techniques, many tasking and maintenance needs are met early on in the workshop, at its close, or throughout the session.

Addressing process throughout the workshop allows most, if not all, of the content to be completed. Ignoring the process will put content in peril.

HUGHism

" Product is the covering,
Process is the uncovering. "

Chapter 12:
Growing Healthy
Relationships

The degree to which I can create relationships which facilitate the growth of others as separate persons is a measure of the growth I have achieved myself.
Carl Rogers

Trainers are great planners.

They can set the daily workshop schedule from the opening warmer upper, to the fifteen well-scripted activities, to the closing inspirational story. They can organize well-timed breaks and excite passers-by with intriguing learning stations. They can arrange for prodigious amounts of audio-visual equipment to arrive on cue. They can research and provide learners with a dozen different luncheon options. They can plan down to the minute, from beginning to end, the complete workshop experience.

So what happens when something comes along that can't be planned for? Yes, that ol' monkey wrench is as much a part of training as a well-rehearsed plan. How do you plan for the reaction a learner will have to your material? How do you organize the level of acceptance and honesty learners may develop amongst each other and with you? How do you schedule for a "prisoner" who will announce her resistance to your material and to others in the room?

Each and every workshop has a human element that defies planning. These elements cannot be contained in a trainer's schedule, but they can be influenced by a leader's ability to communicate effectively. By choosing appropriate communication options, trainers become facilitators as well as planners.

Facilitation is a more open, less predictable process than planning, and it is *the* aspect of training that usually leaves us feeling the most vulnerable. You can always beef up your knowledge and experience base, but how do you bolster the facilitation side of training? Of course experience helps, but no matter how long you've been training, that unpredictable human side of an event cannot be scheduled—no matter how hard you try.

It's clear that as trainers we can't just hope that the group gets it together. We have a proactive role to play in helping the group meet its full potential. We wear the hat of trainer and the hat of facilitator. More than just imparting information, we impact the group with interpersonal skills that help the group to work cooperatively and productively.

In this chapter, I'd like to give you an edge in the facilitation aspects of training. I will begin by looking at the twelve signs of healthy, functioning groups. Then we can use these characteristics to objectively assess the groups you work with. Are they functional or dysfunctional? Healthy or not? Finally, I'll provide you with practical suggestions for effectively managing the human element of training with the use of strong communication skills. These suggestions will teach you how to nurture your learners and "grow" healthy groups.

The Healthy DOZEN

I've led groups that are easy to read. Learners are open and honest. They candidly provide me with feedback throughout a session and help me to gauge where the group is at.

I've also led groups that are difficult to read. Learners don't say much and it's hard for me to tell if they're having a good time or if they're disappointed with the session. Sometimes, I've been sure that a group is dissatisfied with the workshop, only to find out in the evaluations that they enjoyed the session and plan to refer me to other individuals or organizations.

Wanting to take the guesswork out of my ability to assess a group, I've spent a great deal of time over the past few years speaking with and observing learners who are a part of healthy, functional, and productive groups. The following twelve "signs" have been constructed from their responses and my experience.

1. Trust and respect

When individuals trust and respect one another, an abundance of positive feelings and thoughts proliferate through the group and a healthy, productive atmosphere is created. Trust, I believe, is based on what we feel about another person; respect is based on what we think of someone else. Trust is affective; respect is cognitive.

What should you look for to determine whether or not your group is trusting and respectful? Levels of trust and respect are communicated both through verbal and non-verbal behaviours. People simply enjoy being with each other. People will be relaxed yet interactive, accepting yet challenging, cooperative yet comfortable with appropriate competition.

2. Balance between tasking and maintenance

Functional groups usually require a balance of tasking and maintenance. You'll find yourself spending equal amounts of time guiding the group to stay on task and helping it to get along. Both are needed. When you are able to assess and respond to task and maintenance needs in an on-going way, a sort of moving balance comes into play and the group continues to function at an efficient level.

3. Humour quotient

Are we having fun yet? When learners enjoy a joke or a humorous story, the group bonds. Too little humour leads to a dull group that takes itself too seriously. Too much humour and the group can upstage itself; the joking interferes with the training activities. The right balance of humour is magical.

4. Process observing

Individuals who spontaneously observe and articulate the process they are a part of are aware of their own needs and the needs of the group. They help to empower themselves by monitoring group interaction and group progress. The workshop is rich and alive because the learners *themselves* intertwine content with process.

5. Energy level

An appropriate level of energy is vital to group productivity. A stimulating environment helps those who are low key to get involved and keeps those with excess energy in check. Energy vitalizes the learning experience and keeps the momentum healthy. You'll find that a higher-energy group leaves you with more energy than when you came in.

6. Body language

Body language can tell you a lot about a group's ability to function productively. Your healthy group will smile, nod, and have open body stances that suggest comfort and compatibility. By watching the group's body language, you'll have a reliable indicator of the group's ability to function. Closed body language gestures, like crossed legs, folded arms, and lack of eye contact, usually characterize a group that is not open to learning or to one another.

7. Tension indicators

Tension erupts naturally as a group grows. If this tension is used as a constructive force and monitored, it actually helps a group to bond. The tension is vitalizing and strengthens the group as individuals and collectively. Learners emerge strong and stable, due in part to their ability to frame tension as a positive growth force.

8. Cognitive–affective views

Healthy groups have a balance between the head and the heart. Not everything can be objectified or quantified, nor is everything "wow" and fantastic. Groups with a cognitive–affective balance have learned to balance these perspectives. Enlightenment and enthusiasm are both high on the list of group values.

9. Leadership factor

Healthy groups share leadership. They balance dependent tendencies and independent ambitions with an interdependent attitude towards leadership. They recognize that both the instructor and the group are responsible for workshop success. The leadership factor is secure because it is shared.

Initially the leadership role lies more with the trainer. It is expected the trainer will take a lead role in getting the group organized, purpose driven, and subject focused. As the group matures, it relies less on the instructor for leadership and takes on this role itself.

10. Clarity of purpose

Healthy groups articulate a clear purpose early in the training event. They will even monitor activities based on the established purpose. Learners will ask themselves, "Does this activity contribute to the ends we've established, or is it a filler or redundant?"

Obviously, the trainer has an important role at the beginning of the workshop to help the group determine the session's purpose. The trainer will also help members realistically assess what can be accomplished in the time provided. Purpose helps ensure a valuable end product.

11. Conflict Management

Healthy groups have learned to manage conflict in a variety of ways, depending on circumstances. Generally, conflict is managed in one of five ways, as indicated in the following chart. Functional groups realize that, depending on the situation, any of these options may be valid.

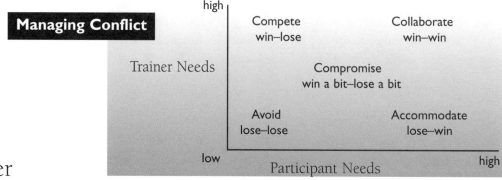

12. Follow through

Healthy groups have members that speak to one another and stay in touch via e-mail following a workshop. With all of the networking that takes place at a session, learners keep in touch by supporting and encouraging one another. Members take on the responsibility of follow-through!

Assessing Group Health

With these twelve indicators as your guide, you can now measure a group's ability to perform in a functional, healthy manner. Use the Group Health Indicator chart below to help you assess the groups you work with. Don't feel you need to evaluate all twelve factors each time, though. I find I can accurately assess a group's health by looking at about six indicators. As much as possible, you're hoping for a group that rates in the middle column.

Group Health Indicators

1. Trust and Respect

| High respect/Low trust | High respect/High trust | Low respect/High trust |

2. Task and Maintenance

| Task heavy | Task/Maintenance balance | Maintenance heavy |

3. Humour Quotient

| Lacking | Balanced | Disruptive |

4. Process Observing

| No checking in | Astute/Timely comments | Excessive checking in |

5. Energy Level

| Suppressed | Stimulating | Harried group |

6. Body Language

| Secretive/Subtle | Open | Exaggerated |

7. Tension Indicators

| Sensitive/Touchy | Dealt with | Dominates group |

8. Cognitive-Affective

| Head first | Blend | Heart first |

9. Leadership-Facilitation

| Instructor dependent | Shared | Group determined |

10. Clarity of Purpose

| No agreement | Established | Instant agreement |

11. Conflict Management

| One option: avoid | Five options | One option: compete |

12. Follow-through

| On their own | Networking | Co-dependent |

Communication: The Key to Healthy Groups

Now that you know what to look for when determining whether or not a group will function in a healthy and productive manner, you're probably wondering what you can do foster this healthiness. What can a trainer do to keep the energy level functioning, the network working, the humour quotient balanced, and the conflict managed? In other words, what can a trainer do to move or keep a group at a healthy level where human needs are met and intellectual challenge and stimulation occur?

I find the key to nurturing a group's health lies in the ways we communicate. By modeling appropriate communication options we foster the healthy growth of groups. And this goes a long way to enriching the learning environment! The three communication options open to you are these:

1. Assertiveness

When you assert yourself as a trainer, you express your needs and wants in a manner that is acceptable to others. For example, you state when class will begin and end and you make a commitment to show up on time and end on time. When you're assertive, your needs are addressed first, and the needs of others, that is, the group members', are addressed second.

When you deliver a lecture, you're also being assertive. You are asking the class to be attentive to the information you are sharing. In the moment of lecturing, the trainer's needs are more important than those of the learners. You need participants to be mentally attuned to your words so they can relate to and connect with the information.

2. Responsiveness

When the focus shifts from the trainer to the learner (or learners), the trainer shifts from assertiveness to responsiveness. For example, when you promote a group discussion, you are responding to the learners' needs to express views and opinions. Even though you could be lecturing (perhaps would even like to be lecturing), you recognize the group's needs are more important than yours in that moment. So you seek input, putting yourself in a responsive role.

The trainer has the right and the responsibility to be responsive. If your voice is the only one heard, one-way communication occurs. Rarely is this necessary. In most cases, time should be given to learner inquiry and discussion.

3. Assertiveness–Responsiveness

Often, assertiveness and responsiveness are needed at the same time. Let's say a participant asks a question right near the end of a lecture. You look at your watch and realize that you only have a few minutes left before lunch. How do you respond? I would say something like, "Thanks for the question. That's a good one. But it's lunchtime in about three minutes, so I'd like to wrap up my lecture and then respond to your question when we come back this afternoon.

Will that work for you?" I've been assertive by thanking the learner and stating that I need to finish the lecture, but I've also been responsive by *asking* the learner if it's okay for me to respond to the question a little later.

the Trainer's EDGE

All the training techniques we use are important to help a group learn effectively. But in and of themselves, the techniques will not help the group to grow, and growth is a must if you want the learning to stick. A positive group experience validates and invigorates your topic. Participants that grow together will connect with the material. The ways you are able to communicate with and facilitate the group are linked directly to the health, vitality, and retention of ideas displayed in your group.

Practice All Three

As you read through these three effective communication options, you'll likely found one more appealing than the others. Chances are this is the mode of communication that you use most often and that you're most comfortable with. But it is important to practice the communication styles that don't come as naturally.

If you are a skilled responsive communicator, you need to practice an assertive communication style, both the verbal and non-verbal aspects. Body language, tone of voice, and mannerisms need to be in synch with the words you speak. If you are a good assertive communicator, you will need to practice a responsive communication style. Some assertive communicators associate responsiveness with weakness. But this isn't true. It takes a lot of courage to be responsive, just as it does to be assertive. Both involve risk; both involve skill. Both are key to fostering healthy groups.

Other Communication Options

As a trainer, three communication options are open to you. But your learners have three more options at their fingertips. This gives them a wider range of choices, but not necessarily a communication advantage. That's because these additional options are *not* effective ways to communicate.

1. Aggressiveness

When learners communicate aggressively, they disregard the rights and dignity of the trainer or of other learners. They are interested only in their own situations. They think they make up 100 percent of the equation and you (or other learners) make up 0 percent. They may be sarcastic or insulting; they may embarrass or humiliate someone.

2. Passiveness

Passive learners abdicate their responsibility and surrender their rights. They deem the trainer's needs or the needs of other learners to be far more important than their own. Unlike aggressive participants, these learners feel that others make up 100 percent of the equation and they're quite fine making up 0 percent. These learners will do what they're told and won't ask questions. Passive learners practically invite others to step in and take advantage of them.

3. Passive-Aggressive

A passive-aggressive style of communication combines these two ineffective ways of interacting with individuals and the group. First the learners will deny they have a problem, say little, and put up with feeling uncomfortable. Then, out of the blue, they'll let off steam by unjustifiably attacking another learner or the trainer. They communicate in extremes. This is a very manipulative behaviour because it is hard to predict and even harder to deal with effectively.

the Trainer's EDGE

It's easy to see why trainers should not opt for these last three ways of communicating. But that doesn't mean it will be easy. If you're tired at the end of a long day, it will be tempting to acquiesce to the group's request to leave early. Or, when a student disagrees with you, you pass off their comment as interesting but fail to address the issue. In most cases, I find passiveness means I don't take responsibility for my actions. Similarly, when I'm tired or frustrated, I find it easier to lose my patience and become sarcastic or aggressive. Whenever I've limited my communication choice to being aggressive, however, I've regretted the decision. Rarely can aggression be justified by the trainer.

The Trainer in You

Walking the Communication Line

When I coach trainers, I encourage them to stay on the line of communication. I demonstrate this principle by laying down about three metres of masking tape on the floor. I stand near one end of the tape and say, "Let's call this end of the tape assertiveness." I walk to the other end of the tape and say, "We'll call this position responsiveness." Then I go to the middle of the tape and say, "The middle of the tape represents assertive–responsive communication."

To demonstrate the off-limits communication options, I first return to the assertive end of the tape, but I keep walking so that I step off the tape. "This," I say, "is being aggressive." I walk to the other end, step off the tape, and say, "And when I step off the line at this end, I'm being passive." Finally, I take a few leaping steps from the passive position and jump to the aggressive spot and call this passive-aggressive.

I explain to my learners that it is very important for trainers to "stay on the line" almost all of the time. (The exception occurs in the rare situation where our physical or emotional safety is at stake.) We are not to step off the line and exercise the three dysfunctional options that do little to dignify the learners or ourselves. By staying on the line, trainers maintain dignity, trust, respect, and the ability to influence. By stepping off the line, we threaten all that we've worked hard to establish.

HUGHism

" " Model appropriate behavior—
Stay on the line of communication. " "

Chapter 13:
Growth Dynamics

Be the change you want to see in the world.

Gandhi

Like people, groups undergo defined growth stages.

Also like people, some groups grow up relatively quickly and smoothly, while others are dogged by erratic starts and stops. I've led groups that advance through the developmental growth stages with minimal struggle. They pick up the usual bumps and bruises along the way, but nothing seems to stop them from progressing. I've worked with other groups that struggle with growth. They can't agree on basic guidelines; they get bogged down by others' opinions, and they find it hard to accept responsibility for their learning.

As a trainer you will delight in the groups that seem to progress through the stages of group development smoothly, and you may struggle with those who have more difficulty with the process. But in both situations, it is important to be familiar with the developmental stages that the group experiences. Your awareness of these stages will provide you with some understanding of what groups and individuals are experiencing at different times throughout a workshop. With this information as your guide, you will be able to choose communication options that are appropriate to the situation, facilitate growth, and model values that contribute to the group's maturity.

Three Stages of Group Development

So, what stages of growth do groups experience? And how can you help a group get through these stages with as few challenges and setbacks as possible? Through personal observation and reflection on the experiences of other trainers, I've learned to distinguish three distinct phases of group development: membership, influence, and authenticity. I've also learned how important my role is in guiding groups through these stages.

Stage One: *Membership*

In the first stage, membership, groups are getting comfortable with you, with other learners, and with the workshop topic.

When a group of learners convenes for the first time, the primary question asked by most participants is "Do I belong here?" Therefore, very early in the session, individuals will begin the task of seeking membership in the group. They will attempt to clarify roles and responsibilities. Some will express their membership needs in an expressive, open manner while others will seek to belong more quietly. No matter the approach they prefer, almost all learners will look for some way to fit into the group.

Supporting Membership

To assist each learner through the membership stage you will need to use both tasking and maintenance skills. The more adept you are at supporting learners at this stage, the more quickly the group will attain a sense of belonging. Try some of the following activities to facilitate this first stage of group development.

the **Trainer's** EDGE

I've found that in longer workshops the need for membership seems more pressing. Membership does not seem nearly as important for a half-day workshop as for a three-day workshop. Keep this in mind when choosing activities that support membership needs. Also, remember that membership will need to be re-established when groups reconvene each day during a longer workshop. Use affiliation techniques that blend a summary of the previous day's learning with the opportunity for group members to interact.

Tasking Activities		Maintenance Activities	
Prior to Workshop	Early in Session	Prior to Workshop	Early in Session
Have manuals, name tags, etc., in place	Start on time	Send invitation to workshop	Implement a warmer-upper activity
Provide refreshments	Help group establish norms/guidelines	Use inviting room arrangements	Personally welcome all participants
Post an agenda	Outline objectives	Post a welcome message	Introduce yourself
	Announce breaks	Provide refreshments	Indicate cooperative intentions
	Announce finish time		
	Point out washrooms and emergency exits		

Stage Two: *Influence*

In the second stage, influence, group members seek a greater degree of interaction with one another.

In this stage, learners work *at* (tasking behaviours) and work *through* (maintenance behaviours) group issues, ideas, and problems. This means it's a busy time for trainers and members. You will be pressed to use your maintenance skills effectively because the human element of the group is most prominent during this stage. Personal and professional needs are expressed in this stage and have to be addressed. As challenging as this time can be, it is also the stage at which groups begin to bond. Through successful resolution of issues and challenges, participants form professional relationships. They assert their interdependence with the group and their independence as individual members.

As with the membership stage, you'll notice that public and private learners seek to achieve influence in different ways. Public learners talk openly to the whole group, to their subgroups, with others during the breaks, and with the trainer. Private learners seek influence by talking one-on-one with others or the trainer.

Supporting Influence

Your role in supporting the influence stage is quite different from the role you played during the membership stage of group development. While you will still rely on tasking and maintenance skills, you will be using your leadership ability to manage learners who are striving to carve out a place of influence, a much more challenging task for learners than gaining membership. Keep the following activities in mind as you guide learners through the influence stage of group development.

Tasking Activities	Maintenance Activities
Reach agreement on agenda (even if this means modifying it)	Help members participate by appointing and encouraging
Model active listening	Accept disagreement as a way to work through conflict or impasse
Keep discussions on track	Assign responsibilities and attach a sense of value and importance to each learner
Manage time proactively	Encourage expression of personal agendas
Enforce (or modify) group norms	Set the stage for cooperation and compatibility

Stage Three: *Authenticity*

In the third stage, authenticity, learners start to "be real" with one another.

When issues have been worked through and norms have been established, the group is ready to be productive. This is the highest and most powerful stage of group development. A level of trust has developed, and, if all has gone well, this will be an emotionally and socially satisfying phase. Learners are no longer limited by the hesitancy of the membership stage or the confusion, conflict, or clarifying that takes place in the influence stage. They have worked at and through group issues, problems, or challenges and are ready to tackle anything that comes their way.

In this stage, public learners will often step forward as the spokespeople for groups, articulating group needs and working visibly on group issues and projects. The private learners will work behind the scenes, ensuring follow-through, guiding task completion, and mentoring others on a one-on-one basis.

Supporting Authenticity

At this stage, the trainer takes a bit of a back seat. The group has empowered itself and will take on some of the trainer's roles. Your job is to encourage the group and help it maintain its high level of performance and its interactions. You will see the fruition of earlier tasking and maintenance efforts, but you will not be as actively involved with the group as you were in the influence stage.

Tasking Activities	Maintenance Activities
Play devil's advocate to encourage thoughtful completion of tasks	Foster humour
Set timeframes for work completion	Help members gain professional intimacy
Support group leaders and individual members	Mentor group members as needed
Provide resources	Share and care

At a recent workshop, I was reminded just how dynamic the stages of group development can be. This particular group jelled very well. In fact, by early afternoon of the first day of the workshop I felt they were already at the third stage of group development—authenticity. Their healthy and happy interactions, combined with a strong work ethic, were making for a great time!

Then, midway though the afternoon, a stranger walked in and took a seat at the back of the room. I soon noticed a very dramatic backward shift in the group. Their spontaneous, easygoing behaviour became stiff, awkward, formal, and non-sensitive.

They stopped responding to my questions. The group energy diminished.

During the break I chatted with the stranger who I discovered was the manager of the group. I also had several conversations with group members. They were anxious about having the manager in the room. She had recently been transferred to their department and had a reputation as a downsizing expert. They felt awkward and self-conscious, and were reluctant to participate for fear of reprisal.

In a brief half hour, this group had regressed from authenticity to membership. They were questioning, do I really want to be here?

Checking In On The A's

With all of this focus on the ways that groups form and interact, we mustn't lose sight of the Eight A's of training. As a matter of fact, the A's are intended to advance group growth. For example, affiliation helps learners gain membership or belonging; the interactive and participatory nature of application facilitates the influence stage; and affirmation is vital to authenticating the training experience. The following table outlines some of the links between the A's and group development.

The A's and Group Development

The A's	Group Growth Stage	Questions Answered
Affiliation and Attention	*Membership:* **Getting comfortable**	Who is in the group? Do I fit here? What is the trainer expecting? Does the agenda fit with my learning needs? Why do I need this training? Will it be interesting? Is it worth my time?
Acquisition and Application	*Influence:* **Working at and working through**	How can I contribute to this group? Will this group accomplish its goals? How are we going to deal with difficult behavior? Am I doing enough networking? Are the workshop guidelines working? Are we going to cover all that was promised?
Action and Affirmation	*Authenticity:* **Being real**	What can we accomplish? What kind of risks am I willing to take? Who will I develop a deeper professional relationship with? What am I going to act on? Am I open with my co-learners? What am I doing and saying that makes a difference to this group? How can I serve this group?

How Does Your Garden Grow?

In our discussion of the various growth stages, I've suggested a few tasking and maintenance activities for you to consider as you guide your groups to healthy interactions. But it's important to have a thorough understanding of the intent of these aspects of a workshop's process. Why will the activities I've suggested succeed? How do they help your garden of learners grow?

In this section I *state the specific trainer skills* that tasking and maintenance activities employ and *comment on the usefulness* of the skills for successfully developing healthy groups. Our job as trainers is to model these skills as best we can. Be assured, your learners will notice proper use of tasking and maintenance skills. If you persevere in developing and applying these skills, participants will adopt them, too.

Tasking Skills: Getting the work done

Initiating

- One of the most important skills early in the workshop

- Occurs when a trainer offers a new idea, suggests a solution, prods the group to action, invites someone to participate

- Energizes the trainer as she provides direction to the group and adds focus

Coordinating

- A powerful skill because it proves that you are an active listener who validates learner ideas

- Occurs when the trainer pulls together ideas, points out relationships between ideas, or refers back to an earlier comment

- Particularly useful for linking similar ideas voiced by different participants

Elaborating

- Teaches the group the importance of adding to ideas that have already been stated

- Occurs when the trainer expands on an idea or fact, or when he takes the time to clear up confusion

- Builds momentum for the group and models active listening

Consensus Testing

- Allows you to "check in" with the group

- Occurs when the trainer asks about the group's position or decision

- Provides focus and builds consensus by asking the group to confirm a position

Summarizing

- A vital skill to help a group review discussion or acknowledge accomplishments

- Occurs when the trainer offers a conclusion or restates and reviews ideas

- Can be used during a lecture, at the end of a discussion, or at an intervening point in a discussion to help the group keep track of shared ideas

- Provides focus

Questioning

- Fosters thinking and inquiry

- Occurs when a trainer asks open-ended or closed questions of the group; open-ended questions are usually more invitational than are closed questions

- See page 104 for more details on questioning

Redirecting

- Allows the group to respond to a question rather than the trainer

- Occurs when you invite group members to respond to a question that has been directed at you

- Establishes more than one credible voice in the group. (Note: Of course, relying too much on this technique can have the opposite effect—the group begins to question your credibility as a trainer.)

Disagreeing

- Playing the devil's advocate is particularly useful when the group is too quiet or too agreeable

- Occurs when the trainer expresses another point of view or contrary observation

- Stimulates deeper thinking, challenges group think, and advances contrasting views

Paraphrasing

- Ensures the trainer has heard the learner correctly and gives the trainer time to respond to a question

- Occurs when the trainer restates what a learner has said, using his own words

- Allows the learner to rethink an observation, validate it with the trainer, or correct a misunderstanding

- Very useful in defusing conflict with difficult learners (See the Trainer's Edge on page 287.)

Maintenance Skills: Helping the group get along

Encouraging

- An invaluable skill!

- Occurs when the trainer accepts learners' ideas at face value and when the trainer is friendly and responsive to others

- A wonderful motivator and energizer for a group

- Groups often model encouraging actions

Gatekeeping

- Requires the trainer to pay careful attention to the group

- Occurs when the trainer helps learners participate and opens lines of communication for all members of the group

- Using a non-threatening manner and empathetic and invitational language, the trainer encourages private learners to participate

Standard setting

- Groups need explicit and implicit norms

- Occurs when the trainer takes the time to set guidelines or point out deviations from guidelines. The group will pick up this skill and remind each other as needed.

- Early efforts to adhere to group standards can prevent problems and issues from arising later on

Harmonizing

- The ability (intuitive or learned) to be comfortable with tension

- Occurs when the trainer reduces tension by reconciling differences or mediating disagreements in a calm, controlled manner

- Confirms that the trainer is able to take the good with the bad, that she can deal with difficulty in a dignified manner

- A very powerful skill to model to participants!

Compromising

- The ability to yield status, admit error, or meet half way on an issue

- An intelligent way to help the group reach a middle ground when extreme views have been the norm

- Occurs when the trainer wants to avoid competition or does not have the time for collaboration

- Implies the trainer is attempting to be fair rather than harsh

Process observing

- Ability to mentally separate yourself from the group to observe what is happening and then process your observations with the group

- Occurs when the trainer points out the processes or problems encountered by a group

- Helps the group move towards more authentic and open communication

---

Dear Hugh,

I attended one of your Workshops on Workshops recently and found myself particularly intrigued by the tasking and maintenance skills you talked about. I came back to the office ready to tackle these skills and apply them in my own training. But it didn't take me long to feel overwhelmed by how much learning I had to do. Any suggestions about how to make this seem like a more manageable task?

Sincerely,
Overwhelmed in Ottawa

Dear Overwhelmed,

Thanks for your note. I remember you from the workshop and believe you definitely have what it takes to "grow" your tasking and maintenance skills. I have a few suggestions for you. First of all, don't feel like you have to tackle everything at once. You're right, that would be an overwhelming task, especially when you consider just how much else you have to remember in training.

Why not first identify the skills you already perform well. Maybe even have a friend or colleague watch you to help determine the skills you seem most comfortable with. Then select one or two skills that you want to get better at and practice them in your next workshop. By limiting yourself to working on one or two skills per workshop, you will slowly but surely develop new habits. One word of caution, though, as you practice new skills: choose some that are tasking and some that are maintenance. Often, our personalities lean toward one or the other and you want to strive for a balance.

Finally, advance your learning curve by watching other, more experienced colleagues. Focus on the tasking and maintenance skills they use. When you observe skills like process observing or consensus testing, you'll not forget the impact they have on a group. Your observations will help cement the skills in your long-term memory, and you'll find them easier to use in your next training event.

Good luck!

Sincerely,
Hugh

People-matter Experts

We've taken a look at the three stages of group development and the trainer skills needed to help foster group growth. As you can see, training is as much about creating the environment in which learners can learn as it is about the learning itself. Trainers are leaders in a topic—subject-matter experts—and leaders of people—people-matter experts!

HUGHism

" You are much more than what you train! "

Chapter 14:
Leading Difficult
Groups

Life without confrontation is directionless, aimless, passive. When unchallenged,
human beings tend to drift, to wander or to stagnate. Confrontation is a gift.
David Augsberger

In chapter 12, I outlined the traits that characterize healthy, functioning groups and I suggested some leadership, facilitation, and communication strategies to foster these types of groups. In chapter 13, I introduced you to the stages of group development and stated that by becoming familiar with these growth stages you'd be better prepared to guide your learners.

But what happens if a group isn't healthy? What can you do if a group finds it difficult to grow? Challenging groups can wear the trainer down, and if too many of them come your way, you may begin to wonder if you want to be a trainer at all! Even experienced trainers begin to resent these groups: the maintenance required and the personal and professional energy demanded numb your talents and your desire to contribute to the group.

In this chapter, I will offer some insights into working with challenging groups. Take heart! As you expand your skills and intuitions with groups, your positive influence will work wonders.

The Three P's

Challenging groups often contain a handful of challenging individuals. It is these individuals who undermine your authority and set the class on edge. If you are able to identify these types of learners, you'll be well on your way to addressing their needs. In general, the learners who come to my workshops tend to fall into three categories: participants, passives, and prisoners.

Participants

Participants are not challenging learners. As a matter of fact, they are the cream of the crop! But for comparison's sake, and to give you an overview of all three types of learners, I've described them here, too.

Participants come to workshops with well-defined intentions, a willingness to learn, and the desire to share. Usually, the timing of the session and the workshop topic both align with their needs and interests. They contribute positive energy to the workshop, manage themselves well when given reasonable guidelines, and are aware of individual needs and the needs of the group. They have little difficulty staying focused and enjoy a flexible work structure. Participants are active learners who enjoy a variety of planned exercises.

In short, these are stellar learners who will teach you many things. Their wisdom and experience will bring you new insights that add value to the product and process of the workshop. When you have a room full of participants, you might not want the workshop to end!

Passives

If passive learners were cars, they'd be stuck in neutral. They are the vacationers in the group. They come with low expectations and appreciate the opportunity to leave the hectic pace of work behind to enjoy a relaxed and fun day with colleagues. Workshops are time-outs for the passive learner. A passive's lack of interest could be the result of being tired, overworked, or thinking that new knowledge will mean more work. Maybe they're just three years from retirement and in retirement mode already.

Usually, passives are pleasant people and present a motivational rather than a management challenge to the trainer. They prefer to play the role of an observer. Their low energy is not a burden to the group, but it can be frustrating to a trainer who is attempting to motivate the group. If you could get inside a passive's head, you'd hear, "Don't bug me; just let me enjoy the class with my colleagues. Yes, it's true I'm using up a space in your class, but I won't create problems for you. If I get one or two good ideas from this workshop, that'll be great."

When you are first getting to know your group, passives will stand out in several ways. First of all, they are sometimes late and seem to have a "my time," not a "group time," mindset. As well, these are the learners who read newspapers, update timers, or even respond to e-mail during a session. Finally, they are often glued to their cell phones or pagers and have told the office to interrupt them if needed. Sound familiar?

Passive learners, like all learners, may be private or public in their approach to learning. The private passive is quiet, unobtrusive, and laid back. He sees the workshop as an opportunity to rest, a respite from a frenetic work atmosphere. The public passive is more sociable. He enjoys the networking opportunities, but doesn't really care if he learns much.

Prisoners

These folks will drain energy from you and the rest of the group. They've shown up at the workshop with enough negative luggage to disrupt the group agenda. Prisoners will surface at workshops for many reasons. Sometimes workshop attendance is mandatory; sometimes low staff morale creates prisoners; sometimes prisoners feel they are subject-matter experts already and that further training is a waste of time; and sometimes personal crises produce prisoners. Whatever their reason for attending, the negative luggage they bring to a training event will play havoc with the group's development and create a challenging learning environment.

Some learners' prisoner status may not be permanent. For example, a one-time participant may become a prisoner if he can't find a parking place, doesn't have the correct change to get a parking ticket, or has to park four blocks away. He arrives late, upset, and frustrated. These types of prisoners can often be persuaded to move back into the participant camp by a caring and observant trainer.

Private prisoners work quietly to sabotage your good work. Public prisoners are visible and usually announce themselves in the workshop. Both types will light bushfires—doing anything they can to distract the group from the intended workshop outcomes.

You won't have much difficulty recognizing the prisoners in your workshops. They usually want to be noticed and demonstrate what I refer to as self-oriented behaviours. This means they are absorbed by their own needs, desires, and problems, and will often take out any frustrations they are experiencing on the trainer or the group.

Self-Oriented Behaviours

I typically associate seven self-oriented behaviours with the prisoners in my classroom. A prisoner may display one or several of these characteristics.

1. Blocking

When prisoners attending a workshop feel overworked, stressed out by unreasonably high expectations, or believe they are under paid, they might see the workshop as an opportunity to get even. They'll do this by blocking group ideas. They'll challenge simple things, like when to reconvene after lunch, or more serious issues, like creating consensus on new company policies and procedures. They will complain or argue at any opportunity. If given full rein, blockers can bring workshops to a stalemate.

2. Dominating

This behaviour occurs when one or more participants talks excessively, interrupts the trainer or other learners, or becomes too forceful. They monopolize discussion periods and impulsively question everything you have to say. Prisoners who dominate usually feel that they know more than the trainer and resent having to attend a session. Dominators can be very stubborn; consequently, their negative influence spreads quickly.

3. Aggression

Aggressive behaviour includes insulting others in the workshop, being sarcastic, criticizing, and showing hostility. It is a high-energy behaviour, but all of the energy is negative. Aggressive prisoners often make other participants feel unsafe or threatened.

4. Playing

Playing may sound like a positive behaviour, but when I talk about prisoners who play I'm referring to class clowns who show off, tell inappropriate jokes, goof around, or take part in side conversations. This type of playing steals energy from the group. It distracts and annoys other learners and leads to an unproductive workshop. Playing is self-oriented and driven by selfish purposes.

5. Withdrawing

Sometimes prisoners are simply distracted by worries, anxieties, and frustrations. By withdrawing from the group, they are able to focus on the troubles that are bothering them. When prisoners withdraw, they daydream, don't pay attention, or seem indifferent to what is going on around them. Your lecture may be fascinating, but to these people it is simply interfering with the time they want to spend absorbed in negative luggage.

6. Self-seeking

When a prisoner tries to make a personal agenda into a public agenda, self-seeking behaviour is at play. Self-seeking occurs when a learner shares personal troubles, insecurities, or needs. Often, these prisoners are public learners who have honed the ability to take centre stage. They love the attention it brings, yet have little motivation to resolve personal issues. Self-seeking behaviour distracts the group from workshop outcomes.

7. Special pleading

Like self-seeking behaviour, prisoners who take part in special pleading are taking personal agendas and making them public. But in this instance, the agenda focuses on causes, political beliefs, or issues that are of special interest to the prisoner. They cannot talk about anything without espousing a stance they feel strongly about. This behaviour distracts the group from its purpose. The prisoners are grandstanding, using the workshop as a platform to inform, persuade, or manipulate other learners.

Inside Scoop

Prisoner Status— Temporary or Permanent?

I remember a recent workshop where a learner came up at break time and told me her husband had just gotten a pink slip. She explained she was absorbed with thoughts about the future—how they would handle the mortgage, how they would buy the kids' school supplies, how they would deal with additional family pressures. She explained that just two days ago she was looking forward to the workshop. But her husband's unexpected dismissal had reshaped that desire. By lunch she had become so absorbed with her family matters that she dismissed herself from the class for the balance of the day. The next day, though, she returned and was ready to be the participant she had originally intended to be.

Frame It Positive

Interestingly, the positive skills associated with tasking and maintenance are close cousins to the self-oriented behaviours outlined here. For example, when the tasking skill of *initiating* is overused, it can become *dominating*. Another tasking skill, *disagreeing*, can be seen as *blocking* when overused. Or the maintenance skill of *encouraging*, when relied on too much, can be interpreted as a way of *self-seeking*. The person doing the excessive encouraging may want others to encourage them.

In a way, the weaknesses identified here are strengths pushed too far. Learners are taking a skill they are normally good at and overusing it. In other words, behaviour, although negative in the moment, often comes from positive intent, from a strength that just happened to get over worked.

Framing difficult behaviour this way allows the trainer to stay cool, to be alert to mediating options, and to respond or assert as needed.

The Three P's at a Glance

Before we look at ways of dealing with challenging individuals and groups, let's take a look at a summary chart that outlines some of the differences between the three types of learners. Before we do this, though, I'd like to add a note of caution. Identifying attendees as participants, passives, and prisoners simplifies what is really a complex topic. I use these categories to help me see the big picture, to get a handle on ways to manage my sessions, especially the difficult ones.

In real life, of course, people cannot be categorized so simply. We are all complex individuals with a variety of motivations, backgrounds, and philosophies. I use the terms participant, passive, and prisoner to help me understand, guide, and manage a learning group more effectively. But—and this is a big but—I always avoid the easy way out of using the three P's as a way to label people. No one likes to be labelled. Use my classifications as a tool to guide your knowledge and understanding of an *individual's* workshop behaviour.

the Trainer's EDGE

The further along the group is in its growth, the stronger it will be socially. During the membership phase the group is vulnerable. Conflict and difficulties usually require active leadership from the trainer. However, a group that has reached the authenticity stage is in a good position to constructively deal with challenges itself. The difficult person is now much more accountable to the group. Utilize the social strength of the group when it has reached a higher level of group development by facilitating the group so that it can manage and monitor itself.

Participants, Passives, and Prisoners

Behaviour	Participant	Passive	Prisoner
Attitude toward the workshop	Expectant	Neutral	Hesitant to resistant
What they want from other learners	Relationship	Friendship	Partnership
Attitude toward the way things get done	Supportive	Non-committal	Disruptive
Measure recognition by	Growth	Giving	Gains
Manage individual need through	Involvement	Guidance	Consistency
Attitude toward workshop outcomes	Positive	Minimal	Negative
Contributions to the group are	Energetic	Pleasant	Tense
Trainer needs to deal with them by	Navigating	Stimulating	Collaborating
Communication style learners prefer	Responsive/assertive	Responsive/assertive	Responsive/assertive

Managing Challenging Learners

Now let's move on to how we can successfully cope with challenging learners. I won't deal with participants here. Any of the myriad techniques and tips for managing effective workshops outlined in this book will work well with participant-learners. All you need to do is actively monitor and manage them. You want them to maintain their participant status throughout the entire workshop.

Instead I will focus on passives and prisoners. Be encouraged that passives and prisoners form only a minority of the typical workshop group. Nevertheless, a minority can upstage training.

Managing Passives

When you identify a passive learner in your workshop, you better take out your motivator's hat and place it firmly on your head! Remember, passives are pleasant folk who are simply not in workshop mode. As with participant-learners, all of the techniques and tips in this book provide useful starting points for involving passive learners; the ones I focus on here are primarily motivational strategies.

1. Connect with work

Take the time to identify a strong connection between the workshop topic and the passive learner's work responsibilities. Completing a thorough audit will help you do this. Promote workshop benefits.

2. Subgroup work

The positive influence of participant-learners may well convert an individual from passive to participant. By putting a passive in a subgroup with four participants (I call this the "4 on 1 Rule"), you may motivate the passive to become a more interactive learner. This is more readily done in a small group than with the whole group.

To make sure a passive doesn't get teamed up with a subgroup of prisoners (who may influence the passive in a negative way), invite people to change subgroups at least once during a workshop day. When asking subgroups to mix it up, I'll say something like, "I'd like to invite you to make new groups. I'll give you a couple of minutes to do this."

3. Shared responsibility

In a non-threatening manner, appoint passives as leaders in their subgroups. For example, during a subgroup activity, say something like, "The next leader at your table will be the person who has the darkest hair. Please find that person now." It just so happens that I've noticed one or more passives and they have the darkest hair at their tables. This subtle approach is better than an authoritarian or insistent manner.

4. Group questions

Instead of relying on individuals to ask question, have subgroups generate two to three questions to be addressed in a Q&A session. By putting the onus on the subgroup, you draw out the passives and encourage them to contribute their queries—again, in a non-threatening way.

Managing Prisoners

Prisoner behaviours are much more disruptive than passive behaviours. As a trainer, you will be testing your facilitation, communication, and collaboration skills as you attempt to persuade the prisoner to play a meaningful role in the classroom dynamic.

When a prisoner disrupts the workshop, begin by asking yourself what impact the behaviour is having on the group. Is the group coping okay or is it sliding backwards, with individuals starting to question their membership in the group. If the prisoner behaviour is having a negative impact on the group, you need to act quickly and decisively. If not, you may want to let the moment pass. Your goal is to preserve group growth, health, and happiness.

I think of a prisoner moment as a bushfire. It may not be serious, but if I let it go it could spread quickly. I may have the resources and equipment to put out a bushfire, but can I contain a forest fire? When you respond to prisoners in a workshop, you'll need to assess the situation and decide whether or not to act. You don't want a forest fire raging through the training room!

I practice two main strategies when managing prisoner behaviours: I diffuse and I depersonalize. I use several techniques when exercising these management strategies.

Diffuse

1. Move from indirect to direct

As a general guideline, when you're working with a difficult learner, move from an indirect (or more preventive) approach to a more direct (or corrective) approach. In other words, move from a responsive to an assertive style of intervention. The responsive approach usually gives the trainer the opportunity to make a connection with the learner. You can draw on this connection at a later time.

2. Avoid arguments—Acknowledge problems

A workshop leader loses every argument. If you do manage to win an argument, chances are you've embarrassed the prisoner you were in conflict with and made the group uncomfortable. Maybe you made your point, but you've alienated individuals and lost their respect. Your goal is not to win arguments; it's to circumvent struggles in the first place.

The most effective way I know of avoiding arguments is by acknowledging the learner's problem. Don't get caught up in stating opposing positions. Instead, hear the problem. Don't downplay it, deny it, or ignore it. Get to the bottom of things by asking questions. You validate the prisoner's point of view by asking things like, "Why is this important to you? Why do you think we should do it that way?" These questions allow you to be hard on the problem but soft on the person involved.

By acknowledging prisoners feelings and thoughts as real, you are not implying your agreement. But you are letting them know that you believe what they are experiencing is valid. This acknowledgement also ensures that you are not making assumptions about the individual's attitude or stance. Resistance is often expressed indirectly and questions help you get problems out in the open. By acknowledging an issue, you are taking the prisoner at face value.

3. Work one on one

Do not give prisoners a stage to perform on. If necessary, diffuse any tendency to upstage the workshop by removing yourself and the prisoner from the room to talk in private or by speaking during breaks.

When you talk privately, take an assertive stance by making a request of the prisoner. With an overzealous person, you could say, "I'm pleased that you've been contributing to the discussion. You bring a wealth of interesting experience to the group. I'd like you to hold back a bit during our next session and allow me to draw out the others. They need to validate their thinking. Will you monitor your comments for the next session, and then we can talk at the next break about where we want to go from here?"

The one-on-one nature of your conversations allows the prisoner the freedom to respond without reprisal from other learners. And did you notice that I prefaced my request with a few positive observations about the individual as a person who added value to the workshop.

When you make a request, be clear, concise, and confident. David Augsburger says, "Confrontation is not a matter of tact, diplomacy, and smoothness of tongue. It is basically simplicity of speech, empathy in attitude, and honesty in response."

4. Refer to ground rules

If you posted and agreed to a set of ground rules during the workshop opening, reminding the prisoner of the guidelines may be all you need to do. However, if workshop guidelines were not established early in the workshop, or the problem arose before you had time to set the guidelines, then it may be appropriate to establish them at this time.

5. The 4 on 1 Rule

In some cases, linking a prisoner with participants in subgroup settings may diffuse the resistance or resentment the prisoner is feeling. Be careful, though, that the linking is not done at the expense of the participants. Monitor subgroups with prisoners and intervene if you find the prisoner is undermining the assignments. Also, avoid having several prisoners together in one subgroup. If this happens, reassign subgroups so that you have only one prisoner in any subgroup. The positive energy of participants will often have sufficient influence on prisoners to help them cope with workshop interactions and expectations.

6. Reflect

When something is bugging you about a learner, ask yourself, "Do I need to do something about it or is it just me? Is this just a minor annoyance that I'm making a mountain out of? Is this affecting just me, or is it influencing the group?"

Sometimes a trainer assumes prisoner behaviour when none exists. By taking a step back and reflecting on the situation, you may decide that the best action is no action. Maybe your own luggage has shaped your perception of a situation. Sometimes you just need to let an issue go. Otherwise it will upstage you and you'll find yourself making an issue out of nothing. The wisdom lies in your ability to discern what to deal with and what to overlook.

7. Physical proximity

Move toward prisoners to show them that they have come to your attention. By positioning yourself closer, you indicate that you have picked up some signals that need to be addressed. This works especially well with dominant and aggressive behaviour. These prisoners like the attention they get from you. At the same time, by moving with positive intent, you help to diffuse the prisoner's desire to take over the group. This also shows that you are prepared to deal with whatever challenging behaviours come your way.

8. Cultivate humour

One of the most effective ways of releasing the tension in a room is through appropriate and well-timed humour. Value and foster humour in your workshop, whether it's through a great laugh, a warm and infectious smile, or a funny story. Whatever the case, cultivate humour in the group so that when a difficult moment comes, you or someone in the group will feel free to use humour to reduce tension. What a delight when you can lighten the moment!

9. Drop the agenda

When a difficult person challenges you or another learner, you may have to drop the agenda. By this I mean you'll have to stop what you're doing (lecturing, leading a group discussion) and deal with the situation. Product has stopped and it is time to process the moment. This can be a turning point in the workshop. Working through the issue can bring clarity not only to the difficult person, but also to other learners. By dropping the agenda, you may forfeit some time in the short term, but more productive learning in the long run will make up for the time spent dealing with the situation.

10. Seek a partnership

When working with prisoners, be collaborative, not competitive. Seek a learning partnership with them. Model the very actions you want from them, such as cooperation, a positive attitude, lots of patience, and good listening ability. To seek a partnership sets up the conditions for the prisoner to save face while looking for more constructive ways to behave.

insidescoop

I remember a prisoner-learner who brought a stopwatch to class. As soon as I announced a break, he would start his stopwatch and then stop it when we reconvened. At the end of the first day, he announced that twelve minutes were lost by overextending our agreed upon break times. Several members thought this was a little much. Their faces reflected disgust and frustration. As a trainer, you have a choice. Do you frame this as a positive or negative opportunity? I requested that if he wanted to continue to keep track the next day that he give me a one-minute warning during our breaks. In this way I could be more accountable to the time contract for group breaks. By the third day, the stopwatch had been put away and the group was managing break time very well.

the Trainer's EDGE

Mutual understanding, not acceptance, is the key with difficult behaviour. Once you understand a problem, you can explain your expectations in relation to it. Active listening skills can help you reach mutual understanding. Active listening is difficult at the best of times, so when you're in the middle of a workshop you can expect it to be even harder. But if you don't take the time to understand a difficult learner, the situation can worsen.

When you actively listen to a learner, follow these four steps, which will then lead to the fifth step where you move from listening to explaining your point of view.

1. Ask about the person's point of view, position, description of the situation

2. Repeat back what you heard

3. Ask the person to fill in the blanks you may have missed

4. Repeat back what you heard until the person feels you understand

5. Now state your position. Speak for yourself. Use "I" statements; do not accuse or blame.

When you reach step five, the leaner will either *respond* or *react* to your request. A response suggests your position has been received positively. Chances are you are going to be able to resolve the issue. A reaction, on the other hand, means your position has been met with a negative reception. Despite your active listening, the prisoner rejects, ignores, or verbally attacks your position. When the learner reacts, you will need to start the active listening process again. This, of course, takes time, so you need to determine what an appropriate demand of your time is in view of workshop agenda, goals, and outcomes. Active listening is a learned skill and, like any skill, the better you get at it, the more efficient use you make of time.

Depersonalize

1. Manage your feelings

One of the cornerstones of training in the moment is the ability to monitor your feelings. You may not want to take the time to step back and reflect on your feelings when you'd rather continue with your workshop plan. However,

Dear Hugh,

While I usually consider myself a patient person, last month I lost my temper with a "prisoner" in one of my training sessions. Of course, no one ended up a winner in that situation, but I just couldn't seem to help myself. Any advice on what to do should this happen again?

Sincerely,
Sorry in Sackville

Dear Sorry,

Sometimes it just happens. We're tired or frustrated with a challenging group or individual and we lose it. Instead of exercising acceptable communication options we respond aggressively (or passively) to prisoner behaviour. I think the most important thing to do is to take responsibility for that behaviour as quickly as possible. This usually means apologizing. Apologizing is an assertive act so we are back "on the communication line" where we belong. By staying on the line we retain our power to influence and inspire.

Then I think you need to identify the situation as a growth moment. Some of your greatest learning as a trainer comes from the insights and intuition you develop as you cope with difficult behaviour. Even when we blow it and do something we regret, we have the opportunity to learn and advance our leadership skills.

Here's to continued growth!

Sincerely,
Hugh

if you don't take the time to assess your emotional status during difficult situations, it is all too easy to take a prisoner's behaviour personally. And doing so just compounds the situation.

When you take stock of your emotional response to a situation, remind yourself that the reasons for a prisoner's behaviour don't usually involve you. Overworked, under employed, stressed out, negative workshop experiences—these are just a few of the possible reasons for a prisoner's behaviour. And none of them apply to you or what you're doing.

Monitoring your thoughts and feelings during difficult moments is one application of process observing—a maintenance skill. As you develop this skill you'll become more self-aware. It will be easier for you to "be" in the moment rather than "be overwhelmed" by the moment. Knowing what is going on inside will help you deal more objectively with what is going on outside, that is, with the group or another individual.

2. Remain calm

Disruptive behaviour can be quite upsetting to you and the group. Stay calm. Remain as objective as possible. The group needs your clear and compassionate thinking. The group wants someone who is able to stay focused on the purpose and goals of the workshop. Remaining calm helps you to depersonalize and avoid blaming yourself. This moment will pass and the calmness of your presence will help it to do so.

3. Strive for interdependence

As trainers, we need to carefully balance the professional and personal. If we're too professional we seem stiff and removed from the group. Too personal and the group wonders if we're training for our own therapy. Rather than appear too dependent or too independent, we need to strive for interdependence. This helps us to stay objective. If we find the right balance between professional and personal, prisoners will find it hard to resist our commitment to their learning.

4. Empathy not sympathy

Empathetic trainers try to understand the situation and remain neutral or non-judgmental in their feelings. Sympathetic trainers can get wrapped up in emotions that cloud objectivity and clear thinking.

the Trainer's EDGE

Dealing with difficult moments is not so much a question of what is the right and wrong thing to do, it is more a question of what is the most appropriate thing to do. Textbooks will give you insights and encouragement, but ultimately how you respond in the moment will be intuitive. In most cases you will do what is appropriate for the moment. Learn to trust your intuition.

Making Connections

When I took my advanced coastal sailing course, we trained in rescue operations. We learned that when someone goes overboard, you don't send someone else into the water to rescue that person. Instead, everyone remains on the boat and helps the MOB (Man Over Board) victim from a position of safety. The main reason for this is that you are in a much better position to help from the boat than if you join the victim in the water. The same is true when attempting to help someone in a workshop. You don't want to get emotionally drawn into the learner's problems or take on the saviour syndrome—the feeling you can help everyone that comes your way. Remain on the boat where you are in the best position to help.

Challenges Are Gifts, Too

Sometimes the workshop experience can be the best thing for a prisoner. With your patience and perseverance, prisoners may park their luggage and become fully engaged with other participants and the program. Maybe the workshop topic actually addresses one or more of the prisoner's concerns, or your strong interest in the topic captivates him. At other times, the prisoner behaviour simply plays itself out during the workshop. The self-absorbed person may find little to be gained from not participating in the workshop experience and decide to join the participants in the room.

But whether or not you're able to help a prisoner, don't forget that the challenges you've faced are ultimately gifts in disguise. As you look back on difficult training moments, ask yourself, "So, what did I do well and what would I change if this happens again?" A question like this led to many of the tips and techniques I've presented here. In other words, frame the experience in a positive light by asking what you have learned and how you will respond more capably to the next challenge.

the Trainer's EDGE

Driven by the Five C's

All of my suggestions for dealing with passive and prisoner behaviours can be summarized by the five C's. These cornerstones of leadership behaviour will serve you well in your interactions with all groups and individuals!

Care	Confront a person because you care. Frame "confronting" as "care-fronting" (Augsberger).
Concern	Focus your energy on the group's needs, not your own. Concern is an outward attitude, not an inward one.
Compassion	Seek to understand an individual's perspective. Be sensitive to the group's needs.
Cooperation	Motivate, invigorate, and bring out the group's best efforts.
Consideration	Frame behaviour in a positive light and be patient, graceful, and trusting of an individual's intent.

HUGHism

"Trainers are subject-matter experts. They must also be people-matter specialists."

References

Augsburger, David. 1980. *Caring enough to confront.* Glendale, Calif.: Rev ed. Regal Books.

Covey, Stephen. 1989. *The seven habits of highly successful people.* New York: Simon & Schuster.

Chapter 15:
Learning Styles

He gives nothing who does not give himself.
French proverb

How do you like to learn?

When you learn something new, do you take a methodical, step-by-step approach? Or do you prefer to immerse yourself in the topic as quickly as possible? Maybe you enjoy discussing and sharing ideas with others? Or perhaps you focus on what you can do with an idea. One thing is clear. When you train, you soon discover that people learn in different ways.

A great deal of research examines the ways individuals learn. In general, this research refers to the different ways in which we learn as learning styles. These learning styles, or learning preferences, have major implications for your success as a trainer and to the trainee's success as a learner. Learning styles are patterned, predictable ways of learning. They are with us from the time we're born; they're innate. We come into this world wired with certain learning style preferences. When these preferences are acknowledged and accommodated in our training experiences, we find learning easier. When preferences are not accommodated, we may get frustrated and discouraged.

The Four Learning Styles

My experience in the training classroom and my knowledge of research done by learning style theorists confirms for me that there are four different learning styles.

I categorize learners into Doers, Influencers, Relaters, and Thinkers. (Using the first letter from each category, I refer to my ideas about learning styles as the D•I•R•T model!) Let's take a look at the traits that are associated with each of these styles.

Doers

Doers excel at completing learning tasks quickly. They will take on a job and stick with it, even if this means sacrificing a more collaborative, people-centred focus. Getting the job done is of prime importance. These learners are blessed with the ability to focus and work with intent.

Motto	Look at my accomplishments!
Emphasis	Get it done
Strengths	Takes initiative Works quickly Independent
Weaknesses	Impatient Stubborn Low tolerance for emotional viewpoints

Influencers

Influencers love to get involved. They value a fast pace and lots of healthy interaction. They see workshops as an opportunity to have fun and interact in an exciting learning environment.

Motto	Hey, look at me!
Emphasis	Get involved
Strengths	Enthusiastic Persuasive Generates ideas
Weaknesses	Lacks follow-through Dislikes planning Makes generalizations

Relaters

Relaters are driven to get along with workshop colleagues. They enjoy discussion and an open workshop environment. They model wonderful listening skills and help build harmony in the training session. They value group work and strive for consensus to define workshop goals and outcomes.

Motto	Everybody likes me!
Emphasis	Get along

Strengths	Ability to listen
	Works well in teams
	Provides service and support to others
Weaknesses	Lacks assertiveness
	Avoids conflict
	Would rather watch

Thinkers

These learners like to get it right. Quality of work is far more important than quantity. They prefer in-depth discussions and a comprehensive examination of ideas. They want ideas to be supported by evidence. Question and answer sessions are important for these learners.

Motto	I am efficient.
Emphasis	Get it right
Strengths	Creative
	Organized
	Problem solver
Weaknesses	Perfectionist
	Critical
	Places high demands on self

Determining Your Learning Style

As you read through the descriptions of the four learning styles in the D•I•R•T model, you may have found yourself trying to figure out where you fit in. I usually find that learners show affinity for two of the four learning styles. The following diagram can be used to help you determine your own learning style. View the diagram, read the explanation provided, and then follow the directions for figuring out your own learning style and learning comfort zone.

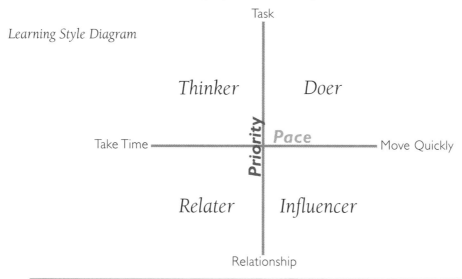

Learning Style Diagram

Diagram Explanation

- The diagram is based on a vertical line—priority, and a horizontal line—pace. These two dimensions are the basis for determining which two D•I•R•T learning styles, as indicated in each quadrant, reflect your natural ways of learning.

- Pace and priority are further defined by the criteria at the end of each line. Learners who emphasize pace may prefer to take their time or to move quickly. Learners with particular learning priorities may emphasize the importance of tasks or of relationships.

Using the Diagram

- The first thing you want to determine is whether you emphasize priority or pace in learning scenarios and which end of the spectrum you prefer.

- Look at the priority line and ask yourself, "When I learn something new, am I primarily task driven or relationship driven? Are the ideas, facts, and information more important to me? Or do I like to focus on sharing ideas and participating?" You may find you come up with an immediate and definitive answer, or you may respond with less certainty. Maybe it depends on the circumstances.

- Now look at the pace line and ask yourself, "What is my preferred learning pace? Do I like to learn at a methodical, step-by-step pace? Or do I prefer a faster pace with brief explanations and minimal details?" Again, you may be able to respond with certainty to these questions or you may be less sure.

- The next step is to decide which of these sets of questions is easier for you to answer. For example, when I ask myself to gauge the importance of priority, I cannot answer decisively. To me, it depends. Sometimes I'm very task driven in my learning, while at other times I really like the interaction. But when I consider the importance of pace, I can answer easily. Without a doubt, I prefer a faster pace. I do not like detail or analysis. I get frustrated when the task takes too long. For me, the pace line elicits the most predictable response.

- What about you? Did you respond more assertively and with greater clarity to the pace line or the priority line? And which criteria most appealed to you? On the diagram, locate the line and criteria that were most predictable for you. The learning styles on either side of the line will show you which two learning styles shape the ways you learn.

- Since the pace line was most predictable for me, and "move quickly" is the criteria that appeals to me, I can determine that I am a Doer and an Influencer, the two learning styles on either side of the "move quickly" end of the pace line.

The four learning styles, as outlined in the diagram, can be summarized this way.

Learning Style	Priority/Pace	Emphasis
Doer	Task/move quickly	Get it done
Influencer	Relationship/move quickly	Get involved
Relater	Relationship/take time	Get along
Thinker	Task/take time	Get it right

Comfort Zone

Another way to view learning style is through the comfort zone lens. The following diagram shows you my learning style comfort zone.

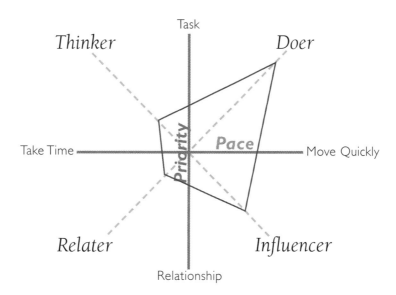

Diagram Explanation

Let's assume the two dotted lines cross at a point with the value of "0." The further outward you move along the diagonal line in each of the four learning style quadrants, the stronger you judge yourself to be in that particular learning style.

As you can see from the diagram, I positioned myself quite far along the diagonal line in the learning style areas I've already identified with—Doer and Influencer. I have not gone very far into the Thinker and Relater quadrants.

What do you think your comfort zone would look like? Once you've indicated your positions along the diagonal lines, link the points as I've done to visually depict your comfort zone.

Learning Style and Temperament

Interestingly, research on human temperaments outlines ideas similar to those associated with learning style. When I examined the literature regarding learning style and temperament, I found a considerable degree of overlap.

The chart below reveals a variety of learning style and temperament terminology. If you've taken any learning style or temperament surveys, you may find this a useful comparison chart.

Comparing Learning Style Terminology

Learning Style Terminology				
Anthony Gregorc Learning Style	Concrete-Sequential	Concrete-Random	Abstract-Random	Abstract-Sequential
David A. Kolb Learning Style Inventory	Converger	Accommodater	Diverger	Assimilator
Hugh Phillips DIRT Model	Doer	Influencer	Relater	Thinker

Temperament Terminology				
DISC	Dominance	Influencer	Steadiness	Conscientiousness
Peter Drucker	Action person	Front person	People person	Thought person
Hippocrates	Choleric	Sanguine	Phlegmatic	Melancholic
Carl Jung	Director	Intuitive	Feeler	Thinker
Merrill & Reid	Driver	Expressive	Amiable	Analytical

Training Implications

When you train, be aware of the variety of learning styles that may characterize your classroom. Plan the session and choose techniques that will acknowledge and address all four learning styles. Consider the following:

1. Strengths and weaknesses

Each learning style is characterized by specific strengths and weaknesses. Review these strengths and weaknesses, as outlined above, before planning your session. Remember that weaknesses are often just an overextension of strengths.

2. Total representation

You can safely assume that most learning groups will have representatives from all four learning styles.

Recently, I was conducting a workshop with a group of professional engineers. It soon became apparent that Thinkers and Doers were vastly over-represented in the room. Sometimes, you won't have an even distribution of learning styles, but this is the exception more than the rule.

3. Difficult learners

In Chapter 14, we discussed leading difficult groups. Sometimes, prisoners are simply individuals who are out of their learning comfort zone. Your ability to read a person's learning style may help you cope with difficult behaviour. Are difficult learners simply trying too hard to get it done, to get involved, to get along, or to get it right?

4. Learner risk

Because learning involves risk, people will tend to learn from a place of strength—their learning style. For example, at the beginning of a workshop, when you ask learners what their expectations are, they will often frame their responses based on their learning style. A Doer will find it easy to focus on the results. An Influencer will comment on the opportunities to interact with others and the instructor. A Relater may wonder if time will be taken for ample discussion. A Thinker will value the quality of learning and will prefer in-depth presentations.

Looking Ahead

Since learning style plays a prominent role in training, it makes sense to focus on what the trainer needs to do to accommodate different learners. In the next chapter, I'll talk about the ways learning style influences trainer behaviour.

HUGHism

"Learning is a matter of style."

References

Gregorc, Anthony F. 1982. *An adult's guide to style.* Maryland, Mass.: Gabriel Systems, Inc.

Chapter 16:
Adapting Your Style

I've learned that we are responsible for what we do, no matter how we feel.
H. Jackson Brown, Jr.

During the summer months, workshop demand decreases. I spend time in my office organizing files, reviewing the work I've completed, and setting goals for the fall. One lazy summer afternoon, several years ago, I was flipping through files, paying particular attention to my planning documents. It didn't take long before I noticed a pretty distinct trend in the training techniques I'd used. About 80 percent of the activities I selected focused on high-energy, fast-paced tasks that clearly emphasized my own preference for quick-moving workshops. My bias was showing. On that quiet summer afternoon, an insight came to me. Subconsciously, I use my learning style comfort zone, which is characterized by the fast pace of Doer and Influencer styles, to select training techniques that favour my preferences for training and learning contexts.

Upon further reflection, it hit me that most trainers probably do the same thing. Our natural tendency would be to train from our comfort zones. Now, this would be okay if all learners had the same comfort zone as the trainer. But, of course, they don't. No wonder some folk had difficulty with my workshops.

As trainers we need to know and understand our own learning preferences as well as those of our learners. We also need to be aware of how differently those learning preferences play out in a training event and how different learning styles affect our ability to achieve workshop outcomes for *all learners*.

Let's look at the strengths and weaknesses of each of the four learning styles and how they impact trainers.

Why would a trainer push a strength too far? I've discovered that when my strength is not working for me I have a choice—try harder or back off. The risk I take when I try harder is that I can overdo it. I try harder because I'm driven to succeed, but I can become self-serving when I focus too much on my needs, my preferences. Remember, a strength pushed too far will be seen by others as a weakness. We generally don't see our own weaknesses as readily as others see them in us. We need to balance our self-awareness with "other awareness."

Trainers and Learning Style

The Doer: Trainer Strengths

Decisive   Moves through the logistics of the program fairly quickly

Provides group norms and leads a short discussion that will, hopefully, lead to general acceptance of these norms

Establishes time frames and an agenda

Learners always know what to expect of the trainer

Practical   Focuses on what works and how to get results

Avoids too much theory (which leads to discussion, not action)

Provides time to create an action plan, a concrete list of tasks for the learner to accomplish

Determined   Sees learning as an event that involves a healthy amount of risk, so makes the effort to help learners accomplish goals

Knows learners have personal agendas, but keeps group goals in mind, too. Wants the class to set the learning outcomes that will give them purpose and focus.

Persistent	Uses time efficiently
	Sticks with learners if they are having difficulty with a task or concept
	Sees the pursuit of learning as a worthy goal
	Believes all learners can accomplish goals if they try hard

The Doer: Trainer Weaknesses

Dictator	Feels agitated if quick pace is not achieved; as a result, will become more directive in managing the group
	Frequently reminds the group of time frames to ensure everything is completed on time
Unimaginative	Values bottom lines
	Sets aside questions that can get group off track and instead focuses on solutions
	Avoids too much out-of-the-box thinking
Narrow	Doesn't want to digress from agenda
	Needs to stay on topic to gauge if time is well spent
	Bothered if all of the material in the learner manual is not covered
Stubborn	Understands people issues are important, but doesn't think they should get in the way of getting work done
	Wants to stick with tried and true methods until it's been proven that something else might do just as well

The Influencer: Trainer Strengths

Enthusiastic	Is passionate about training and content
	Wants each workshop to be a worthwhile experience for the learner
	Creates an exciting learning environment
	Sees learning as most valuable when it is fun and fulfilling
Personable	Acknowledges and shares stories about life beyond the training event
	Uses anecdotes to create a personal connection between the topic and life
	Uses own experiences as teaching tools

Optimistic	Believes learning has not occurred unless behaviour has changed
	Sees the learning experience as an opportunity to learn better ways of feeling and doing
	Wants training to have an impact on learners' futures
Outgoing	Likes to interact with learners
	Hopes learners will find time to interact with one another outside the workshop experience
	Sees the workshop as a give-and-take event. Learners give what they can to the experience and take what they need

The Influencer: Trainer Weaknesses

Tiring	Gives so much of self that training can be exhausting
	Expects same level of involvement from the class
	Believes that in order for training to make a difference, everyone needs to commit completely
In your face	Can go too far and "get in people's faces"
	Rationalizes in-your-face attitude because learning matters, so you must get learners motivated at any cost
	Wants event to be memorable, not just another training event
Phoney	Strong interaction with class may seem put on
	Can overdo giving recognition to participants
Unrealistic	Helps learners set big goals that can really make a difference, but may not be achievable
	Seen as a hope merchant. Feels that if learners don't dream about tomorrow then they'll never get beyond where they are today

The Relater: Trainer Strengths

Willing	Has an "I'm here to serve you" philosophy
	Truly enjoys helping learners so they can benefit from training
	Believes cooperation and caring create a healthy learning environment
Agreeable	Likes standard operating procedures that make for a healthy, comfortable learning environment
	Believes in the importance of jointly-created ground rules. This may take some time but will pay off in the end

Reliable	Is dependable
	Has a "we're all in this together" attitude
	Believes learners and trainer must value and respect each other
Supportive	Knows that if human needs are met, learning goals will be achieved
	Has the courage to ask for help and the conviction to offer it
	Wants to bring out the best in learners

The Relater: Trainer Weaknesses

Doormat	Doesn't say no very easily
	Focuses on what the learner needs to accomplish, not on own needs
	Minimizes risk, but sacrifices growth in the process
Yes Person	Is driven to get along with everyone
	Will say yes in order to avoid conflict
	Unwillingness to take a stand means disagreements can escalate into conflicts, and conflicts weaken learning
Predictable	Wants to do things the same way, so it is easier for learners and trainer to count on one another
	Doesn't want the risks associated with an unpredictable environment
	Feels people don't deal well with change, so sticks with what is known and safe instead of new and risky
Smothering	Can be over protective, in order to ensure learners succeed
	Can do too much for learners rather than let them assert their interdependence

The Thinker: Trainer Strengths

Orderly	Can adeptly analyze and break down training topic
	Trains in an organized, methodical manner that leads to insight and understanding
Thorough	Provides in-depth coverage of a topic
	Takes the time to uncover and discover
	Sees discovery as one of the greatest rewards of learning
	Believes in the lifelong nature of learning for self and trainees

Industrious	Works hard
	Sets high expectations for self and participants to make learning worthwhile
Creative	Can look at an idea in more than one way
	Takes the time to explore theories and ideas
	Encourages learners to keep minds open to new ideas
	Welcomes new ideas and is willing to explore their meaning

The Thinker:	**Trainer Weaknesses**
Perfectionist	Sets the bar too high
	Assumes those who don't achieve are not trying their hardest
	Emphasis on order leads to inflexibility and little adaptability
Workaholic	Focuses on task to the point of excluding the human element in training
	Emphasizes competence and independence over teamwork and cooperation
Intense	Doesn't have much time for humour
	Believes learners need to be intellectually, not socially, engaged
	Wants to be serious with learners because the topic is serious to the client
Lack of progress	Can get bogged down because wants to be 100 percent sure of understanding
	Can get sidetracked during Q&A sessions because there is so much to understand

Adaptability

Now that we know how our own learning styles affect the ways we train, how do we learn to balance our own natural abilities with learners' needs? We need to be adaptable. I divide adaptability into two components: attitude and conviction.

With a positive attitude, which is shaped by a willingness to accept the validity of other learner preferences, we will be receptive to the ways others learn. We will put the trainee's intellectual comfort ahead of our need to train from our comfort zone. Our positive attitude leads to the desire to become more accommodating of other's needs.

When we train with conviction, we have the courage to leave our comfort zone and adapt to the learning preferences of others. We meet learners where they are at. Our own intentions are no longer our sole focus. We act to help people satisfy their learning needs.

It's one thing to say, "I value adaptability." It's another to become an adaptable trainer. Leaving your comfort zone takes more than good intentions. Why?

When you train, you are performing. You want each class to be a great class. You want to accomplish the goals you've set out so carefully. You want to maintain a sense of professional pride and enhance your reputation. The easiest way to accomplish these dreams is to stay in your comfort zone because that's where you excel. It makes sense to rely on your natural abilities. You know this is where you are strong.

But to go *where the learners are strong,* and to appreciate their comfort zones, takes even greater strength. Remember, some learners will have the same learning style as you. They're in the same comfort zone. But many other learners will be wired differently than you. If you can adapt by moving out of your comfort zone and into theirs, you will help them learn.

Are you up to the challenge? The next chapter outlines an easy-to-use strategy to help you make the transition away from your comfort zone. And as impossible as this may seem, you can become comfortable with this transition. You can do it!

HUGHism

"Learning is self-discovery.
Training is mutual discovery."

Chapter 17:
Planning With Style

Watch me, repeat, then forget what you saw me do. Find your own way.
Trust your body, it remembers.
Chungliang Al Huang

It's always good to watch other trainers

That's exactly what I intended to do when I signed up for a three-day Faculty of Extension course on group dynamics at the University of Alberta. It was early in my training career and I wanted to learn more about group interaction. I also wanted to observe another trainer in action. What he did, when he did it, how he did it, and maybe even discover why he did it. I thought taking a course would be a good way to enhance my understanding of group dynamics while watching an experienced trainer.

I arrived early the first day, keen to learn more about group dynamics. Imagine my disappointment when, by 10:30, all we had accomplished were two warmer-upper activities! I had enjoyed getting to know my classmates, but I was anxious to start learning about group dynamics. After the morning break, John, the workshop leader, asked a few open-ended questions about the two activities. This led to quite a lively discussion about the value of warmer-uppers. John patiently and adeptly guided the group as he kept us focused and respected the variety of opinions shared. But to my dismay, lunchtime was upon us and we still hadn't been presented with any real content. Where was the product? I decided to bring my concerns to John.

As the class was leaving for lunch, I made my way up to the front to talk with John. I let him know that I didn't feel we had accomplished much that morning. I told him I was looking for content. I wanted to learn about group dynamics. I wanted him to tell me what he knew. John listened intently and then invited me to sit down and share more. I reluctantly agreed, wondering what he was up to.

We continued our conversation. John's gentle, kind manner and steady eye contact put me at ease. As we spoke, I felt reassured. It seemed to me we both had similar hopes for the workshop, just different ideas about how these hopes would be fulfilled. My anxieties were abating. I was ready to focus on observing John's training style—which was so different from my own—and learn what I could from him about group dynamics.

That afternoon I watched John more carefully. I could see that he was a very fine trainer indeed. Why, I wondered, had I been so quick to criticize his style early in the session? Then, a flash of insight came to me that shook my assumptions and presumed wisdom. John's strengths were my weaknesses! His patience, approachability, slow but intense pace, openness, perseverance, and accommodating nature contrasted sharply with my approach. His training style was exactly the opposite of my own! My early impatience was simply my own misunderstanding of something I was unfamiliar with. He was a strong Relater and Thinker; I am a Doer and Influencer.

In the remaining days of the workshop, I watched John carefully. I saw how he handled questions, paced the day, reinforced his lectures, introduced new topics, responded to objections, and maintained a comfortable atmosphere—all while he remained clearly focused on our purpose. I could see I had a lot to learn from the Relater and Thinker way of doing things. Incorporating aspects of his style into my sessions would definitely take me out of my comfort zone, but it would also open me up to more of my learners. I knew that adapting my training style would not be easy. I also wondered how I could encourage trainers, in practical ways, to intentionally and comfortably incorporate the four learning styles into their workshops. No quick solution was apparent.

Later . . .

Weeks later, as I prepared for a new workshop called Coaching for Peak Performance, it happened. I stumbled upon the perfect way to adapt my own learning style and give other trainers a foolproof strategy for adapting their styles, too.

In my preparations, I knew that participants in Coaching for Peak Performance would have to practice new skills by actually coaching another learner. I did not want to substitute first-hand experience with simulations, case studies, or discussions. Hands-on learning was key to the workshop's success. I reviewed the techniques available to me and, somewhat grudgingly, realized that role play would provide learners with the perfect opportunity to practice coaching skills. Yet, I hesitated to use it. Why?

I saw role-playing as a technique that took too much time and yielded results that were difficult to measure. I felt the time spent setting up, staging, implementing, and debriefing would be better spent on more practical exercises. As a matter of fact, up until this point in my training career, I had avoided role-playing when at all possible. But, try as I might, I couldn't find a better means to prepare learners for the world of coaching.

To my surprise, learners consistently provided me with positive feedback on the role-play aspect of the workshop. Through their eyes, I was able to see role-play as a productive, fun, and beneficial technique. As I thought about this, it dawned on me that role-playing was an activity ideally designed for the Relater: it takes a lot of time and it is a very people-centred technique. Going a step further, I thought to myself, "If role playing is especially suited to the Relater, then other techniques must be especially suited to the other learning styles." Bingo! I had come up with a strategy for preparing trainers to adapt other learning styles into their sessions.

That day I began to assess the many techniques I use (or hesitated to use). I employed the same diagram I used to determine my own learning style, but focused the questions to help me determine the learning style that would best suit each of the techniques. Sound tricky? Not at all. In the next section, I'll walk you through the process I followed for matching learning styles with two different techniques. You can use this same process to assess the techniques that you use. (Refer to the diagram on page 293 as you read through the examples.)

Matching Techniques and Learning Styles

Case Study

- As with assessing my own learning style, the first thing I did was determine whether the Case Study technique emphasized *priority* or *pace* and which end of the spectrum seemed most characteristic of the activity.

- I looked at the priority line and asked myself, "What is the priority of a case study? Is it task driven or is it relationship driven?" Because case studies attempt to relate what was learned earlier in training to an actual case or event, I felt the focus was on reading and analyzing. The priority was "task."

- Then I looked at the pace line and asked myself, "What is the pace of a case study? Does it take time or does it move quickly?" Most case studies I've conducted or participated in have taken at least twenty minutes to complete. Learners read an article, respond to a series of questions, and then discuss the answer with the trainer. The pace is "take time."

- Using the "take time" and "task" criteria to guide me, I determined that the Case Study training technique matches the Thinker learning style best.

Name Tent

- Again, the first thing I did was determine whether the Name Tent technique emphasized *priority* or *pace* and which end of the spectrum seemed most characteristic of the activity.

- I looked at the priority line and asked myself, "What is the priority of the name tent exercise?" This technique is used to make participants feel welcome at the beginning of the workshop. Each person responds to about five questions on the back of the name tent and then circulates around the room, exchanging answers with other participants. The focus of this activity is to meet people, so the priority is on relationship.

- Then I looked at the pace line and asked myself, "What is the pace of the name tent activity?" Typically, learners are asked to meet four to five people in five minutes. The technique does not work well if learners take too much time. Therefore, the pace is quick.

- The name tent technique has "relationship" as its priority and "moves quickly" as its pace. Therefore, it favours the Influencer learning style.

Ensure Accurate Matching

As you can see, spending a bit of time reviewing a technique can lead to a relatively quick and easy assessment of its suitability for a learning style. Keep the following three points in mind, though, to ensure your assessments are accurate.

1. Process is important

A technique can be employed in a variety of ways. Let's take story telling, for example. When I tell stories in a workshop they are usually short—less than five minutes—and most of them are people based. Clearly, my story-telling style is quick and relationship oriented, so it best reflects the Influencer learning style.

However, stories can be told in different ways. A friend of mine, who also trains, likes to embellish stories and may take ten or more minutes for the telling. Her stories are well presented, powerful, and usually focus on people. Her stories are best suited to the Relater learning style.

Clearly, process affects a technique's learning style assessment.

2. Powerful techniques

Some techniques suit more than one learning style. For example, the Think•Pair•Square•Share technique encompasses all four learning styles. Let me explain.

The "Think" component of this technique requires participants to generate data in less than three minutes. This is a task-driven, quickly completed activity, so best suits the Doer.

In the "Pair" component, participants take the data they've generated and compare their findings with another participant. Participants may add their colleagues' ideas to their list if they want. The pairing up is done quickly and learners find themselves affirming one another's ideas, so this component matches best with the Influencer style.

In the "Square" component, learners reconvene with their subgroups and take seven to ten minutes to construct a composite list of the seven best ideas. This is a task-driven activity and takes more time, so it appeals to the Thinker.

Finally, in the concluding "Share" component, one summary list from all of the subgroup lists is generated. The entire group's ideas are brought together and the group shares ownership of the ideas. This activity takes time and builds learner compatibility. It best suits the Relater learning style.

As you assess new techniques, remember that they may incorporate more than one learning style.

3. Revising process

A note of caution. Because trainers naturally lean toward areas of strength, you may find yourself reworking an activity to match your learning style. If you're going to change an activity, ensure that it matches the needs of the learners first, not your own learning preference.

For example, I've taken case studies and shortened them so that the exercise goes quickly. In essence I've changed the case study from a Thinker activity to a Doer activity. It certainly made me feel more comfortable with the case study technique, but as I look back I think that rushing the process sabotaged the results. One of the benefits of the case study is that it takes time to fully explore the implications of decisions made and assess the consequences of those decisions.

Matching the A's

Below, I outline the matches I've made between training techniques and the four learning styles. Keep in mind that my assessments reflect the process of each technique as described in this book; the process you follow, however, may be somewhat different. If so, you will need to assess the technique yourself and thereby ensure a proper match with the learning style.

A

	Learning Style	Affiliation Technique
Affiliation	Doer	Ray of Sunshine, Workshop Guidelines, Live Audit
	Influencer	Name Tent, Gang Up On, Welcome Letter, Solo Introduction
	Relater	Needs, Group Résumé
	Thinker	Progress Chart
Attention	Doer	Prop, Gap Analysis, Immersions, Mind Mapping
	Influencer	Story Telling, Humour, Skit
	Relater	Tick Box, Think•Pair•Square•Share, Video
	Thinker	Questions, Quotations
Acquisition	Doer	Five Plus, Checklist, PINing, Top Ten
	Influencer	Iconing, Hot Seat–Hot Tips
	Relater	Affinity Diagram, Acrostic Challenge, Banking
	Thinker	Full Card, Checking In, Tutoring
Application	Doer	The Jigsaw, Project, Drills
	Influencer	Games, Behaviour Modeling, Learner Feedback, Video Analysis
	Relater	Role Play, Diad Hum
	Thinker	Case Study, Quizzes, What's In A Number
Action	Doer	Skill Tool
	Influencer	Icon Summary, Puts and Calls
	Relater	Buddies, Manager Follow-up
	Thinker	Looking Back, Then and Now
Affirmation	Doer	Awards
	Influencer	Recognition Letter, Motivational Stories & Quotes, Visualization
	Relater	Sharing Circle, What I Remember About You, Significant Others
	Thinker	Learner Letter

HUGHism

"Understanding your uniqueness makes you special.
Acknowledging differences makes learners important."

Chapter 18:
The POWERtool

Homines, dum docent, discunt. (We learn while we teach.)

Seneca

Wow!

We've covered a lot of material in this book. In Part One, I introduced you to my ideas about the Eight A's training cycle; in Part Two, I shared over seventy creative training techniques. Then we spent time looking at ways to manage groups and recognize the stages of group development. Finally, we discussed the importance of learning styles and the ways these preferences and predispositions impact learning and training.

Now you're probably asking yourself, "Okay, Hugh, so now what? There's so much information. How can I possibly integrate it all into a well-designed, dynamic workshop?" I struggled with this question myself for several years as I strove to deliver increasingly effective Train the Trainer workshops. When I eventually hit on the answer, it took shape as one of my most versatile training tools—the POWERtool!

By purchasing this book, you have acquired your very own POWERtool. I'm convinced that you will find it a useful timesaving tool for developing dynamic and inclusive workshops. In this chapter, I will provide you with the information you need to take advantage of all the tool has to offer. Let's begin!

A POWERtool Overview

The POWERtool is divided into three parts: an *Organizer, a Techniques Matrix,* and *a Planner*. Each component contributes to the overall versatility of the tool and serves its own unique purpose. As I discuss each of the components in these next pages, please refer to your POWERtool.

The Organizer

The Organizer is, for the most part, a reference aid. It outlines five key training concepts and enables the trainer to see the links between these concepts. The training concepts it summarizes comprise the following:

1. The three aspects of training that are essential for completing a workshop plan
2. The Eight A's of the training cycle
3. The questions answered by each phase of the training cycle
4. The purpose of each A
5. The stages of growth a group experiences over the course of a workshop

Use the Organizer whenever you start to plan for a training event. It will allow you to see the big picture before you get into the details.

The Techniques Matrix

The Techniques Matrix provides an at-a-glance listing of the more than seventy training techniques described in this book. Each training technique is categorized according to the eight A training cycle and learning style. As you plan for a workshop, you can use the Techniques Matrix to help you determine which technique will work best for your group. Page numbers are provided so you can find out more about the techniques you are interested in.

Example

Let's say you're starting to plan for a new workshop. You've already reviewed the Organizer part of the POWERtool to refresh your knowledge about the various aspects of planning a successful training event. You've conducted an audit and, as you develop your learning modules, you want to choose some training techniques for the session. What next?

- You want to choose an interactive welcoming technique that will guide participant interaction as they meet one another for the first time. You know you are looking for an affiliation technique, so you turn to the Techniques Matrix.

- You notice the first heading in the first column is Affiliation, so you scan across the row and see a wide selection of affiliation techniques.

- You choose a technique that sounds appealing and that accommodates a learning style you know will be present in the group.

- Then you turn to the page indicated to see if the technique you've chosen fits with other workshop factors you have to consider: amount of time available, size of group, workshop purpose.

- If the technique looks like it will work, you go on to find an activity for the next phase of the workshop. Or you may decide you can find an affiliation technique that is more suitable.

- When you move on to choose an attention technique, try to select one that accommodates a different learning style than your affiliation technique. For example, if you chose the Name Tent affiliation technique, which accommodates the Influencer learning style, you'll want to choose an attention technique that accommodates the Doer, Relater, or Thinker styles.

- As much as possible, you want to adapt your style to match the variety of learners in your group. One of the overall purposes of the POWERtool is to encourage and assist trainers to create inclusive workshops that accommodate all four learning styles.

The Planner

This component makes up the bulk of the POWERtool and guides trainers as they design interactive workshops. It is organized into five sections: Before The Workshop, Getting Started, Learning Modules, Strong Endings, and After the Workshop. Each section helps you build an effective workshop, one step at a time. I think the best way to walk through this component is to apply each of the five sections to a training scenario.

Training Day Example

Let's say you have a training day to plan. You know you will begin with an affiliation exercise, end with an affirmation exercise, and use four learning modules to cover (and uncover) content. You also know you want to conduct an audit prior to the workshop and do some follow-up with the group after the workshop is complete. In other words, you are planning a one-day training event that includes the Eight A's. You pull out your handy, dandy POWERtool, turn to the Planner component, and get started.

Part One: Before The Workshop (Audit)

This section summarizes the elements of a standard audit. We know how important it is to find out about the learners who will be attending your session. You will be able to determine appropriate pace, techniques, and examples once you know the audience's needs, interests, and concerns.

To use the *Before The Workshop* section of the Planner:

- Review the elements of an audit (Demographics, Experience, Expectations, and Venue) and develop an audit interview sheet that includes pertinent details. (The page number indicated refers to the sample audit in this book. You can use it to generate further questions for your audit.)

- Arrange to meet or speak with your contact person (or designate). The information you glean about your audience will provide a context for the decisions you make about the training program.

- Use the information you've gathered to develop workshop outcomes or goals. Remember that these outcomes need to address the three H's: head, heart, and hands. The head outcomes address what you want trainees to know and understand by the end of training. The heart outcomes address what you want the trainees to believe, feel, or appreciate. And the hands outcomes address what you want the trainees to be able to do after training is over.

Part Two: Getting Started (Affiliation)

You want to get your workshop off to a good start with a strong opening module. The intent of this opening is to build an effective and participatory learning climate. Remember that the affiliation phase operates on several dimensions: Learner Affiliation techniques help learners get comfortable with one another; Topic Affiliation techniques help learners get acquainted with the training topic and develop workshop expectations; and Trainer Affiliation techniques give the learners the opportunity to learn more about you, the trainer. (These dimensions are discussed in more detail in Chapter 5.) If you have the time, feel free to use more than one affiliation technique. You are creating a strong foundation for learning in this part of your plan.

To use the *Getting Started* section of the Planner:

- Complete the "Topic" column by noting the dimensions of the affiliation phase (learner, topic, and trainer) that you would like to include in your workshop.

- Complete the "Technique" column by selecting techniques that address the affiliation dimensions you've chosen. Use the Techniques Matrix to guide your decisions.

- Complete the "Style" column by indicating the learning style that each affiliation technique suits the best. This information is included in the Techniques Matrix. If you are using more than one affiliation technique, choose techniques that accommodate different learning styles.

- Complete the "Time" column by jotting down how much time the activity will take. This information is located on the reference page indicated in the Techniques Matrix.

- Complete the "Equipment" column by listing the AV and learning equipment you will need for the technique. This information is also located on the reference page indicated in the Techniques Matrix.

Part Three: Learning Modules
(Attention, Acquisition, Application, Action)

A learning module is a self-contained unit in a training program. While a learning module stands alone because it focuses on one main topic, a series of sequential modules makes up a training program. For example, in the one-day training program in this example, you are planning to have four learning modules. These modules are separate from the opening module of the affiliation stage and the closing module in the affirmation stage because learning modules deal primarily with content.

This section of the POWERtool Planner allows you to create a detailed outline for your training session. When I plan a workshop, my learning modules usually include one attention technique, one or more acquisition and application techniques, and one action technique. As I plan each module, I follow the same process.

To use the *Learning Modules* section of the Planner:

• Begin by referring to the left hand column of Learning Module One. (You'll notice that all of the Learning Modules are set up the same way.)

• The first heading in the left hand column is "Attention." You will use this row to record your plans for the attention phase of the training process. The information you will provide for the attention phase is the same as the information in the Getting Started module that marked the affiliation phase. So...

• Complete the "Topic" column by writing down the topic, issue, or question that you will be addressing during the attention phase of this module.

• Complete the "Technique" column by selecting an attention technique(s) you will use to hook the learners. Use the Techniques Matrix to guide your decisions.

• Complete the "Style" column by indicating the learning style that each attention technique suits the best. This information is included in the Techniques Matrix. If you are using more than one attention technique, choose techniques that accommodate different learning styles.

• Complete the "Time" column by jotting down how much time the activity will take. This information is located on the reference page indicated in the Techniques Matrix.

• Complete the "Equipment" column by listing the AV and learning equipment you will need for the technique. This information is also located on the reference page indicated in the Techniques Matrix.

• The attention technique you choose will ignite learner interest in the module's topic. Now you're ready to teach learners what they need to know (acquisition), give them some time to practice what they've learned (application), and reinforce their learning (action). Respond to the same questions identified above to complete the acquisition, application, and action rows on the Module One Planner.

• Then implement the same process to complete the remaining three modules for your one-day session.

Sample Learning Module

Here's a sample Learning Module One from my one-day Train the Trainer workshop. This is a one-hour module. Notice that all four learning styles are accommodated in the techniques I chose.

Learning Module One

A	Topic	Technique	Style	Time/Equipment
Attention	How the A's were discovered	Story telling	Influencer	10 min. Prop
Acquisition	Using the A's	Checking In Lecture	Thinker	20 min. Desktop/Learner Manual
Application	Where the A's fit in training	The Jigsaw	Doer	20 min.
Action	Develop a sample Module	Buddies	Relater	10 min. Handout

Sample Learning Module—Expanded

In the following version of the same module, I include two acquisition techniques and two application techniques. I would use this version of Learning Module One for a two-day Train the Trainer workshop. The module is now an hour and a half long (instead of an hour). I still choose techniques that accommodate all four learning styles.

Learning Module One: Expanded

A	Topic	Technique	Style	Time/Equipment
Attention	How the A's were discovered	Story telling	Influencer	10 min. Prop
Acquisition	Using the A's	Checking In Lecture	Thinker	20 min. Desktop/Learner Manual
Application	Where the A's fit in training	The Jigsaw	Doer	20 min.
Acquisition	Sample lesson module explained	Tutoring	Thinker	15 min. Prop
Application	What if?	Game	Influencer	20 min. Post-it Notes /Flip Chart
Action	Sample lesson plan	Buddies	Relater	10 min. Handout

Part Four: Strong Ending (Affirmation)

This section of the Planner addresses the trainer's need to provide thoughtful and supportive closure to a training event. Remember the affirmation phase operates on several levels: Learner Affirmation techniques give learners the opportunity to endorse one another's achievements and contributions; Topic Affirmation techniques will inspire and motivate the learner to dig deeper, to learn more about the training topic, or to envision a desired future; and Trainer Affirmation techniques support and encourage the learner upon their return to work. If you have the time, feel free to use more than one affirmation technique.

To use the *Strong Ending* section of the Planner:

- Follow the same steps as identified in the Getting Started section, but use affirmation techniques rather than affiliation techniques (see above).

Part Five: After the Workshop (Assessment)

This section of the Planner ensures you conduct follow-up activities so you can find out what went well and what you might change about the workshop should you conduct it again. You will consult learners from the session and your contact person (or designate). Some assessment can take place during the workshop with In-the-Moment surveys (see page 46). Other assessments can be conducted at the end of the workshop (see page 48), and still others can be conducted three to four weeks after the session has been completed using a Follow-up Questionnaire (see page 51).

To use the *After the Workshop* section of the Planner:

• Complete the "Timing" column by indicating when you will conduct an assessment: during the workshop, at the end of the workshop, or after the workshop is complete. Remember you can select more than one of these options.

• Complete the "Details" column by noting aspects of the workshop on which you want feedback. Be sure to include questions on these aspects in your assessment.

• In the "Completed by" column, indicate who will be completing the assessment: trainees, managers, and/or contact people.

Tips for using the POWERtool

1. Go with the Flow

Refer back to the expanded learning module sample on page 321. You'll notice I didn't work through the four A's in consecutive order. I started with an attention technique, then moved on to an acquisition activity, followed by an application exercise. But then I used another acquisition technique followed by another application exercise. I concluded the module with an action technique.

Using the A's does not have to be a linear process. Sometimes you'll want to break up the acquisition phase and intersperse it with application exercises. Or you may decide to drop the action phase from earlier modules and just use it near the end of a session. Maybe you'll use an application technique like Role Play as an attention getter earlier in the module. All of these scenarios work. Go with the flow.

2. Combine the A's

When I conduct half-day workshops or participate in large conventions that often have a series of short (e.g. ninety-minute) sessions, I combine A's to save time. For example, I've combined the attention and acquisition phases by telling a story that wove together my four key points. When the story was finished, I moved right into an application exercise. I not only saved time, but this technique seemed perfect for such short sessions!

3. Multiple Techniques

Who says you should use only one attention technique in a module? Recently I was providing a ninety-minute presentation to 150 people starting at 7:00 pm Given the large group size and the late hour, I knew I would have to use several attention techniques to get them interested. So I used a prop, an open-ended question, and a role-play. It worked! The audience got involved right away and most stayed with the session for the entire hour and a half!

4. Specialty Groups

Some professions attract certain learning styles. For example, when I conduct workshops with engineers, I know I will have an abundance of Doers and Thinkers. So, I begin with several Doer and Thinker activities to get the group comfortable with each other, with me, and with the topic. As the workshop progresses, I include Relater and Influencer techniques when appropriate. This works because I've established trust by starting in the comfort zones of most of the group. Later in the workshop, when I ask learners to engage in an activity outside their comfort zones, they are usually willing to take that risk.

5. Adjusting a Training Plan

Chances are you have already created a training plan without the benefit of the POWERtool. If so, you can still use the POWERtool to ensure your plan is inclusive. Do the techniques you've included reflect all four learning styles? Does your plan incorporate all Eight A's? If so, way to go!! If not, it's time for some adjustment.

6. Leaving Your Comfort Zone

By deliberately selecting activities that are not in your comfort zone, you learn about the value and benefits of new techniques. In fact, you may be surprised by the way these new techniques increase learner interest and involvement. Training becomes more exciting for you because you've put yourself in the position of the learner—you're taking a risk and surviving it!

7. Changing the Learning Style Focus

By changing the way a technique is implemented, you can change its learning style classification. For example, the case study technique has been classified as a Thinker learning style activity. However, if you decide to abbreviate the process and condense the discussion time and questions, you may well have a Doer activity. In this example, the case study still has a task as its priority, but the quickened pace no longer requires as much time.

HUGHism

" It's not what you do but how you do it that determines the ultimate use of any training technique. "

Appendix One:
Sample Room Arrangements

The U Shape

What it looks like

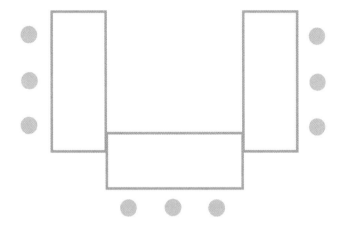

Advantages

- Very inclusive; everyone can see one another
- Good for open discussion and debate
- Subgroups can be formed easily

Disadvantages

- Limits the number of learners
- Side talking and distractions can occur
- Solo or individual work is not easily accommodated

Half Rounds

What it looks like

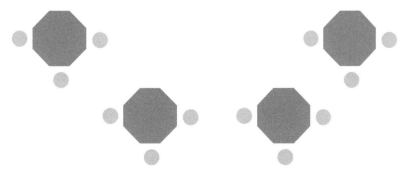

Advantages

- Very open and interactive
- More control for participants
- Round tables are more inclusive than square or rectangular tables

Disadvantages

- For a controlling instructor, this arrangement can be threatening
- Requires more meeting room space to accommodate the tables and chairs
- If using a lecture style presentation, there is little purpose to this set-up

Classroom Style

What it looks like

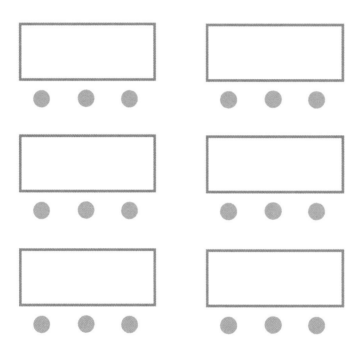

Advantages

- More control for instructor than participants (if instructor needs it)
- Good for lectures
- Can accommodate large numbers in a limited space

Disadvantages

- A return to the typical classroom we've used for so long
- "Problem" learners tend to gravitate to the back
- Sight lines not good for people near the back

Appendix Two: Visual Aids

The techniques described in this book often require a trainer to use one or more visual aids. While these aids are pretty straightforward to use, plenty of practice has given me some insights into using them effectively and efficiently. I hope you'll be able to put my suggestions to good use in your own workshops when you use flip charts, overhead projectors, desktop projectors, and learner manuals.

Flip Charts

I enjoy the spontaneity inherent in using flip charts! A fresh, blank piece of paper just waits for recording the wisdom of group ideas, the concise notes of a presenter, or a humorous saying. So, what do you need to keep in mind to make the best use of the world's number one visual aid? Here are some of my ideas.

1. Paper or plastic?

Do you want to use newsprint or white paper? White paper costs more, but may be easier for some learners to read. If you choose white paper, do you want lined or unlined? The almost invisible grid of blue lines makes it easier to print neatly, draw circles, and create other assorted shapes.

Perhaps you prefer the plastic flip charts called "static images," which come in rolls of twenty-five. These are relatively inexpensive and reusable. The static created by the plastic sheets allows them to cling to almost any wall surface. You can use overhead markers, permanent or erasable, with these sheets.

2. Choosing markers

I like to have the popular, scented markers on hand. I use yellow, orange, and red markers for highlighting and other colours for printing and drawing. You should always have a package of unscented watercolours just in case someone is allergic to the scented ones.

3. Include notes to self

I write my key points in pencil in the top right or left corner of the flip chart before the presentation, so I can refer to them if necessary. This allows me to be spontaneous but also ensure I don't forget anything.

4. Practice your printing

Richard Brandt outlines four aspects of good printing: consistency, motion, position, and time.

To be consistent, only print; do not write. Use either block letters or lower case.

An effective motion means your strokes are fluid and sharp. Position refers to the best place to stand. If you are right handed, position yourself on the left side of the flip chart and vice versa if you're left handed. To use time effectively, don't try to write everything you hear from learners. Focus on key words or phrases, which usually occur at the beginning or end of the learner's comment.

5. Key hole technique

This technique involves duplicating and enlarging the client's logo to a 4 x 4 inch size. Then, tape the logo near the top and centre of the flip chart page that is ten pages in from the front page. Cover the logo with a piece of cardboard. Using an exacto knife, cut a square hole about 4 x 4 inches through the first ten pages. Uncover the logo. The logo is now visible during your use of the ten flip chart pages.

6. Formatting

Bullets: Use bullets, such as round dots, squares, arrows, check marks, asterisks, and small circles to indicate points. I rarely use numbers to record points unless they involve prioritized or sequenced data.

Borders: Use simple borders to highlight the content on a flip chart. I tend to use citrus colours, like orange and yellow, to make borders. Borders can take on any creative design you wish as long as they help the learner focus on the content and not on the border itself.

Recently, I took a few minutes before a workshop in Calgary for an oil and gas corporation to employ the key hole technique. At the noon hour, the vice president came up to me and commented, "You not only personalized the program for us, you even customized the flip chart!"

7. Storage of flip charts

Use cardboard tubes (3 inches in diameter) to store and dramatically extend the life of prepared flip charts. Tubes can be bought at stationery stores.

8. Survival kit

I always keep the following items on hand when I know I'll be using a flip chart:

- 1-inch masking tape
- Scissors
- Hold-it putty
- 1-inch, double-sided sticky tape
- Small glue stick
- Several dozen felt markers (water based)

- Pencil sharpener
- Stick pins
- Post-it Notes of assorted sizes
- Post-it Note tape flags

- Paper clips
- Small one-hole punch

Overhead Projectors (OHPs)

Useful for groups of ten or a thousand, OHPs are versatile, simple to use, and easy to maintain. Here are a few tips and techniques to help you make effective and impressive use of the overhead projector.

1. 5 x 5 rule

I can't emphasize how important this rule of thumb is. When putting content onto your overhead transparencies, only use five lines of words with up to five words in each line. Use any more than this and you will frustrate learners with too much information. Learners will be thinking, "Look, I can't listen to you and read all of those words at the same time. So I have to make a choice. Either I listen to you and ignore the visual or visa versa." So keep to a twenty-five-word maximum.

2. Flapper technique

When changing transparencies, you may want to darken the screen to avoid showing the motion of straightening and aligning each transparency. You can do this by turning the machine on and off (which is a bit distracting) or you can use the flapper technique. Cut out a 5- x 7-inch piece of dark cardboard. Tape the top edge (that is the 5-inch side) to the leading edge of the overhead projector head mirror. When you want to darken the screen, simply lower the flap over the mirror. The machine is on but the screen is dark. Take off the transparency, put on the next one, and then turn the flap up. Quiet and classy!

3. Use frames

Frame your transparencies, especially if you're going to use them more than once. You can put your notes on the frames to remind yourself of the key points, stories, or questions you want to use with each transparency. Frames also prevent the spillover of light onto the screen from the overhead.

4. Watch for key stoning

When you tilt the head of the OHP up to elevate the image on the screen you cause the light to disperse. The image ends up slightly pie shaped—bigger at the top, smaller at the bottom. This is called key stoning. To prevent this with portable projection screens, use the arm extension to tilt the screen until the image is uniform. With a fixed projection screen, affix the bottom edge of the screen on the wall or tilt up the front base of the projector.

5. Keep lights on

One big advantage of an OHP is that you can use this machine without having to dim room lights. The audience can see you and your visuals.

6. Use colour

Use of colour transparencies or clear transparencies with colour overlays will help you to make your points visually. Be selective in your use of colour. More than three colours on a transparency can be distracting (unless you're using colour in graphs or charts to delineate categories or sections).

7. Turn it off

When you have time gaps between transparencies, turn off the machine. You want to make sure the overhead is a visual aid, not a visual distraction. Keep it on only for as long as you need it.

8. Number the transparencies

Should you drop the transparencies, it's good to know that you won't waste audience time sorting through them. Numbers will also help you keep your transparencies organized.

9. Screen in the corner

I prefer to position the screen in the front corner of the room, rather than in the front centre. In the corner, the projector is out of the way and I'm not always stepping around the machine or over cords. The audience generally has good sight lines as well.

10. Avoid overhead striptease

Avoid showing bits and pieces of information at a time. Learners may feel they're being treated like inattentive children. If you must use this technique, explain why.

11. Survival kit

I keep the following items on hand when I know I'll be using an OHP:

- Spare bulb
- Duct tape (to conceal electrical cord)
- Swizzle stick or pointy miniature hand
- Extension cord
- Laser pointer

Desktop Projectors (DTPs)

As with personal computers, technology is leading to smaller, brighter, and cheaper DTPs! Here are some general tips to keep in mind when using a DTP as a visual aid.

1. Darken the screen, not the room

While the brightness rating in DTP lamps (ANSI lumen capacity) has increased significantly, you still need to darken the screen to get maximum colour contrast. Also, be aware that most DTP lamps last up to 2000 hours. You can check on the number of hours used and anticipate when you'll need to replace the lamp. With most DTPs, you need assistance to change the lamp.

2. Software options

The two most common software options are Apple Keynote and Microsoft Power Point. Both programs have similar capabilities, pricing, and power. I prefer the Apple Keynote because of its novel templates and ease of use.

3. Protective travel bags a must

Your DTP requires a major capital investment, so you need to protect it with a suitable travel bag. Ensure your bag meets airline baggage size regulations for under-the-seat or compartment storage. You don't want your DTP to end up in the baggage compartment.

4. Colour transfer from computer to DTP

When you design your slides on the computer, you'll have thousands of colour combinations to choose from. But when you show the same image on the screen using a DTP, your program does not have as many colours to choose from. The DTP will automatically select comparable colours, but these will not be as deep or true as the colours you saw on the computer screen. Be selective and experiment with your computer and DTP to identify what colours show up best.

5. Darken the screen when not in use

When you're done with the computer presentation, turn off or mute the DTP or put the computer in sleep mode. The DTP can become a distraction when it is left on for no apparent reason.

6. Use the DTP remote

DTPs come with remote controls. These handheld devices allow you to move around the room, advance or repeat slides without touching the computer, even pull down commands on your menu to change program options. Most remote controls come with a built-in laser pointer or magnification feature that highlights images on the screen.

Learner Manuals

Learner manuals are used in class but many learners also use them as a reference tool when the workshop is over. Here are some suggestions for making the most of this useful tool.

1. Opportunity to summarize

Learner manuals are the perfect place to highlight (or have learners highlight) workshop content. Summary notes highlight the key ideas and principles of your presentation and these can be included in the learner manuals as fill-in-the blank exercises, short articles, instruction sets, or bulleted points.

2. Visual appeal

A visually appealing learner manual will be used over and over again. Synthesize your ideas and concepts using diagrams, flow charts, and checklists. Personalize the manual by using drawings, clip art, shapes, lines, even scanned photos. You can also make the manually visually attractive by including lots of white space. A cluttered or crowded manual can overwhelm learners.

I also make a point of using sans serif font styles (that is, those without tails) to facilitate reading. Limit yourself to three font sizes in your manual.

3. Background information

Because it will be used as a reference tool, use the learner manual to provide learners with background and related information. For example, a bibliography that includes both the latest publications, along with some of the classic, time-proven works, can also include relevant Web sites, glossaries, lists, and statistical data that will all be useful to learners.

4. Forms

The learner manual is a perfect place to insert a workshop evaluation form. Or, if you have products such as videos, audiocassettes, and CDs, you can insert order forms, too.

5. Contact information

At the front and/or back of the manual, you should provide current contact information. I include my name, company name, e-mail address, Web site, and phone and fax numbers with area codes.

6. Introductory material

Introduce yourself to the learner by including a brief biography and/or a welcome letter in the learner manual. The bio provides another way to market yourself and the welcome letter gives you the opportunity to thank, encourage, and assure learners that you want the best learning experience for them!

7. Quotations

Scatter humorous, thoughtful, or inspirational quotes throughout the manual. Be sure to identify the author and source. If possible, include the quote on a page with pertinent content.

8. Notes

Provide extra pages (at the back or spaced throughout) for note taking and journal entries.

9. Design

Provide front and back covers to the manual. When you are making decisions about binding, remember a stapled manual quickly falls apart. Use cirlox or tape binding. It's quick, inexpensive, and provides a professional look for the manual. The tape comes in different colours, too.

References

Brandt, Richard C. 1986. *Flip charts: How to draw them and how to use them.* San Diego, CA: Pfeiffer & Company.

Appendix Three:
Q & A

I keep six honest and serving men. They taught me all I know. Their names are
What and Why and When and How and Where and Who.
Rudyard Kipling

Managing Learner Questions

Throughout any training event, you will be asked many questions. Questions are important. They help learners clarify content and explore new ideas. As a trainer, you need to let learners know that you value their questions. You also want to make sure learners have the opportunity to ask questions by planning Q&A sessions throughout the workshop.

Whether questions arise in planned Q&A sessions or are asked spontaneously, it is important to respond appropriately. Remember, learners are taking risks when they ask questions. You need to respect this and also remain aware of the needs of the entire group. Use the following guidelines when responding to learners in your sessions.

Direct or indirect

When you respond to learners' questions, you can provide the answer yourself, you can use other expertise in the class, or you can defer the question. When you respond yourself, you are using a direct approach; when you use others or defer, you are using an indirect approach. You should use the direct approach about 70 percent of the time (or even more often if your time is limited, or if the expertise in the group is not confirmed). Here are the options:

Direct: Answer the question concisely and clearly. If a more lengthy answer is required, ensure the question is of interest to the group and then proceed by letting the group know you will be taking a few extra minutes to respond.

Reframe: If the question is unclear, take the time to reframe the question so you can make a clear connection with the lecture. You can also ask learners to rephrase questions. Or, if they have made a comment rather than ask a question, you can ask them to rephrase the comment as a question so you can respond to it.

Relay: Relay the question back to the group for a response. Add your comment if necessary to develop the answer.

Reverse:	Invite the learner to respond to the question himself. This technique is especially effective if you suspect the learner may know the answer but is curious about your view.
Designate:	Ask an expert in the group to respond to the question. Manage the time available.
Delay:	Indicate that the question will be covered a bit later in the lecture. Ask the learner to record the question on a Post-it Note and place it on the parking lot flip chart.
Research:	If you don't know the answer, and others in the class do not know but the question is relevant, indicate that you will find out the answer and get back to the group.
Deny:	With a loaded question, one that is perhaps designed to put you on the spot, respond by indicating you'll pass. Be tactful yet firm.

Improving Q&A participation

Have you ever invited learner questions but been met with silence? Be prepared for this and exercise one or more of the following options

Prepare Questions:	Bridge the moment with a prepared question. Say something like, "One question I often get asked about this training concept is…." After you pose the prepared question, answer it and then ask for other questions.
Practice patience:	Wait patiently for ten to fifteen seconds. Be comfortable with the silence, even smile as you anticipate questions.
Plant:	Plan ahead and write the questions you want to respond to on index cards. Give these cards to the learners before the lecture and invite them to ask the questions at a specified time.

Dear Hugh,

I've noticed that some trainers will repeat a learner's question before responding to it. Is this a technique that you use?

Sincerely,
Querulous in Quesnell

Dear Querulous,

Sometimes it's a good idea to repeat a question. If it was not worded clearly, was spoken too softly for everyone to hear, was rather long winded, or came out of right field, a quick recap is useful. Be careful though. Always repeating a question can be tiresome and irksome for the audience.

Truly,
Hugh

| Teams: | At the end of a lecture, organize participants into subgroups of four or five learners. Provide each subgroup with a few index cards and give them three minutes to generate one to three questions. Host a Q&A session. |

Learner resistance to answers

Sometimes a learner will either openly disagree with your answer or challenge you on it. When this happens, try these options.

• Refer to your professional experience and give an illustration or example. Personal stories often help clear the air and reduce resistance.

• Acknowledge the resistance tactfully and then move on. Avoid making an issue out of it.

• Acknowledge that the information you find relevant may not be relevant to the learner's situation and let them know they can ignore or adapt your answer. It simply may not be applicable to all situations.

• Be proactive by indicating at the start of the session that your views may not be held by all in the group or may not be applicable to some.

• If the question revolves around policy, programs, or procedure, advise the group that your role is not to defend or justify the company's decisions. Don't get trapped into taking sides. Address this up front rather than wait for this type of resistance to crop up. Be tactful, fair, and clear about your purpose as a trainer.

Developing and Delivering Trainer Questions

As a trainer you will ask many different questions for many different reasons. Sometimes you will use questions to gain learner attention, at other times you will ask questions to encourage learner thinking, or you may simple want to find out more information about something.

No matter the reason for your questions, you will want to use them effectively. Asking effective questions is a learned skill. It requires practice and patience. You need to continually experiment with the different purposes and kinds of questions you ask. I use these four simple steps when asking questions and responding to answers.

| Ask: | Phrase your question concisely, clearly, and sensitively. Think through the questions before your ask it. When you ask a question, phrase it in a non-threatening, casual manner—especially when dealing with sensitive issues. A loaded emotional word in a question can create challenges for you. If necessary, prepare questions ahead of time. |

| Pause: | Waiting patiently for a response can be tough. Be patient and disciplined here. Don't rush responses to the question or pass over the question if you don't receive a response. Wait for ten |

seconds. If you jump in with the answer yourself, you are letting the group off the hook. A little pressure is okay. At the same time, you need to give individuals the opportunity to pass and not respond to a question.

If you don't receive a response after ten seconds, rephrase the question. If you still don't receive a response you may want to deal with the lack of group responsiveness. You could state, "I need your help here. I don't seem to be able to generate discussion on this topic. Is there something I need to do differently?"

Listen: Listen actively to the response. Learn to listen in order to understand, not to judge or evaluate. Ask yourself what prompted the response. Decide if you need to ask another question. Keep alert and seek clarity if the response doesn't make sense to you.

Respond: Use one of the options listed in the direct or indirect section (above).

the **Trainer's EDGE**

What Types of Questions Can I Ask?

I like Robert Jolles' assessment of the four different ways to frame or orient a question. He divides questions into four types:

Fact-based: Also called closed questions. They have a right and wrong answer. They can potentially put participants on the spot, so they need to be used carefully. Inexperienced trainers often overuse closed questions. Closed questions usually end up with the leader talking, directing, and controlling the workshop.

Opinion-based: Also called open-ended questions. They require subjective answers that are neither right nor wrong. These questions are less intimidating than fact-based

questions. They also allow for a more natural flow to the session and often take the learners in new or unpredictable directions.

Comparison-based: These questions invite learners to discuss the similarities and differences between methods, procedures, and other concepts. They help the learner think more deeply, more reflectively.

Conclusion-based: These questions require workshop participants to apply learning from the workshop. Responses may involve theories, methods, or models provided in the training session. These questions make a subtle transition into the application phase of training.

Frequently Asked Questions About Questions

When I work or meet with novice trainers, they tend to have the same types of questions about questions. Here's what I usually hear and how I respond.

1. Is it okay to challenge the group with questions?

Yes! Helping a group or individual to examine an idea, to explore a concept more deeply, or to reflect upon their assumptions can be productive. Your goal is to help learners think through an issue or problem, become more specific with their examples, or see possibilities that are only remote ideas at this point.

Remember, though, a strong rapport with the group needs to exist if you want challenging questions to work. If you are trusted and accepted, challenging questions will encourage the group to go beyond the obvious. Without rapport, your challenge may backfire.

2. What do I do if someone gives an incorrect answer?

One of my early mentors in training advised, "Always dignify the response." In other words, you want the person answering the question to know you appreciate the effort taken in responding. One way I do this is to ask others in the group what they think of a response. This provides those who may know an acceptable or correct answer to respond. It takes the burden of always being right off an individual and encourages group resourcefulness.

3. Is body language important in Q&A?

Yes. When someone asks you a question, face the individual and look directly at her. When possible, sit with the group when facilitating Q&A so you're at eye level. This will help develop rapport more quickly and set you and the group at ease. When you answer the question, respond to the entire group (not the questioner only) by shifting your body stance and eye contact away from the questioner to address the others in the room. As you're answering the question, check in on the questioner by looking at her briefly.

4. What if the learner is taking too long to answer the question?

Play this one by ear. Be reasonable. Maybe the group needs to spend time on the question. If, however, it seems the responder is simply having trouble expressing himself, you may want to intervene and summarize the response for the group or ask someone from the group to summarize the response.

5. What if someone asks a question that you covered a short while ago? Should you respond?

If a short answer will suffice, then respond. If a longer answer is needed, ask the group if anyone else is wondering about this point. If so, respond. If not, indicate to the questioner you'll meet with him at the next break to respond.

References

Jolles, Robert L. 1993. *How to run seminars and workshops: Presentation skills for consultants, trainers, and teachers.* New York: John Wiley & Sons.